Sizzle & Drizzle

The Green Edition:
Over 100 Essential Bakes,
Recipes and Tips

NANCY BIRTWHISTLE

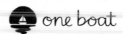

First published 2020 by Nancy Birtwhistle
This edition published 2024 by One Boat
an imprint of Pan Macmillan
The Smithson, 6 Briset Street, London EC1M 5NR
EU representative: Macmillan Publishers Ireland Ltd, 1st Floor,
The Liffey Trust Centre, 117–126 Sheriff Street Upper,
Dublin 1, D01 YC43
Associated companies throughout the world
www.panmacmillan.com

ISBN 978-1-0350-4449-8

1 3 5 7 9 8 6 4 2

A CIP catalogue record for this book is available from the British Library.

Illustrations by Ruth Craddock

Typeset in Adobe Caslon Pro by
Palimpsest Book Production Ltd, Falkirk, Stirlingshire
Printed and bound by CPI Group (UK) Ltd, Croydon, CR0 4YY

MIX
Paper | Supporting
responsible forestry
FSC
www.fsc.org   FSC® C116313

Visit **www.panmacmillan.com/bluebird** to read more about all our books
and to buy them. You will also find features, author interviews and
news of any author events, and you can sign up for e-newsletters
so that you're always first to hear about our new releases.

It cannot be denied that an improved system of practical domestic cookery, and a better knowledge of its first principles, are still much needed in this country; where, from ignorance, or from mismanagement in their preparation, the daily waste of excellent provisions almost exceeds belief.

Eliza Acton, from *Modern Cookery*, 1860

Contents

Foreword

Nancy first leapt out of the TV and into my heart when I saw her slay the competition on *The Great British Bake Off.*

Long before I was on *Queer Eye*, I was cheering on Nancy as she breezily knew when to employ the use of a microwave to her Bake-Off Championship. And so, when I later became friends with her through Instagram, I was ecstatic.

Since then, Nancy has been one of my most gratifying Instagram friendships. From baking, to gardening, to organization, resourcefulness and just her incredible energy, I look forward to seeing what Nancy is up to every day. She creates art out of everything in her life and takes so much joy in the process.

I know that all of us who read this book will become smarter and cleverer when it comes to caring for ourselves, our families and our homes.

Keep slaying, Nancy!

– Jonathan Van Ness
TV personality, grooming consultant, writer,
comedian and host of *Getting Curious* podcast

A Letter from Nancy

I wonder why I wasn't given the name Prudence.

Cooking and home-making – making my own, growing my own, making do, mending and generally using every last scrap from the fridge and cupboards – became part of my life at an early age. My grandmother was a huge influence – she had lived through two world wars and during those times people learnt resilience, prudence, self-sufficiency and pride. She taught me how to sew, knit, cook, bake and, as she described it, 'keep house'. My grandad taught me how to grow food, when to sow, how to identify and solve problems, when to harvest and how to preserve everything to make sure there were enough provisions to carry us through the winter. As a working mother on a tight budget, I've always been resourceful and felt a responsibility to avoid unnecessary waste and have always baked and cooked to feed the family.

I love food and everything it involves, from growing, cooking and baking, to eating! When I retired, baking became an obsession. Reading recipes, practising, failing, then succeeding became the norm. Before long, I was baking most days (and was glued to *The Great British Bake Off*!). When my first application to appear as a contestant on the show failed at the second audition, I was devastated but not undeterred. I applied again a year later, for Series 5, and the rest is history. Winning *Bake Off* changed my life.

I am often asked, 'Where did you learn this?' or, 'How do you know that?' Now I'm older, I want to share my wealth of experience and knowledge. In 2017, I decided to embrace social media. It took a little time to find my way around but when I announced I would share a hint, tip, 'how to' video or free recipe every day for a whole year I started to gather a 'following', and I have been sharing problems and solutions, recipes and tips ever since. The response has been tremendous and here I am, many years on, still visiting thousands of followers' screens every morning. Within these pages you'll find the best of my daily posts, along with QR codes that link to the videos which have become an integral part of my work. To use the QR codes in this book, simply open the camera on your phone, hold it over the code (as though you are taking a photo) and click on the link that appears, which will take you to my website.

Those friends who have been following me on social media will know what this book is about because you have been asking for it. I previously published this book myself and I'm now so excited to bring you the green edition, featuring the same classic recipes and tips from my original edition but in the style of my other books!

I am always thinking about the next meal. Am I cooking from scratch today? Will it be something out of the freezer that I made in bulk earlier? Or will it be a quick omelette or snack? Whatever it is, I always know what will be on the menu. My hope is that this book will help you in so many ways, with everyday meals and baking. I am going to teach you how to make the best pastry and avoid those pitfalls that often lead to soggy bottoms and tough crusts. A sinking cake and split buttercream will be a thing of the past. Breads and biscuits feature too, with tips to ensure success every time. And you will find life-changing tips to make your baking and cooking experiences easier and simpler: these nuggets of knowledge have proved to be super popular among my followers and I have woven them throughout the book.

I have also included a whole 'free from' chapter containing gluten free, fat free, low sugar, dairy free, vegetarian and vegan options for readers whose food allergies or dietary needs can make cooking and baking a little more challenging.

Last, but no means least, is my life changer in the kitchen! How many times have you picked up a recipe only to find you don't have the right size tin? The recipe says 23cm (9 inch) but you have 20cm (8 inch) and 25cm (10 inch) – does it matter? Yes, it does. Don't stress though, because I have included a table which will calculate for you how you need to adjust your ingredients to achieve the perfect bake in the tin that you own.

I thank each and every one of you for inspiring me to write this book and for keeping me energized and happy!

Love,
Nancy

GETTING STARTED

ESSENTIAL EQUIPMENT

Whether I am gardening, sewing, knitting, drawing, cooking or baking, it is essential I have the right tools for the job.

When it comes to kitchen equipment the number of tools, tins, pans, appliances, gadgets and general clutter are too many to mention and I feel so many of them are unnecessary. Don't be tempted by a 'full range' of anything. Choose something that you like and stick to it.

In this book I keep equipment to a minimum and those items I recommend are used over and over again.

SAUCEPANS, CASSEROLE DISHES AND FRYING PANS

There is an enormous range to suit every kind of kitchen and hob. Choose the best you can afford.

Non-stick saucepans are fantastic as long as metal utensils are not used with them (these can scratch and eventually damage the non-stick coating).

Glazed cast-iron casserole dishes are my favourites as they can be used on the hob and then transferred to the oven for long, slow cooking. They can be expensive and heavy but invest in a large casserole dish and it will last you a lifetime and can be used for so many recipes.

When choosing a **frying pan**, select one you can use on the hob and transfer to the oven if necessary with a metal handle rather than plastic. The advantages of this type of frying pan are many, one being that it is perfect for frying a full English breakfast on the hob but then, on another occasion it can be filled with apples and pastry, popped into the oven and double up as a baking dish to produce my delicious Tarte Tatin (page 296)!

MIXERS

Tabletop (stand) mixers have a place in many kitchens and as they can be purchased in a variety of colours have become part of the modern kitchen's look and décor. They are expensive and for that reason I rarely refer to them in my recipes. I use mine for bread making but for most cakes I use a hand-held electric whisk. The exception to this is when I am making a large wedding cake or my Christmas Cake (page 150), when I use my tabletop (stand) mixer.

Hand-held electric whisks can be purchased for not very much money and make cake-making so much quicker and easier than making by hand.

A **food processor** – now that's a different story. I always make pastry in mine and I wouldn't be without it. It carries out a whole range of tasks efficiently – blending, chopping, grating, whisking, slicing. Like everything, top of the range models are expensive but a good one will last you years. I have a good-quality basic model and it has served me well for thirty years. It is still going strong so I find no reason to change it. It's worth saving up for one or, better still, put one on your Christmas list.

BAKING TINS

Tins can be expensive and even though I have a huge collection which have been bought over the years, I still seem to stick to my regular-sized favourites.

How many times have you picked up a recipe book, looked at a photograph of a cake, dessert or pastry you want to make but found you don't have the right size tin? You go out and buy the tin, make the cake (which by the way doesn't look at all like the one in the fancy studio photograph), then never use that tin again. This won't be the case with my recipes: for each one, where practicable, my 'cake tin calculators' on page 13 will calculate for you the revised quantities to fit the tins that you already have.

For sandwich cakes, I prefer to use tins with a loose bottom for easy release. For deeper celebration cakes, I use a springform loose-bottom tin.

Do invest in a couple of 450g (1lb) **loaf tins** – I use them a lot. They are used for bread, of course, but also for my Lemon Drizzle Cakes (page 130), Malt Loaf (page 205), Brioche (page 110) and Summer Pudding Terrine (page 224).

Deep 12-hole **muffin tins** are used regularly throughout this book, for buns and muffins and supporting paper cases for small cakes. Equally, I find them ideal for shaping and baking deep-filled pies. My Luxury Mince Pies (page 261) and Picnic Pork Pies (page 277) are both baked in a deep muffin tin.

Biscuits and scones are baked on **flat metal baking sheets**. Buy two if you can afford it, but one good one is better than two cheap ones. I have made the mistake of buying a cheap sheet, only to have it bend and buckle in the oven. Buy one good one and when a recipe calls for a second one, turn a roasting tin upside down and bake on the underside.

WEIGHING SCALES

For years I used my grandmother's balance scales and I still treasure them but they are now a kitchen ornament and souvenir rather than a trusted piece of kit. A set of **digital weighing scales** simplifies and speeds up baking preparations.

I routinely place my mixing bowl on the scales, zero its weight, weigh in my butter, zero its weight then add the sugar and so on. You can see that using this method you will save on using extra bowls.

I realize my US readers are fond of cup measures and I have included a conversion chart for liquid measures if that is your preferred system, as well as imperial conversions within each recipe. I strongly recommend that because baking is 'exact' in its nature that the digital weighing scales are a must.

MEASURING SPOONS

These are used in most recipes and their measurements are not to be confused with tableware. Teaspoons for example come in all sorts of shapes and sizes, whereas a proper 'teaspoon' **measuring spoon** will give you the exact 5g / 5ml amount – essential when working with flavourings, spices, extracts and raising agents such as baking powder.

CUTTERS

These are an essential and inexpensive piece of kit for biscuits, scones and tarts. There are so many on the market but a good starting point (and all you'll need for this book) is a pack of **double-sided pastry cutters** in metal or plastic. They come in various sizes – one side fluted and the other side plain.

BOWLS AND JUGS

Bowls and measuring jugs are used throughout this book. I tend to use Pyrex glass or glazed earthenware jugs rather than metal, simply because I can pop them into the microwave when necessary. A small, medium and large mixing bowl should be added to your kitchen collection.

SPOONS AND SPATULAS

Can you believe my favourite **spatula** is a plastic one I received as a free gift with a magazine? It is small and handy, gets into every nook and cranny, and I love it. Even though I have a full set of different sizes I always reach for the little one. Similarly, a **large spoon** – a metal one is my favourite and will always be used for folding in the flour when cake making.

A **bench scraper** is handy when bread making or if you have made a mess on the work surface and need to clean it down quickly. I have a metal one and a plastic one – I tend to reach for my plastic one for all sorts of jobs, including smoothing buttercream.

A **small-angled palette knife** is great too, for spreading and smoothing.

WOODEN UTENSILS

My **rolling pin** must be 40 years old. It is shiny, well used and rarely gets a wash. After use, I wipe clean it with a damp cloth if necessary.

Wooden spoons are great for non-stick pans as they will not damage non-stick coatings. Always wash wooden spoons by hand – a dishwasher will shorten their life dramatically.

SIEVE

If you don't already have a **sieve** and wonder which sort to buy, get a metal one. I have both plastic and metal; they both work well but of course boiling liquids are best passed through a metal sieve rather than a plastic alternative.

A FEW REUSABLES!

Reusable baking parchment: If you haven't yet tried reusable baking parchment, I urge you to invest in a sheet or two. I bake biscuits, flapjacks and scones on it, roast potatoes on it, line baking tins with it, then simply wash it between uses. My sheets are several years old now – they are now very well used, dark in colour but still going strong. No more scrubbing off baked-on deposits.

Piping bags and nozzles: I used to be a real fan of disposable piping bags but in my drive to reduce the amount of single-use plastic I now only use reusable washable ones. Going back to the old ways really! I have a selection – a huge one for meringue and smaller ones for royal icing and buttercreams. There are hundreds of piping nozzles but to start with, a plain and star nozzle (plastic or metal) will be all that you need.

Shower caps: Hang onto shower caps and use them as bowl covers in place of cling film. They are particularly good for rising and proving bread – the shower cap actually does a better job than cling film as it provides some expansion space which cling film doesn't. Or buy reusable bowl covers.

Sugar thermometer: I have one and use it rarely but there are a few recipes in this book where monitoring temperature is essential. I use it so infrequently I remove the battery before popping it back in my drawer so that it always has life!

LET ME SHOW YOU . . .

My Equipment Video

||||||||||||||||||||||||||||||||||||||||||||||||||||||||||||||||||||||||||||||||||||||||||||||||||||||||||||

Nancy's lining paste
Simply take equal quantities of vegetable shortening or soft butter, plain flour (or gluten-free flour) and vegetable or sunflower oil. I use 100g (3½oz) of each then store in a jar in the fridge. Whisk together the soft fat and flour until you have a smooth paste then add the oil. Brush this thick paste inside your cake tin to save paper lining. Don't worry, it won't leave a residue on your baked cake or bread.

||||||||||||||||||||||||||||||||||||||||||||||||||||||||||||||||||||||||||||||||||||||||||||||||||||||||||||

CAKE TIN CALCULATORS

These tables look complicated at first glance but once you get your head around the concept you will discover they are a fantastic 'ready reckoner' when you want to adapt your favourite recipe to fit a different-sized tin. I have tried to simplify them but have found that they just become harder to explain. Instead, I will describe a few scenarios to help you navigate the rows and columns of the tables.

EXAMPLE 1

The recipe is for a 20cm (8 inch) round tin but my tin is 23cm (9in) (although it is round).

Find the table for the 20cm (8 inch) round tin – this is written at the top of the table and represents the recipe you have. Look under the Round Tin column, find your 23cm (9 inch) and you will see the recipe needs to be multiplied by 1.3 in order to achieve a cake of the same height.

Example: your recipe states 180g (6¼oz) soft margarine or butter

Multiply 180 × 1.3 = 234, so 234g soft margarine or butter needed.

What to do about eggs? If the recipe states 3 eggs:

Multiply 3 × 1.3 = 3.9 eggs (round up to 4 eggs)

EXAMPLE 2

The recipe is for a 15cm (6 inch) round tin but my tin is 20cm (8 inch) and is square.

Find the table for the 15cm (6 inch) round tin – this is written at the top of the table and represents the recipe you have. Look under the Square Tin column in the table, find your 20cm (8 inch) and you will see the recipe needs to be multiplied by 2.2 in order to achieve a cake of the same height.

Example: your recipe states 125g (4¼oz) soft margarine or butter

Multiply 125 × 2.2 = 275, so 275g (9¾oz) soft margarine or butter is needed.

What to do about the eggs? If the recipe states 2 eggs:

Multiply 2 × 2.2 = 4.4 eggs (use 4 eggs plus 1 tbsp milk)

Calculating eggs
If your calculations come out at more than 0.5, add another egg. If your calculations come out less than 0.5, add 1 tablespoon of milk.

Calculating baking times
You will find that for sponge cakes the baking time will be about the same because the finished sponge is the same height. If your recipe states that your 20cm (8 inch) cake needs to bake for 20–25 minutes you will find that your adjusted cake – if adjusted to be smaller – will be nearer the 20 minutes and if larger may need up to 25 minutes. Either way, baking times are not substantially different. Always check that your sponge

is just leaving the sides of the tin, is well risen, springy to the touch in the centre and golden in colour (unless it is chocolate of course).

When it comes to rich fruit cakes, again the baking times are not vastly different. If you follow my Christmas Cake recipe on page 150 you will see that a 23cm (9 inch) cake bakes for a long 10 hours. I made a smaller 18cm (7 inch) cake and baked it for just 1 hour less.

SIZE CONVERTOR FOR ROUND TINS

Recipe Round Tin 15cm / 6 inch

Round		Square	
		15cm / 6 inch	x 1.3
18cm / 7inch	x 1.4	18cm / 7inch	x 1.7
20cm / 8inch	x 1.8	20cm / 8inch	x 2.2
23cm / 9inch	x 2.2	23cm / 9inch	x 2.8
25cm / 10inch	x 2.7	25cm / 10inch	x 3.5
28cm / 11inch	x 3.3	28cm / 11inch	x 4.2
30cm / 12inch	x 3.8	30cm / 12inch	x 5.1

Recipe Round Tin 18cm / 7inch

Round		Square	
15cm / 6inch	x 0.7	15cm / 6inch	x 0.9
		18cm / 7inch	x 1.3
20cm / 8inch	x 1.3	20cm / 8inch	x 1.7
23cm / 9inch	x 1.7	23cm / 9inch	x 2.1
25cm / 10inch	x 2.0	25cm / 10inch	x 2.6
28cm / 11inch	x 2.5	28cm / 11inch	x 3.1
30cm / 12inch	x 2.9	30cm / 12inch	x 3.8

Recipe Round Tin 20cm / 8inch

Round		Square	
15cm / 6inch	x 0.6	15cm / 6inch	x 0.7
18cm / 7inch	x 0.8	18cm / 7inch	x 1.0
		20cm / 8inch	x 1.3
23cm / 9inch	x 1.3	23cm / 9inch	x 1.6
25cm /10inch	x 1.5	25cm / 10inch	x 2.0
28cm / 11inch	x 1.9	28cm / 11inch	x 2.4
30cm / 12inch	x 2.2	30cm / 12inch	x 2.9

Recipe Round Tin 23cm / 9inch

Round		Square	
15cm / 6inch	x 0.4	15cm / 6inch	x 0.6
18cm / 7inch	x 0.6	18cm / 7inch	x 0.8
20cm / 8inch	x 0.8	20cm / 8inch	x 1.0
		23cm / 9inch	x 1.3
25cm / 10inch	x 1.2	25cm / 10inch	x 1.6
28cm / 11inch	x 1.5	28cm / 11inch	x 1.9
30cm / 12inch	x 1.8	30cm /12inch	x 2.3

SIZE CONVERTOR FOR SQUARE TINS

Recipe Square Tin 15cm / 6inch

Round		Square	
15cm / 6inch	x 0.8		
18cm / 7inch	x 1.1	18cm / 7inch	x 1.4
20cm / 8inch	x 1.4	20cm / 8inch	x 1.8
23cm / 9inch	x 1.8	23cm / 9inch	x 2.3
25cm / 10inch	x 2.2	25cm / 10inch	x 2.8
28cm / 11inch	x 2.6	28cm / 11inch	x 3.4
30cm / 12inch	x 3.1	30cm x 12inch	x 4.0

Recipe Square Tin 18cm / 7inch

Round		Square	
15cm / 6inch	x 0.6	15cm / 6inch	x 0.7
18cm / 7inch	x 0.8		
20cm / 8inch	x 1.0	20cm / 8inch	x 1.3
23cm / 9inch	x 1.3	23cm / 9inch	x 1.7
25cm / 10inch	x 1.6	25cm / 10inch	x 2.0
28cm / 11inch	x 1.9	28cm / 11inch	x 2.5
30cm / 12inch	x 2.3	30cm / 12inch	x 2.9

Recipe Square Tin 20cm / 8inch

Round		Square	
15cm / 6inch	x 0.4	15cm / 6inch	x 0.6
18cm / 7inch	x 0.6	18cm / 7inch	x 0.8
20cm / 8inch	x 0.8		
23cm / 9inch	x 1.0	23cm / 9inch	x 1.3
25cm / 10inch	x 1.2	25cm / 10inch	x 1.6
28cm / 11inch	x 1.5	28cm / 11inch	x 1.9
30cm / 12inch	x 1.8	30cm / 12inch	x 2.3

Recipe Square Tin 23cm / 9inch

Round		Square	
15cm / 6inch	x 0.4	15cm / 6inch	x 0.4
18cm / 7inch	x 0.5	18cm / 7inch	x 0.6
20cm / 8inch	x 0.6	20cm / 8inch	x 0.8
23cm / 9inch	x 0.8		
25cm / 10inch	x 1.0	25cm / 10inch	x 1.2
28cm / 11inch	x 1.2	28cm / 11inch	x 1.5
30cm / 12inch	x 1.4	30cm / 12inch	x 1.8

LET ME SHOW YOU . . .

My Ready Reckoner Video

INGREDIENTS

You will come across many recipes, especially online, that encourage you to use a certain brand of butter, sugar, flour or flavouring. Remember these are probably sponsored sites and the recipe writer will have been paid to promote that particular product. I would suggest you buy the best version of ingredient you can afford. If you are new to baking, are you really going to want to spend your money on top-end ingredients when you are experimenting for the first time? I certainly didn't.

BUTTER OR MARGARINE?

There are many out there that would never use soft margarine in cake making. In fact, this reminds me of a particular occasion on Week One in that famous *Bake-Off* tent.

Our Showstopper Challenge was to make thirty-six mini cakes. Our recipes had been submitted in advance and our ingredients were put out before us on our bench. I looked around the twelve benches and everyone apart from me had requested butter for their cakes. I was the only person with soft margarine. My confidence was wobbling but then I reminded myself that the cakes I was about to make were good – and they were very good as it turned out.

Star Baker was awarded to me!

Soft margarine creams easily, is less likely to curdle, is cheaper than butter and produces a light sponge. However, if you have concerns and questions about what goes into making margarine then choose butter. Butter is absolutely delicious but do make sure it is at room temperature before you start to cream (see below).

If you decide to use butter some recipes suggest baking with salted, some specify unsalted. For me, it makes absolutely no difference. I buy salted butter, rarely unsalted, because the butter I buy is used at the table as well as in baking. There will be chefs who disagree with me, but I have yet to be convinced that unsalted butter is better for baking than salted.

How to get cold butter up to room temperature

It has probably happened to us all. You need room-temperature butter, but have forgotten to remove it from the fridge (or maybe your kitchen is as cold as the fridge). Whether you need soft butter for baking, cooking or simply for spreading on bread here is a simple and effective way to soften your butter in a matter of minutes.

Take a microwave-proof bowl or glass that is large enough to cover the butter you need to soften. Rinse the glass or bowl under cold water, don't dry it. Pop the wet glass or bowl into the microwave and heat for 1 minute on full power. Take the hot bowl from the microwave (use a cloth to protect your hands) then invert it over your piece of cold butter. Leave it for 5 minutes then remove the bowl and your butter will be soft enough to use without any oiliness or melting.

SUGAR

When I was first married, I only ever had granulated sugar in the cupboard. Caster sugar was more expensive. Granulated sugar, while being great sprinkled over cornflakes or used to sweeten tea or coffee, is coarse in texture and slow to dissolve when creamed with butter or margarine for a cake. Caster sugar has finer grains and will combine readily with the fat.

How to make caster sugar from granulated sugar
If you have run out of caster sugar or bake infrequently and only have granulated sugar, you can grind your granulated sugar in a food processor. Simply pop the granulated sugar in the bowl of your machine with the blade attachment attached then blitz for 2–3 minutes. Your sugar will grind down to fine crystals, which are just perfect for baking!

Rich fruit cakes and many dark moist cakes such as gingerbread are better made with brown sugar. Brown sugar (light, dark, muscovado etc.) have a soft texture but once the packet is opened, if not sealed really well afterwards will suffer as the humidity gets to it. The next time you reach for your packet of dark brown sugar instead of being soft and flowing it will have formed into a brick. The sugar can be rescued but remember next time to put your bag of opened brown sugar into an airtight container to keep it soft and easy to use.

Your solid brick of brown sugar can be rescued. Place
the required amount for your recipe in a non-metallic
bowl. Take a sheet of kitchen paper and dampen it with
cold water from the tap. Fold the kitchen paper and lay
it over the sugar in the bowl. Pop into the microwave
oven for about 1 minute (for 150g/5½oz sugar). Take
the bowl from the microwave – the sugar will have
softened and is good to use. More sugar will need a
longer time, but increase it just a few seconds at a time,
as you don't want your sugar to melt.

EGGS

Where would we be without eggs? Many of my readers will
know I keep chickens and have done now for some fifteen
years. It is a delight to collect eggs each day. Obviously, having
my own chickens means I have no 'use by' dates on my eggs.
I write the date on the shell in pencil every day and I have
calculated that my eggs remain good for about six weeks out
of the fridge. Supermarket and bought eggs will have a date
stamped onto them so the user is well aware of the shelf life.
All eggs referred to in this book's recipes are large eggs, unless
specified otherwise.

If you are given eggs without a date (I sometimes find a
random egg or have omitted to write the date on one), how
do I know it is good to eat?

How to know if eggs are fresh

Fill a large jug or bowl with cold water. A fresh egg carefully placed in the water will sink to the bottom and lie on its side. An egg that is old but still good to eat will still sink to the bottom but will stand up. A bad egg or an egg not fit to eat will float and is best thrown away. Older eggs (the ones that sit upright but still sink) are perfect for hard boiling because the shells come away much more easily.

Retrieving eggshells from a mixture

Ever dropped a shard of eggshell into your mixing bowl? Try as you might it will refuse to be caught. It will slide off a spoon, will slither away from your finger and will run away from you however you might try to remove it. Take one of the eggshell halves and take it to that slippery character and without any effort whatsoever you will see it gently swim into that empty shell. Amazing really, but it works!

LET ME SHOW YOU . . .

My Fresh Eggs Video

FLOUR

I buy self-raising flour for cake making. There are many brands on the market, just buy the best flour you can afford. Even though self-raising flour these days is supposed to not require sifting I still do it as a matter of course – just habit I suppose. I believe it makes for a lighter, more airy sponge.

I will explain how I mix a sponge on page 119 – the mixing is all important. I rarely use additional raising agent partly because I can taste it (a kind of bitter aftertaste) yet I see many recipes using self-raising flour plus baking powder. It really is not necessary if the mixing is right.

How to make self-raising flour

If you are out of self-raising flour you can make your own but don't be tempted to just make enough for your recipe. Make a batch of 500g (1lb 2oz) because then you will know the amount of baking powder added is just right. Take 500g (1lb 2oz) plain flour (or all-purpose flour) and add 15g (½oz) baking powder (often a sachet weight). Sift the two together, give a really good stir then transfer to a jar and use as necessary.

LET ME SHOW YOU . . .

My Browned Flour Video

COOKING CONVERSION CHARTS

Weight

Imperial	Metric
½oz	15g
1oz	25g
2oz	57g
3oz	90g
4oz	110g
5oz	140g
6oz	170g
8oz	225g
10oz	283g
12oz	340g
13oz	370g
14oz	400g
15oz	425g
1lb	450g

Temperature

Fahrenheit	Celsius
100 °F	37 °C
150 °F	65 °C
200 °F	100 °C
250 °F	120 °C
300 °F	150 °C
325 °F	170 °C
350 °F	180 °C
375 °F	190 °C
400 °F	200 °C
425 °F	220 °C
450 °F	230 °C
500 °F	260 °C
525 °F	274 °C
550 °F	288 °C

Measurement

Cup	Ounces	Millileters
8 cups	65oz	1900 ml
6 cups	48oz	1420 ml
5 cups	40oz	1180 ml
4 cups	32oz	960 ml
2 cups	16oz	480 ml
1 cup	8oz	240 ml
¾ cup	6oz	180 ml
⅔ cup	5oz	150 ml
½ cup	4oz	120 ml
⅜ cup	3oz	90 ml
⅓ cup	2 ½oz	75 ml
¼ cup	2oz	60 ml
⅛ cup	1oz	30 ml
1/16 cup	½oz	15 ml

BISCUITS AND SCONES

BISCUITS

A clue to the origin of the biscuit is probably in the word, which is French for 'twice cooked'; 'bi' meaning two and the verb 'cuir' to cook. As far back as the twelfth century, reference is made to bread being baked for a second time to dry it out completely.

Fast forward to the twenty-first century and there are so many biscuits in the shops that you may question why there is the need to make them.

The recipes in this chapter are my favourites. Biscuits are great to make with children and if you are feeling particularly patient, they can decorate them for Christmas or Easter. Biscuits have a longer shelf life than cake or pastry and make excellent gifts. A few spiced shortbread biscuits beautifully wrapped will delight even the most difficult person to buy suitable gifts for.

I routinely reduce the sugar in my baking and biscuits are no exception.

As a general rule, biscuit dough needs to be on the dry side. The piece of dough may crack a little at the edges when rolling but when cut out it should hold together nicely. A dry but firm dough will bake well, have a good texture and will not spread during baking. If you have made biscuits in the past and taken time to cut out a number of interesting shapes only to find they have spread and become totally unrecognisable in the oven, then the dough has been too wet. I always mix biscuit dough by hand because I find a machine overmixes it and the biscuits can then be hard.

When your dough is mixed, rolled out, shapes cut and spread onto a baking sheet pop them into the fridge to firm up while your oven comes to temperature.

SCONES

You can't beat a scone. Whether you put your jam or cream on first, however you pronounce the word - they are an absolute staple in my house. I've included some of my favourite sweet and savoury recipes for you to try out, I hope you love them as much as I do.

———

How to stop dough sticking to the work surface
How many times have you seen a work surface covered in flour ready to roll out the rested dough? I no longer do this because I want to keep the flour and fat quantities exact. I roll out the dough between two sheets of food-grade plastic (which I re-use again and again – washing between each use) so no extra flour is needed for rolling, the dough doesn't stick to the surface when rolling out, and the biscuit 'project' can easily be popped into the fridge for a few minutes to firm up before cutting out. I save cereal packet liners for this, cut to make two separate sheets – they are absolutely perfect, as are freezer bags: cut down one side and across the bottom and you have your first sheet. Repeat with a second bag.

———

Creating an additional baking sheet

Biscuits are usually baked on a flat baking sheet and although you may have one or two to hand, a batch of biscuits may call for more. Create an additional baking sheet by simply turning a large roasting tin upside down then grease the base or, alternatively, lay over a piece of reusable baking parchment. Spread your cut out biscuits on this newly created flat surface and bake as normal.

LEMON SHORTBREAD BISCUITS

MAKES: 40–50 BISCUITS, DEPENDING ON CUTTER SIZE

These are delicious at any time of the year, but are a favourite in our family at Easter time. They are easy to make and serve plain, or why not use the leftover egg white and half a lemon to make a royal icing and release your piping skills!

FOR THE BISCUITS

200g (7oz) plain flour
finely grated zest of 1 lemon
80g (2¾oz) icing sugar, sifted
140g (5oz) butter, diced, at room temperature
1 tbsp lemon juice
½ tsp Sicilian lemon extract (optional)
1 egg yolk

FOR THE ICING

1 egg white
200g (7oz) icing sugar, sifted
1 tbsp lemon juice
food colour gel (optional)

Equipment: 1 or 2 baking sheets lightly greased or lined with reusable baking parchment biscuit cutter, cooling rack

Place the flour, lemon zest and icing sugar in a roomy mixing bowl then rub in the butter with your fingertips until the mixture resembles breadcrumbs. Adding the lemon zest at the outset releases lemon flavour as the zests are rubbed together with the flour. I prefer to do the rubbing in by hand as I believe the final biscuit is much lighter than from a mix made in a machine.

Add the lemon juice and extract (if using) to the egg yolk, stir briefly, then pour into the butter and flour mix. Stir the egg into the crumbs with a metal knife then bring the mixture together using your hands to form a ball.

Place the dough between two sheets of plastic and roll out into a circle about the thickness of a £1 coin. Chill the dough in the fridge for a minimum of 20 minutes.

Remove the chilled dough from the fridge, remove from the plastic and cut out biscuit shapes, then transfer to two greased or lined baking sheets. When all the dough has been used – after rolling and re-rolling the trimmings – pop the baking sheets into the fridge and leave to chill until the oven comes up to temperature.

Preheat the oven to 200°C/180°C (fan)/400°F/gas 6. Bake for 8–10 minutes (I like to bake one tray at a time), until the biscuits are set with just the slightest hint of colour.

Remove from the oven and lay the sheets on a cooling rack. Allow the biscuits to cool before removing them from the sheets – they may break otherwise. If you decide to ice your biscuits, make a royal icing.

Beat the egg white in a small bowl until frothy, then start to add the sifted icing sugar, and whisk well after each addition, until the mixture forms soft peaks. Add lemon juice if the icing is too thick. Whisk well for about 5 minutes until you have a smooth, shiny icing. When the biscuits have cooled completely decorate them as you wish. The biscuits will keep well in an airtight tin for at least a week.

LET ME SHOW YOU . . .

My Lemon Shortbread Biscuits Video

SPICED CHRISTMAS SHORTBREADS

MAKES: 100 SMALL BISCUITS

These spiced shortbreads are easy and quick to make, inexpensive, delicious, and make excellent little gifts.

50g (1¾oz) chopped nuts (mixed chopped nuts or nuts of
  choice), lightly toasted
1 tsp ground cinnamon
110g (4oz) butter, at room temperature
50g (1¾oz) caster sugar
175g (6oz) plain flour
50g (1¾oz) fine semolina
a little milk, to bind
icing sugar, for dusting

Equipment: food processor, hand-held electric whisk, 1 or 2 baking sheets lined with reusable baking parchment, small biscuit cutter (I use 2.5cm/1-inch novelty Christmas cutters)

Blitz the nuts and cinnamon in a food processor until you have a fairly fine crumb. Do not overdo it or the nuts will turn pasty and glue-like.

Cream the butter and sugar in a bowl with a hand-held electric whisk until light and fluffy. Work in the flour and semolina with a wooden or metal spoon then add the nut crumb. Bring the mixture together into a ball using your hands. The dough should be quite dry (this will help prevent your biscuits spreading in the oven), however if you find it really difficult to knead the dough into a ball, add a couple of table-spoons of milk to bind.

Roll out the dough between two sheets of plastic to the thickness of a £1 coin then slide onto a lined baking sheet and chill in the fridge for 30 minutes.

Remove from the fridge, peel away the top plastic sheet then cut out the shapes with a small biscuit cutter, re-rolling the trimmings. Place the biscuits onto the chilled baking sheet(s).

Preheat the oven to 170°C/150°C (fan)/325°F/gas 3. Chill the cut-out dough in the fridge on the baking sheet until the oven has reached its temperature then bake the biscuits for 25–30 minutes until pale.

Remove from the oven and allow to cool on the sheet, then carefully transfer to a cooling rack and dust with icing sugar.

Store either in a tin or parcel up into little airtight
gift bags. These shortbreads will keep easily
for up to two weeks.

LET ME SHOW YOU . . .

My Spiced Christmas Shortbreads Video

VANILLA SHORTBREAD BISCUITS

MAKES: 20–22 BISCUITS

These little shortbread biscuits are easy, inexpensive to make and tasty, especially if you take the time to dip them in (or drizzle them with) a little melted chocolate.

100g (3½oz) plain flour
40g (1½oz) icing sugar
70g (2½oz) butter, diced, at room temperature
½ tsp vanilla extract
1 egg yolk

TO DECORATE (OPTIONAL)
50g (1¾oz) dark chocolate, broken into pieces

Equipment: 1 or 2 baking sheets greased or lined with reusable baking parchment, 5cm (2 inch) biscuit cutter

Put the flour, sugar and butter in a medium bowl and rub with your fingertips until the mixture resembles breadcrumbs. Stir the vanilla into the egg yolk then add to the dough and stir everything with a metal knife. Bring the mixture together to form a ball using your hands.

Roll out the dough between two sheets of plastic to about the thickness of a £1 coin then slide onto a greased or lined baking sheet and chill in the fridge for 20 minutes.

Remove from the fridge, peel away the top sheet of the plastic then cut out shapes – I use a 5cm (2 inch) cutter. Re-roll the trimmings. Place the biscuits onto the chilled greased or lined baking sheet.

Preheat the oven to 200°C/180°C (fan)/400°F/gas 6. Chill the cut-out dough in the fridge on the baking sheet until the oven has reached temperature then bake the biscuits for 6–8 minutes until just starting to colour. Remove from the oven and allow the biscuits to cool on their tray.

If you want to dip the biscuits in melted chocolate, melt the chocolate in the microwave in a non-metal bowl in 30-second bursts, stirring between each blast. You don't want it too runny or too thick. If you have a sugar thermometer, 35°C is just about right. Dip the biscuits in the chocolate, or drizzle the chocolate over them, and allow to set on a sheet of foil.

The biscuits will keep in an airtight tin for at least a week.

LET ME SHOW YOU . . .

My Vanilla Shortbread Biscuits Video

FLAPJACKS

MAKES: 16 PIECES

This is a thrifty family favourite. These little bars will keep for weeks in a tin but in my house, they don't last that long. They're great for kids when they come in from school, or as a packed lunch treat and are perfect with a cuppa in the afternoon. I have included two flavour variations – both are delicious.

FOR CHERRY AND COCONUT FLAPJACKS

- 100g (3½oz) margarine or butter
- 3 tbsp golden syrup
- 90g (3oz) granulated sugar
- 40g (1½oz) desiccated coconut
- 160g (5½oz) porridge oats
- ½ tsp almond extract
- 20 glacé cherries, roughly chopped (I use dark morello glacé cherries which are packed with flavour)

FOR TROPICAL FLAPJACKS

- 100g (3½oz) margarine or butter
- 3 tbsp golden syrup
- 90g (3oz) granulated sugar
- 40g (1½oz) desiccated coconut
- 160g (5½oz) porridge oats
- 20g (¾oz) dried mango, cut into pieces with scissors (about currant size)
- grated zest and juice of 1 lime
- a generous grating of nutmeg (about 1 tsp)

Equipment: rectangular baking tin (mine is 26 × 18cm/ 10½ × 7 inches and about 4cm/1½ inches deep), base and sides lined with reusable baking parchment

Preheat the oven to 200°C/180°C (fan)/400°F/gas 6.

Melt the margarine (or butter) and golden syrup in a medium saucepan, then take it off the heat and stir in the sugar then the coconut and finally the oats, almond extract and cherries (or the dried mango, lime zest and juice and nutmeg, if making tropical flapjacks). Mix well so that all the dry ingredients have absorbed the moisture.

Transfer to the prepared tin and smooth the mixture with the back of a spoon or an angled palette knife. Bake in the oven for 20 minutes until golden brown. Remove from the oven and leave for 5 minutes then, while still warm and with a sharp knife or pizza cutter, score 16 pieces. Leave to cool completely then remove from the tin, peel off the parchment and cut along the scored lines for neat even pieces. The flapjacks will keep in an airtight tin for up to 2 weeks.

LET ME SHOW YOU . . .

My Flapjacks Video

BRANDY SNAPS

These brandy snaps are easier to make than you think and can be eaten by young and old alike as a biscuit, or filled with raspberries and cream for a retro dessert.

60g (2¼oz) butter
60g (2¼oz) soft dark brown sugar
60g (2¼oz) golden syrup
60g (2¼oz) plain flour
½ tsp ground ginger

Equipment: 2 baking sheets lined with reusable baking parchment

---

My brandy snaps break when I try to mould them
If the brandy snaps cool and become brittle before you have time to mould them, pop them back into the oven for 1 minute and they will soften again.

Put the butter, sugar and syrup in a saucepan and stir over a fairly low heat until the butter melts and the sugar dissolves. Don't allow the mixture to boil.

Take the pan off the heat and sift in the flour and ground ginger. Bring everything together using a wooden spoon then put in a bowl and cool. Chill in the fridge for about 30 minutes.

When ready to bake your biscuits, preheat the oven to 210°C/190°C (fan)/425°F/gas 7.

Cut the chilled paste into about 20 even-sized pieces. I prefer to weigh mine and then you have identical sizes for your brandy snaps and identical baking times. My pieces weighed 12g (just short of ½oz) each. Roll each piece into a ball and space out five on each lined baking sheet.

Bake one sheet at a time – they take only 4–5 minutes. The brandy snaps are baked when the mixture has spread, is a dark golden brown, bubbling and looking like little lace doilies. Remove the baked brandy snaps from the oven and leave for 2–3 minutes or until cool enough to handle but still warm to the touch and pliable.

Place the textured side to the outside and wrap around the handle of a metal kitchen utensil or suitable clean mould. You can mould them around the bottom of a pudding basin if you want to make little baskets. Leave until completely cool then take away the mould support.

Repeat with the other sheet(s) until you have your 20 brandy snaps.

If you want to fill them with cream and raspberries do this just before serving otherwise your brandy snaps will lose their crispness.

LET ME SHOW YOU . . .

My Brandy Snaps Video

ROSE AND CHOCOLATE MACARONS

Once you have mastered the art of macaron making, you'll be finding any excuse you can to magic some up. They are naturally gluten free, keep well, make marvellous gifts and while perfect on their own can also be used to enhance a celebration cake or dessert.

100g (3½oz) ground almonds
100g (3½oz) icing sugar
2 × 40g (1½oz) egg whites (about 3 egg whites)
100g (3½oz) caster sugar
40ml (1¼fl oz) water

FOR ROSE AND CHOCOLATE
½ tsp rose water
pink food colour gel

For filling and decoration
100ml (3½fl oz) double cream
100g (3½oz) dark chocolate, broken into pieces
30g (1oz) dark chocolate, melted, for decorating (optional)

FOR MOCHA
3 tsp instant espresso powder
1 tsp coffee extract

For filling and decoration
    100ml (3½fl oz) double cream
    100g (3½oz) dark chocolate

FOR LEMON
    ¼ tsp lemon extract
    yellow food colour gel

For filling and decoration
    100g (3½oz) white chocolate, broken into pieces
    50g (1¾oz) lemon curd

Equipment: food processor, sugar thermometer, hand-held electric whisk, 2 piping bags fitted with 5mm–1cm (¼–½ inch) plain nozzles 2 baking sheets lined with reusable baking parchment

Mark circles on your parchment as a guide for the macarons if you wish.

Blitz the ground almonds and icing sugar in a food processor to break down any lumps in the almonds and sugar (this will help ensure your finished macarons are smooth and shiny). Sift into a bowl. Add 1 × 40g (1½oz) of egg white and stir until everything comes together.

Add the rose water and food colour (or colour and flavour of choice). The colour needs to be quite deep as it will be made paler when the meringue is added, so don't be afraid to go dark.

Set this bowl aside and make the meringue. Dissolve the caster sugar in the water in a saucepan and once the mixture is clear increase the heat, bring to the boil and allow the temperature to reach 119 °C (don't stir).

While the syrup is heating, whisk the other 40g (1½oz) egg white to soft peaks in a clean, dry bowl with a hand-held electric whisk then, when the sugar has reached temperature, pour it into the beaten whites in a slow steady stream continuously whisking. Continue whisking until the mixture has cooled and when you pop a finger in it, it feels neither warm or cold.

Using a spatula, incorporate about a third of the meringue into the almond paste (to loosen it) then gently incorporate the rest. This is the most important step – fold carefully and thoroughly to make sure all the colour is evenly spread but don't beat so quickly or fiercely that the mixture becomes thin and runny: you want to avoid destroying the air bubbles in the meringue mix. If this happens you may as well start again. The mixture should be quite thick.

Spoon the macaron mix into a piping bag fitted with a plain nozzle then pipe even rounds, each about the size of a coin, onto your parchment-lined baking sheets. As it is piped, the macaron mix will leave a little nipple or point as the nozzle is lifted away. This is exactly right – when you look again you will see the circle has settled, the nipple has disappeared, and the finish is smooth and shiny. The macarons now need to dry for 30 minutes. If the environment is humid, I find placing them in the oven with just the fan on works well (just remove them before you heat the oven for baking).

After 30 minutes, test to check whether your macarons have skinned over: gently touch them and if the mixture doesn't stick to your finger you are ready to bake. If the mix is still sticky leave it for 15–20 minutes longer.

Preheat the oven to 140°C/120°C (fan)/275°F/gas 1. Bake the macarons in the oven for 18–24 minutes (I bake each tray separately, one at a time) until risen – while they are still in the oven, try lifting one from the sheet. If they are smooth and dry underneath then they are baked through, if the underneath is still soft and wet, bake for a further 10 minutes.

Take the sheet of macarons out of the oven and put the sheet on a dampened cloth on your work surface – this will make it easier to remove the shells. If your macarons crack on the top, then your oven is too hot so reduce the temperature a little before baking the next batch. The perfect macaron shell is smooth on the surface, has a little ruffle skirt around the bottom and a solid smooth base.

When all the macarons are baked, make the rose and chocolate (or mocha) filling. Bring the cream to the boil in a small saucepan, then pour it over the broken chocolate in a heatproof bowl. Stir until the chocolate melts, leave to cool and thicken, then place in a piping bag. The ganache needs to have cooled to the consistency of buttercream before filling the shells. Once filled, decorate them with a little melted chocolate piped over the shells if you like.

For the lemon filling, simply melt the white chocolate in a small non-metal bowl in the microwave in 15-second bursts then stir through the lemon curd. Leave until completely cold and thick then fill the shells as above.

LET ME SHOW YOU . . .

My Macarons Video

BABY CHERRY, CHOCOLATE AND ALMOND BISCOTTI

MAKES: 30 PIECES

These crunchy, twice-baked Italian biscuits are delicious and just happen to be fat free. I often make several batches at Christmas time, wrap them in gift bags and give them as presents. They keep for 2–3 weeks in an airtight tin.

1 egg
75g (2½oz) caster sugar
125g (4¼oz) plain flour, plus extra for dusting
½ tsp baking powder
50g (1¾oz) morello glacé cherries, washed, dried and
    quartered
1 tsp almond extract
75g (2½oz) flaked almonds, lightly toasted and roughly
    chopped
50g (1¾oz) dark chocolate, roughly chopped, or choc chips

Equipment: hand-held electric whisk, baking sheet lined with reusable baking parchment

Preheat the oven to 200°C/180°C (fan)/400°F/gas 6.

Whisk the egg and sugar in a mixing bowl with a hand-held electric whisk until thick and creamy – when you lift the whisk from the mixture it should leave a trail (this is ribbon stage).

Sift the flour and baking powder into the egg and sugar mix and fold in briefly, then add the cherries, almond extract, almonds and chocolate. You will have a ball of fairly sticky dough.

Turn the dough onto a floured work surface and simply form it into ball – don't be tempted to knead the dough – then divide in half. Shape each half into a sausage shape about 25cm (10 inches) long and about 5cm (2 inches) wide. Transfer the sausage-shaped pieces of dough to the lined baking sheet and bake in the oven for 15–18 minutes. The bake will be lightly coloured, slightly risen and firm to the touch.

Remove the baked dough from the oven and leave for 5 minutes, then use a serrated bread knife to cut each roll of dough into slices about 1cm (½ inch) thick (about 15 slices from each piece of baked dough). Place the slices back onto the baking sheet and bake in the oven for 4 minutes. Take them out, turn them over and pop back in the oven again for a further 3 minutes.

Remove from the oven and leave to cool on the baking sheet.

LET ME SHOW YOU . . .

My Biscotti Video

HOBNOBS

If you like Hobnobs then you will love these. My recipe is a cross between a biscuit and a cookie, crunchy on the outside but squidgy on the inside. I often double up the quantities and bake them on 4 baking sheets.

pinch of salt
¼ tsp bicarbonate of soda
75g (2½oz) plain flour
60g (2¼oz) mixed nuts, finely chopped (or nuts of choice)
90g (3oz) butter
½ tsp ground cinnamon
60g (2¼oz) soft dark brown sugar
40g (1½oz) granulated sugar
½ tsp vanilla extract
1 egg, lightly beaten
125g (4¼oz) porridge oats or medium oatmeal

Equipment: food processor (optional), 2 baking sheets lined with reusable baking parchment

In a small bowl mix together the salt, bicarbonate of soda and plain flour. Set aside.

Place a small frying pan over a medium heat, then add the chopped nuts and dry toast, swirling the nuts around so that they toast evenly. Once they are golden brown, turn them out onto a cold plate. In the same frying pan melt the butter then cook it until it starts to become golden and smells nutty, but don't allow it to burn. Pour it into a large clean heatproof bowl, capturing all the cooked solids from the butter – that's where the flavour is.

If you have a food processor you may want to blitz your porridge oats with the toasted nuts before making the biscuits mix – I think it makes a better biscuit.

Add the cinnamon and sugars to the melted butter and mix well, then add the vanilla and the beaten egg followed by the flour, oats and nuts. Stir together until well combined. I often pop the bowl into the fridge for 30 minutes or so, so the dough firms up a little.

Divide the mixture into 18–20 even pieces, taking a large spoonful of mixture and forming it into a ball with your hands for each one. Place each piece onto lined baking sheets. They spread a little during baking, so I allow 9 per baking sheet. Use a damp cold hand to flatten each ball of dough. Each disc needs to be about 5cm (2 inches) in diameter.

Pop the sheets into the fridge and leave while you heat your oven to 210°C/190°C (fan)/425°F/gas 7.

Bake the biscuits in the oven for 8–10 minutes until they are deep golden brown around the edges, then remove and leave to cool slightly before transferring to a cooling rack.

These cookies will keep for up to a week in an airtight tin.

LET ME SHOW YOU . . .

My Hobnobs Video

RYE AND FENNEL THINS

MAKES: 36–40 THINS

These little oatcakes – short and light, with a hint of fennel – are truly delicious and you may remember seeing a version of these on *Bake Off!* I have a friend, a real cheese addict, who always raves over the flavour pairing of this oatcake with her favourite cheese.

2 heaped tsp fennel seeds, crushed with pestle and mortar
    or blitzed in a spice grinder
60g (2¼oz) oat bran
140g (5oz) rye flour
140g (5oz) plain flour
1 tbsp caster sugar
1½ tsp baking powder
¾ tsp sea salt
1 tsp celery salt
½ tsp chilli powder
160g (5½oz) butter, diced, at room temperature
75ml (2½fl oz) milk, to bind

Equipment: 3 baking sheets lined with reusable baking parchment, 6cm (2½ inch) round biscuit cutter

Combine all the dry ingredients in a large mixing bowl then rub in the butter with your fingertips until the mixture resembles breadcrumbs. Add the milk to help the mix bind together to make a fairly stiff dough.

Roll out the dough between two sheets of plastic to a thickness of 3mm (⅛ inch). Slide the dough onto a baking sheet and chill in the fridge for 30 minutes.

Remove from the fridge, peel the top sheet of plastic away, then use a 6cm (2½ inch) plain cutter to cut out 36–40 rounds and place on 3 lined baking sheets. You will have to re-roll the trimmings to get 40 thins. Prick each biscuit with a fork or skewer and chill for 15 minutes or so while you preheat the oven to 210°C/190°C (fan)/425°F/gas 7.

Bake each sheet of biscuits one at a time for 8–10 minutes until the edges are just beginning to brown. Remove from the oven and place on a cooling rack.

The thins will keep for up to 10 days in an airtight tin.

LET ME SHOW YOU . . .

My Rye and Fennel Thins Video

LEMON AND CARAWAY SCONES

MAKES: 6 SCONES

A well-made scone is light, springy and delicious, and these scones, flavoured conservatively with lemon and caraway seed, are sublime. My inspiration for this recipe came from the lemon and caraway seed cake my grandmother used to make. When jam and cream are added – this is Cream Tea at its very best.

Scones are best served fresh and eaten the same day they're baked. The recipe below therefore is for just six scones – you need to eat them all in one sitting. This recipe is low in fat and sugar so don't be afraid to apply plenty of clotted cream and jam!

1 tsp caraway seeds
grated zest and juice of 1 lemon
130ml (4½fl oz) whole milk
225g (8oz) self-raising flour, plus extra for dusting
45g (1½oz) butter, at room temperature
35g (1¼oz) caster sugar
½ tsp vanilla extract

Equipment: baking sheet lined with reusable baking parchment, 7cm (2¾ inch) round fluted biscuit cutter

I always make scones by hand: the secrets of success with scone baking is make sure the mix isn't too dry, avoid over-handling the dough, and ensure the oven is very hot.

Heat a dry frying pan over a medium heat, add the caraway seeds and toast gently for a minute or two just to release their nutty, fragrant flavour. Don't burn them or they will be bitter.

Grate the zest from the lemon into a medium mixing bowl.

Pour the milk into a small jug or glass then squeeze the lemon juice into it (the lemon should yield about 20ml/1⅓ tablespoons) and set aside to thicken and curdle.

Place the self-raising flour into the bowl containing the zest then add the butter and use your fingertips to rub the mix together until it resembles breadcrumbs. Stir in the sugar and toasted seeds. Add the vanilla extract to the milk mixture then add enough of the milk to bind the dough together (keep some back to brush the tops of your scones). I use a metal knife initially, then my hands. The dough needs to be just sticky: not so wet that you can't handle it and not so dry that it crumbles and doesn't hold together.

Turn the dough out onto a lightly floured work surface then smooth out using a rolling pin or simply the palm of your hand. The dough needs to be quite thick – about 2.5cm (1 inch).

Using a 7cm (2¾ inch) cutter dipped in flour to prevent the dough sticking, cut out six scones. When cutting out scones don't be tempted to twist your cutter. A simple straight up and down will give them an even rise. You will need to reuse the trimmings.

Place your scones on a lined baking sheet then pop them into the fridge and preheat the oven to 240°C/220°C (fan)/475°F/ gas 9.

When your oven has reached temperature, take your scones from the fridge and brush a little of the leftover milk mix on the tops. Avoid letting any run down the sides as this will impede the rising. Pop straight into the hot oven and bake for 10–12 minutes until well risen and golden. Do not overbake them – the base of your scone should be golden brown, not dark brown or black!

Leave to cool on a cooling rack and serve the same day.

LET ME SHOW YOU . . .

My Lemon and Caraway Scones Video

CHERRY BAKEWELL SCONES WITH HOMEMADE CLOTTED CREAM

MAKES: 8 SCONES

This is one of the quickest bakes and one of the most delicious. I am always playing around with flavours and ingredients and these Cherry Bakewell Scones are perfect spread with jam and topped with a blob of homemade clotted cream!

FOR THE CLOTTED CREAM
   300ml (10fl oz) double cream

FOR THE SCONES
   50g (1¾oz) morello glacé cherries
   225g (8oz) self-raising flour, plus extra for dusting
   1 tsp baking powder
   50g (1¾oz) butter, diced, at room temperature
   35g (1¼oz) caster sugar
   1 egg, beaten with 6 tbsp leftover clotted cream liquid (or milk)
   1 tsp almond extract

Equipment: medium gratin dish for the clotted cream, baking sheet lined with reusable baking parchment for the scones, 5cm (2 inch) biscuit cutter

You will need to start the clotted cream the day before you bake the scones. Simply pour the cream into a shallow ovenproof dish (I use a medium gratin dish) and bake in the oven at 50°C (non-fan)/120°F for 12 hours. I cook mine overnight.

The next morning, remove the cream from the oven and let it cool uncovered at room temperature. When cool, cover and pop into the fridge for at least 6 hours.

Remove the cream from the fridge and you will find that the cream has formed a very thick skin. Carefully peel off this skin and transfer to a clean bowl. Keep the residual thin liquid as this will be used to make the scones. Using a fork, beat the skin so that everything is well combined then cover and chill until ready to use. The cream will keep for up to 1 week in the fridge.

When you're ready to make the scones, rinse the cherries in cold water to remove the sticky glaze, dry them, then chop them to about the size of a raisin. Pop the cherries into a small bowl then add 1 tablespoon of the flour to be used to make the scones. Toss them around to coat, then set aside (this flour coating prevents the cherries sticking together in the mix and allows them to be evenly distributed).

Sift the flour and baking powder into a roomy mixing bowl then rub in the butter with your fingertips until the mixture resembles breadcrumbs. Add the sugar and prepped cherries and stir everything through with a metal knife.

In a small jug mix together the egg, reserved clotted cream liquid (or milk) and almond extract. Pour some of the liquid into the dry mix and start to bring the mixture together to a fairly sticky dough. Finish with your hands. You will not need all of the liquid – keep some back to brush the tops of your scones. A scone dough does not like to be handled much, so don't over-knead.

Turn the dough out onto a lightly floured work surface then smooth out using a rolling pin or simply the palm of your hand. The dough needs to be quite thick – about 2.5cm (1 inch).

Using a 5cm (2 inch) cutter dipped in flour to prevent the dough sticking, cut out eight scones and place on a lined baking sheet. Re-roll the trimmings as necessary and don't twist the cutter – just press straight down and straight back up. You will get a better rise.

Place your scones on a lined baking sheet then pop them into the fridge and preheat the oven to 240°C/220°C (fan)/475°F/ gas 9.

When your oven has reached temperature, take your scones from the fridge, brush the tops with the leftover egg mix then bake in the oven for 10–12 minutes until well risen and golden.

Remove from the oven and leave to cool on a cooling rack. Serve the same day, with your homemade clotted cream.

LET ME SHOW YOU . . .

My Clotted Cream Video

APPLE AND CINNAMON SCONES

MAKES: 8 SCONES

I love these little scones and, like any scone, they can be made in a jiffy. My addition of apple and cinnamon gives them an interesting twist. They can be topped with butter and jam, of course, but I also enjoy them with a slice of cheese.

225g (8oz) self-raising flour, plus extra for dusting
1 tsp baking powder
50g (1¾oz) butter, diced, at room temperature
25g (1oz) dried apple, cut into pieces the size of a currant
½ tsp ground cinnamon
35g (1¼oz) caster sugar
3 tbsp plain yoghurt
1 egg
3 tbsp milk

Equipment: baking sheet lined with reusable baking parchment, 5cm (2 inch) fluted pastry cutter

|||||||||||||||||||||||||||||||||||||||||||||||||||||||||||||||||||||||||||||||||||||||||||||||||||||||||

Dust the cutter with flour between cutting each
scone then they will release easily.

|||||||||||||||||||||||||||||||||||||||||||||||||||||||||||||||||||||||||||||||||||||||||||||||||||||||||

Sift the flour into a bowl with the baking powder then rub in the butter using your fingertips until the mixture resembles breadcrumbs. Dust the dried apple with the cinnamon then stir it into the flour and butter mix with the sugar, using a metal knife. Stir in the yoghurt then beat the egg and milk together and add enough of it to the mix to form a reasonably wet dough (keeping some back for brushing). The dough needs to be more sticky than pastry but not so sticky that you need lots of flour to work with it!

Handling the dough as little as possible, turn the dough out onto a lightly floured work surface then smooth out using a rolling pin or simply the palm of your hand to a thickness of about 1.5cm (½ inch). Cut out eight scones with a 5cm (2 inch) fluted cutter (dipped in flour to prevent the dough sticking). When cutting out scones don't be tempted to twist your cutter. A simple straight up and down will give them an even rise. You will need to reuse the trimmings.

Place your scones on a lined baking sheet then pop them into the fridge and preheat the oven to 240°C/220°C (fan)/ 475°F/gas 9.

When your oven has reached temperature, take your scones from the fridge and if you have any milk mix left, give them a little brush with the egg and milk mix just on the tops. Bake in the oven for 10–12 minutes until well risen and golden.

Leave to cool on a cooling rack and serve the same day.

LET ME SHOW YOU . . .

My Apple and Cinnamon
Scones Video

CHEESE SCONES

There are times when a slice of cake just will not do, and a savoury bite is required in order to satisfy my cravings. This little cheese scone is packed full of flavour and I have added caraway seed which lifts the deliciousness!

- 125g (4¼oz) self-raising flour, plus extra for dusting
- 25g (1oz) rye flour (if you don't have this, use all self-raising)
- ½ tsp baking powder
- ¼ tsp salt
- 25g (1oz) butter, at room temperature
- 75g (2½oz) strong Cheddar cheese, finely grated
- 1 tsp caraway seeds (optional)
- 1 egg
- 2–3 tbsp whole milk
- 1 tsp English mustard

Equipment: 6cm (2½ inch) cutter, baking sheet lined with reusable baking parchment

---

How to store grated cheese
If using bags of ready grated cheese, take what you need for the recipe, reseal the bag and pop into the freezer. Then simply use what you need straight from the freezer next time you need it. This will keep for at least 3 months.

Sift the flours, baking powder and salt together into a roomy mixing bowl then add the butter and rub the mixture together with your fingertips until it resembles breadcrumbs. Add most of the cheese (keep back 1 large tablespoon to sprinkle over the scones before baking) and the caraway seeds (if using) and stir to combine using a metal knife.

Make a well in the centre then, in a cup or small jug, mix together the egg, milk and mustard. Pour this into the well in the mixture and bring together using the knife, then use your hand to form the dough into a soft, fairly moist ball.

Transfer to a lightly floured work surface and roll out lightly to a thickness of 2cm (¾ inch). Use a 6cm (2½ inch) cutter to cut out 6 scones, re-rolling and cutting until all the dough is used. Transfer to a baking sheet then pop them into the fridge and preheat the oven to 230°C/210°C (fan)/450°F/gas 8.

When your oven has reached temperature, take your scones from the fridge, brush with a little milk and scatter over the remaining grated cheese. Pop straight into the hot oven and bake for 15–18 minutes until the scones are risen, dark golden and smelling amazing!

Remove from the oven and leave to cool on a cooling rack. They are best eaten the same day.

LET ME SHOW YOU . . .

My Cheese Scones Video

BREAD

'Nancy, remember you need a light hand for pastry yet a heavy hand for bread' – My nan's words still echo in my ears.

I started making bread regularly about 20 years ago when I bought a bread-making machine. I thought it was fantastic. I put all the ingredients in the pan, switched it on and in 5 hours I had a loaf. I was unsure of the process but knew I was in control of every ingredient. After a few years, the machine got tired, the paddle stopped working and the loaves it produced were unrisen. I had a dilemma – do I buy another machine, or do I learn to make bread myself?

I have made many hard brick-like loaves, bread that was edible the day of baking but so inedible the next that even the chickens ran away when I threw chunks for them. Bread, for me, was the most difficult baking discipline to get right and it was because I didn't understand the importance of kneading, the right amount of liquid to use and the difference between under- and over-proving.

Home-made bread gives such pleasure to the senses! The smell of bread straight out of the oven is probably one of the most comforting aromas in the kitchen, not to mention the taste and feel of a soft fresh loaf. Interestingly, whenever the grandchildren visit, they always ask me for bread rather than cake or sweets.

When I was a child, many people made their own bread and there were plenty of independent bakers in most towns who served the population with fresh bread every day. This is still very much the case in France, where the daily baguette is actually subsidised and price fixed by the government so that it is still available to everyone.

Bread making first became 'automated' back in the 1960s and scientists discovered a new way of producing our daily loaf which became known as the Chorleywood method. We are now all too familiar with the white sliced loaf. This new bread replaced the home-baked loaf in many homes because it was softer, cheaper, uniform in size and lasted twice as long as home-made bread. It was a new innovation and Britain's bread was the cheapest in the world. Unfortunately, this put many small bakeries out of business as large factories popped up to get on with churning out the nation's bread at a fast, cheap, uniform pace.

The high amounts of yeast, enzymes and chemicals being used to speed up the making of mass-produced loaves could be a contributing factor in such breads being difficult for some people to digest, and might explain why more and more people are switching to a gluten-free diet. Let us examine the ingredients that go into our homemade loaf of bread.

Did you know that about a million loaves of bread bought in Britain are thrown away every year?

BREAD INGREDIENTS

FLOUR

My bread recipes call for strong white flour, but what does 'strong' mean? The strength is not referring to the flavour or smell – it is the amount of protein (gluten) that it contains. How 'strong' a flour is will depend on the variety of wheat and the climate in which it was grown. For example, wheats grown in extreme climates, like that in Canada, produce flour with a higher gluten content, which means the dough will expand and stretch better: strong flour is perfect for bread making.

YEAST

The wonder of yeast. It is mysterious and magical, natural and, for me, the one living thing above any other that contains the most enthusiasm!

Yeast is available in three forms: fresh, dried and granular, or dried and powdered in handy 7g (¼oz) sachets or small tins. I find powdered yeast the most convenient as it can be sprinkled straight onto the flour, but if you can get hold of fresh yeast then simply double up the yeast quantity quoted in the recipe. Fresh yeast should be moist and firm, with a pleasant smell. If it is dry and crumbly with an acidic unpleasant aroma, then it is probably stale and will not work well. Fresh yeast will keep in the fridge for about a week. If you buy fresh yeast, weigh it into portions (about 20g/¾oz) then wrap and freeze. It will keep in the freezer for up to 3 months.

LIQUID

Water is the most common liquid used in basic bread making but when making enriched dough a mixture of egg, milk and water is used. Many recipes call for tepid or warm water but if I'm making bread in a machine, I use room-temperature water as I find the machine's work and agitation warms things up perfectly. When bread-making by hand, I use tepid water. Half water and half milk will result in a softer loaf (see the 'Fat' paragraph below).

SALT

Salt is required for taste, but salt and yeast are arch enemies. Sprinkle salt directly onto the yeast and you could kill it. Measure salt carefully. I always use fine sea salt and add it after all the other ingredients.

SUGAR

Sugar is not essential as an ingredient but 1 tablespoon of honey, brown sugar (for wholemeal bread) or white sugar can add flavour and improve the keeping quality of your loaf.

FAT

I often add a knob of butter or 1 tablespoon of oil, particularly sesame oil, to my bread for extra flavour. Fat helps the bread keep fresh for longer but too much again will retard the yeast.

DOUGH ENHANCERS

Potato starch

Yeast and potato starch are great pals and I routinely add 1 tablespoon of potato starch (I bought a bag online) with my yeast when making bread. The potato starch helps the yeast to be more active. Potato starch creates an outer casing on the gluten bubble, preventing it from popping easily. I read in an old cookery book that women used to save their potato boiling water for bread making for this very reason. I save potato water from time to time; it does make a difference to your finished loaf. Remember not to salt the cooking water.

Ground Ginger

Yeast loves ginger and ¼ teaspoon ground ginger added to your bread flour during mixing will enhance your dough and give the yeast a boost. Because you have used such a small amount there is no ginger taste.

Milk powder

When making an enriched dough for hot cross buns, Chelsea buns and croissants, milk, eggs and sugar are added. When you make your routine loaf of bread try adding 1 tablespoon of dry milk powder to the flour. The dry milk produces a softer loaf, helps the crust to brown and adds flavour.

HOW A LOAF OF BREAD IS MADE

Make your dough easier to handle: spray a little oil on your hands and rub them together as you would with hand cream. Your dough will not stick to your hands.

KNEADING

Once the bread ingredients have come together into a shaggy dough, the kneading starts. Many recipes will suggest kneading for about 10 minutes until the dough is smooth. That, for me, is always an understatement. I do not think it is possible to over-knead by hand, and 10 minutes for someone new to baking seems an awfully long time. Pushing and pulling this sticky mess seems not really worth the effort, and the temptation always is to add more flour. My advice is to keep it going, refrain from adding more flour and eventually that dough will start to leave you alone. It will become as smooth and soft as the finest cotton pillow. In the past, I would cut short this process and add more flour to help make it workable – the dough still rose but the finished bread was hard.

If you have a tabletop (stand) mixer fitted with a dough hook, then this process is super easy. If your dough has formed a ball and is simply moving around the bowl in a solid lump, then add more water. The dough hook needs to be pulling and stretching at that dough, flexing that gluten. The dough needs to be thick and sticky and then after about 10 minutes in the machine it will turn to a stretchy, soft smooth mass.

RISING AND SHAPING

Your beautifully smooth, soft dough now needs a warm place to rise. The top of a radiator is too hot. Some ovens have a bread-proving setting which is probably around 36°C (about 96°F) but if like me you don't have that facility then just turn on the oven light in your electric oven. This will generate just enough heat to rise your dough perfectly. Grease your bowl with a spray of oil (otherwise the dough will stick) then add the dough and cover with a shower cap (I have been using the same shower cap for six months and it is still going strong). I stopped using cling film on 1 January 2019!

Many recipes will suggest leaving your dough for about 1 hour, or until doubled in size. The time taken to rise will depend on temperature and humidity but 1–1½ hours is just right.

|||||||||||||||||||||||||||||||||||||||||||||||||||||||||||||||||||||||||||||||||||||||||||||||||||||||||||||||||||||||||

Slow down your bread making
If your breadmaking is interrupted, the rising of the dough can be slowed down by popping it into the fridge. You can go out for several hours and your dough will come to no harm. Dough can even be mixed the night before and popped into the fridge overnight then continue the next morning (chilled dough will need some time to return to room temperature and then it will continue its rise).

|||||||||||||||||||||||||||||||||||||||||||||||||||||||||||||||||||||||||||||||||||||||||||||||||||||||||||||||||||||||||

Once your dough has risen until it has almost doubled in size then it is time to 'knock it back'. I always consider this a harsh term, but it is necessary to ensure your finished loaf has an even rise (no huge air bubbles inside). I treat my risen dough with respect and carefully ease it out of the greased bowl onto a lightly floured surface. I then push out any bubbles of gas by folding it in on itself over and over again, tightening the dough as I go. The dough returns almost to its pre-risen size and begins to feel tight and firm rather than lying flat and limp as it did when it came out of the bowl.

You can now decide how your dough will be shaped. It can be transferred to tins (greased or brushed with my lining paste, see page 12), shaped into a bloomer, formed into rolls or a plait, or placed into a ridged bread basket – the possibilities are endless.

How to make a shiny glaze on a loaf

I have childhood memories of a huge cone-shaped earthenware glazed bowl which sat by the fire containing bread dough. It was covered in a damp tea towel (no plastic or cling film then) undergoing its first rise. My grandmother would shape it into two 450g (1lb) loaf tins then it would be proved, baked and glazed by simply using a saved butter paper wrapper while it was still piping hot – I still use this butter paper method now.

Make enough for 2 loaves

I carry on our family tradition and regularly bake a tinned loaf. When I prepare the dough, I make enough for two loaves: one I bake straight away, the second loaf I pop into the freezer risen, knocked down and shaped and placed in the tin but unproved, so that I always have a loaf handy. When I want to bake it, I take my frozen dough, in its tin, pop it into the oven with just the light on (I cover the frozen dough with a shower cap) and following a long five-hour thaw and prove, I remove the shower cap, preheat the oven to 240°C/220°C (fan)/475°F/gas 9 and bake (see page 79).

PROVING

Your dough now needs to prove. Many recipes will state 30 minutes, some just say, 'until the dough has risen'. I have spent so many years perfecting proving and I think 30 minutes is never long enough. Placing your shaped loaf in the oven with just the light on will generate sufficient heat (creates a temperature of 25°C/77°F to perfectly rise your dough, taking 50 minutes exactly).

How do you know whether your loaf is under-proved, over-proved or just right? If the weather or your kitchen are warm, then you can prove your bread at room temperature, but it will need to be covered so that it doesn't dry out. A shower cap is perfect for covering your dough. Alternatively, a slightly damp piece of muslin will work perfectly. If doing the prove in the oven which is closed to the air, then covering your dough is not essential. I sometimes place my loaf in the microwave and keep the door shut – it keeps the air out and saves having to cover the bread.

An under-proved loaf will burst its crust during baking – it will taste fine but the shape will be affected. A previously perfect-looking bloomer could come out of the oven bearing a crack at one side showing escaped baked dough or a loaf baked in a tin will have its roof blown off to one side and dislodged as dough has tried to escape from the side.

An over-proved loaf will not rise during baking. Instead of being soft and pillowed it will be quite hard and exactly the same size as it was when it went into the oven. The yeast did its work before it went into the oven and has nothing left to give.

After the prove, if you press the dough and your finger leaves a mark and the dough looks deflated – a little like a balloon that is starting to lose its air – it is probably over-proved and rather than bake it and risk failure, reshape it again and wait for it to rise up once more. Your finished bread will not be as fine as if this had not happened, but you will have a risen loaf.

The perfectly proved dough will, after 50 minutes, feel firm yet soft to the touch. The dough will still be smooth and have some resistance when you press it gently with the finger. I like to spray it with a fine water spray then put it straight into a very hot oven (240°C/220°C (fan)/475°F/gas 9).

It is better to over-bake than under-bake bread. An under-baked loaf will be pale and dense inside, an overbaked loaf of bread will have a much darker crust (which I love) but the crumb inside will be a perfect consistency.

Once out of the oven, place your bread on a cooling rack. Leaving bread to cool in a tin or on a flat surface will result in steam getting trapped and the base will be wet and soggy.

Rubbing your newly baked bread while still hot with a butter paper will leave a long-lasting shiny glaze.

LET ME SHOW YOU . . .

My Bread Finish Video

Increase the humidity in your oven when making bread
Bread loves a steamy environment and it results in a better rise during baking – many modern ovens have steam injection feature for this very reason. If, like me, you have an old oven or an Aga then you can still create a steamy environment for your bread. If your oven is electric, have a small tin at the bottom of the oven (mine is a miniature loaf tin) to preheat with the oven. When you put the bread in to bake, drop an ice cube into that tiny tin. If you bake with an Aga, then as the bread slides onto the base of the top oven throw an ice cube to the back of the oven at the same time.

LET ME SHOW YOU . . .

My Bread Enhancer Video

SOFT WHITE BREAD

MAKES: 1 BLOOMER OR 3 X 450G (1LB) TIN LOAVES

A loaf of white bread fresh from the oven – the smell, the taste, the sight, the touch and the sound as the bread crackles as it cools – delights all of the senses. Once you have made your own bread using a handful of simple ingredients, you will realize that the ultra-processed, mass-produced equivalents will never again hit the spot.

500g (1lb 2oz) strong white flour, plus extra for dusting
7g (¼oz) salt
7g (¼oz) dried yeast
15g (½oz) butter or lard, at room temperature
150ml (5fl oz) milk, at room temperature
150–170ml (5–5¾fl oz) tepid water spray oil for greasing

Equipment: tabletop (stand) mixer (optional), lightly greased baking sheet or 3 x 450g (1lb) loaf tins (optional)

If you are mixing your dough by hand, put the flour, salt, yeast and fat in a roomy mixing bowl then add the milk and 130ml (4½fl oz) of the water and mix to a rough dough. The dough will be quite dry so add the rest of the water little by little until you have a sticky, stretchy dough. Knead for at least 10 minutes until it becomes stretchy, smooth and non sticky.

If you are using a tabletop (stand) mixer, fit it with a dough hook and place the yeast into the bottom of the bowl then add the flour, salt, fat and finally the milk and water. Add 280ml (9½fl oz) of the liquid then mix on the lowest speed for 5–6 minutes until the dough forms a ball. Add the rest of the liquid a little at a time. The dough ball will bang around in the mixer in the newly added liquid which makes a much better job of mixing than adding all the liquid at the start. Continue to knead the bread dough, increasing the speed slightly and mix until the dough leaves the sides of the bowl, the bowl is clean and the dough smooth and stretchy – avoid adding extra flour. This kneading will take about 10 minutes.

Use spray oil to grease a bowl, transfer the dough into the bowl, cover with a shower cap and leave in a warm place until doubled in size. This usually takes 1–1½ hours.

When the dough has risen, turn it out onto a lightly floured surface, knock it back gently, eliminating any air bubbles, then shape into a bloomer and transfer to a lightly greased baking sheet. To shape the loaf, I fold the dough in on itself to form a ball then turn it upside down and twist so that the dough tightens before turning it upside down so that the 'key' of turned dough is uppermost before firmly rolling the dough into a thick sausage 'bloomer' shape. The tightening of the dough in this way will encourage it to prove upwards rather than outwards and flat, resulting in a better shape of loaf.

Leave to prove in a warm place for 50 minutes until the loaf has doubled in size. Shortly before the end of the proving period, preheat the oven to 240°C/220°C (fan)/475°F/gas 9.

Spray with a fine mist of cold water and a dusting of flour, neatly slash with a sharp knife then bake in the oven for 30 minutes until dark golden brown.

Transfer to a cooling rack and leave to cool completely before slicing.

LET ME SHOW YOU . . .

My Soft White Bread Video

CRUSTY-TOPPED BLOOMER

MAKES: 1 TIGER LOAF OR 12 INDIVIDUAL ROLLS

This simple white bloomer loaf has a tasty, crunchy top. Once you have tried it, I assure you, you will be hooked. A dusting of bread flour on the shaped dough, followed by a quick slash with a very sharp knife, will result in a beautiful artisan-looking finished bake.

FOR THE DOUGH
- 500g (1lb 2oz) strong white bread flour, plus extra for dusting
- 7g (¼oz) salt
- 7g (¼oz) dried yeast
- 1 tbsp rapeseed oil
- 300–320ml (10–11fl oz) tepid water
- spray oil for greasing

FOR THE CRUNCHY TOP
- 50g (1¾oz) rice flour
- 4g dried yeast
- 1 tsp sugar
- 1 tbsp toasted sesame oil
- about 2 tbsp water

Equipment: tabletop (stand) mixer (optional), 1 or 2 lightly greased baking sheets

If you are new to bread baking, then make just the
bloomer without the topping, proving it for 50 minutes
in the oven with the light on.

If you are mixing your dough by hand, place the flour,
salt, yeast and oil in a roomy mixing bowl then add 280ml
(9½fl oz) of the water and mix to a rough dough. If the dough
is very dry, add the rest of the water little by little until you
have a rough sticky dough. Knead the dough for at least 10
minutes until it becomes stretchy, smooth and non sticky.

If you are making the dough in a tabletop (stand) mixer, fit it
with a dough hook, place the yeast into the bottom of the
bowl first then add the flour, salt, oil and finally the water.
Add 280ml (9½fl oz) of the water then mix long enough for
the dough to form a ball then add the rest of the water a little
at a time. Continue to knead the bread dough for a further
10 minutes or so, on low speed, until smooth and stretchy –
avoid adding extra flour.

Use spray oil to grease a bowl, transfer the dough into the
bowl, cover with a shower cap then leave in a warm place until
doubled in size.

While the dough is rising, make the topping. Put all the
ingredients in a small bowl, adding enough water to mix into
a thick paste about the consistency of whipped double cream.
Set aside.

When the dough has risen turn it out onto a lightly floured
surface, shape into a bloomer and transfer to a greased baking

sheet (or two sheets if making individual rolls). To shape the loaf, I fold the dough in on itself to form a ball then turn it upside down and twist so that the dough tightens before turning it upside down so that the 'key' of turned dough is uppermost before firmly rolling the dough into a thick sausage 'bloomer' shape. The tightening of the dough in this way will encourage it to prove upwards rather than outwards and flat, resulting in a better shape of loaf. To shape into rolls, divide the dough into 12 pieces – you may want to weigh the dough to ensure even sizes. Shape each piece of dough as with the bloomer above, turning the dough in on itself until a ball is formed and using a cupped hand to work the dough in circular motions until the dough is tightened and a perfect ball.

Spread a thick coat of topping paste over the shaped dough with your hand then add a generous sifting of flour.

Leave to prove for about 1¼ hours uncovered at room temperature (not in the oven with the light on as in other recipes). You will see that the paste top will start to crack as the dough expands. Shortly before the end of the proving period, preheat the oven to 240°C/220°C (fan)/475°F/gas 9.

Bake in the oven for 30–40 minutes until the top is crisp and brown. (If you're baking smaller rolls, bake for 25 minutes.)

LET ME SHOW YOU . . .

My Crusty-Topped Bloomer Video

CRUSTY DARK RYE AND FENNEL DINNER ROLLS

MAKES: 12 ROLLS

These dark coloured, delicately fennel-flavoured rolls have a slightly sour taste, crusty top and are superb! They will be well received at a meal with friends: for sandwiches, with soup or cheese. I make them often as they are so delicious.

FOR THE DOUGH

- 300g (10½oz) strong white bread flour, plus extra for dusting
- 200g (7oz) dark rye flour
- 10g (⅓oz) salt
- 7g (¼oz) dried yeast
- 1 tbsp black treacle
- 1 tbsp oil of choice
- 1 dessertspoon fennel seeds (I like to blitz the seeds to a powder in a grinder, but they can be left whole)
- 300–320ml (10–11fl oz) tepid water

FOR THE CRUST

- 60g (2¼oz) rice flour
- 1 tsp caster sugar
- 1 tsp dried yeast
- 1 tbsp toasted sesame oil
- about 2 tbsp water

Equipment: tabletop (stand) mixer (optional), 1 or 2 lightly greased baking sheets

Either by hand, or using a tabletop (stand) mixer fitted with the dough hook, combine the dough ingredients and add 300–320ml (10-11fl oz) water, enough to form a dough. Knead until the dough is smooth and elastic – this will take about 10 minutes in a machine or 15–20 minutes by hand. Grease a roomy mixing bowl, pop the dough into it then cover with a shower cap and put in a warm place to double in size. This will take about 1–1½ hours.

While the dough is rising, mix the crust ingredients. Simply mix all the ingredients in a small bowl with enough water to form a thick paste. Set aside.

When the bread has risen, turn it out of the bowl and divide it into 12 equal pieces – each one should be about 70g (2½oz). Shape the rolls and place on one or two baking sheets. To shape into rolls, shape each piece of dough as with the bloomer rolls on page 84, turning the dough in on itself until a ball is formed and using a cupped hand to work the dough in circular motions until the dough is tightened and a perfect ball.

Using your hands, gently cover each roll well with a layer of paste, then sift over a layer of white bread flour. Prove uncovered in a warm place for 1½ hours. During the prove, the tops will start to crack as they rise and look quite interesting.

Shortly before the end of the proving period, preheat the oven to 240°C/220°C (fan)/475°F/gas 9. Pop the bread in the hot oven and bake for 20 minutes until brown and crispy on the top.

LET ME SHOW YOU . . .

My Crusty Dark Rye
and Fennel Rolls Video

Storing bread

Bread left out, uncovered, will soon turn stale. I used to
store mine in a plastic bag until I made my own
beeswax bread bag. An airtight yet breathable wax bag
is just perfect for keeping your bread fresh.

WHOLESOME LOAF

MAKES: 1 LOAF

This incredibly tasty loaf has a real feel good factor about it. I like to give it a quick and easy butter glaze when it comes straight from the oven to enhance its rustic charm!

300g (10½oz) strong white bread flour, plus extra for dusting
100g (3½oz) dark rye flour
100g (3½oz) wholemeal bread flour
2 tbsp mixed seeds (pumpkin, sunflower, sesame, poppy)
10g (⅓oz) salt
7g (¼oz) dried yeast
1 tbsp black treacle
1 tbsp toasted sesame oil (or vegetable oil)
280–320ml (9½–11fl oz) tepid water
used butter paper, for the glaze

Equipment: tabletop (stand) mixer (optional), baking sheet lined with reusable baking parchment

Either by hand or using the dough hook of a tabletop (stand) mixer, combine all the ingredients then add 280–320ml (9½–11fl oz) water, enough to form a dough. Continue kneading until the dough is smooth and elastic – this will take about 10 minutes in a machine or 15–20 minutes by hand.

Grease a roomy mixing bowl and pop the dough into it then cover it with a shower cap or tea towel and allow to double in size in a warm place. This will take about 1–½ hours.

Take the risen dough from the bowl and reshape into a circle, twisting the dough so that it tightens more and more into itself. This way you will achieve a round loaf rather than a flat one. Place the dough ball on the lined baking sheet and leave to prove for 50 minutes.

Shortly before the end of the proving period, preheat the oven to 240°C/220°C (fan)/475°F/gas 9. Spray the dough with water then pop into the hot oven and bake for 30 minutes until well browned.

Remove the loaf from the oven and rub the surface with used butter paper – the glaze is amazing!

LET ME SHOW YOU . . .

My Wholesome Loaf Video

HOT CROSS BUNS

MAKES: 12 BUNS

I adore a fresh hot cross bun, eaten slightly warm with butter. Many recipes finish with a sticky glaze applied after baking while the buns are still hot. This for me can be messy, too sweet and then impossible to toast the next day without burning. My glaze is a slightly sweetened frothed egg white which is applied before baking and before the traditional crosses. The result is a dark, glossy, sweet glaze which isn't sticky to the touch.

FOR THE FRUIT MIXTURE
    75g (2½oz) sultanas or mixed dried fruit and peel
    1 tsp mixed spice
    grated zest and juice of 1 small orange

FOR THE DOUGH
    30g (1oz) butter, melted
    150ml (5fl oz) warm water
    50g (1¾oz) caster sugar
    100ml (3½fl oz) milk
    1 egg yolk (keep the white for the glaze)
    10g (⅓oz) dried yeast
    7g (¼oz) salt
    500g (1lb 2oz) strong white bread flour, plus extra for
        dusting

FOR THE GLAZE
   1 egg white
   1 tsp caster sugar

FOR THE CROSSES
   2 tbsp plain flour

Equipment: tabletop (stand) mixer (optional), piping bag fitted with a small icing (writing) nozzle, 2 lightly greased baking sheets

||||||||||||||||||||||||||||||||||||||||||||||||||||||||||||||||||||||||||||||||||||||||||||||||||||||||||||||||

Don't discard stale buns
Leftover hot cross buns make a fabulous Bread and Butter Pudding (see recipe on page 312)

||||||||||||||||||||||||||||||||||||||||||||||||||||||||||||||||||||||||||||||||||||||||||||||||||||||||||||||||

If you have time (and you remember), put the dried fruit, spice, orange zest and juice in a small bowl then cover and leave overnight (or minimum 2 hours) in a warm place. The fruit will absorb the flavours and the juice and the resulting taste is truly luscious! Rather than covering the bowl with cling film lay a plate over it.

Put the butter in a heatproof jug then pour over the measured warm water and add the sugar. Stir well until the sugar has dissolved, pour in the milk and add the egg yolk. Beat briefly with a fork then add the dried yeast. Stir to combine.

In the bowl of a tabletop (stand) mixer fitted with a dough hook place first the salt then the flour. Pour over the warm milk and egg mix then start your machine at its lowest setting and mix for 3–4 minutes or until the dough has started to come together but is scraggy. Add the fruit and keep the machine going until the dough comes together but is still quite sticky. Don't be tempted to add more flour. Mix for a further 5 minutes until the dough starts to leave the sides of the bowl and becomes smooth and elastic. You can make the dough by hand in a large mixing bowl instead if you don't have a tabletop (stand) mixer.

Tip the dough out onto a lightly floured surface and knead into a ball then place in a greased bowl, cover with in a shower cap and leave to rise in a warm place for 1–1½ hours until doubled in size.

Once risen turn the dough out onto a lightly floured work surface and divide into 12 equal pieces. I like to weigh the dough pieces as this produces uniform buns. 80g (2¾oz) per piece should be about right. Shape each piece of dough into a ball then space out on two lightly greased baking sheets – six per sheet.

Leave to prove for 40–50 minutes until doubled in size. I place my buns in a closed oven with just the electric light on. This provides an airtight environment with just sufficient heat to prove the bread.

After the proving time, carefully remove the buns ready for the glazing. Preheat the oven to 220°C/200°C (fan)/425°F/gas 7.

Beat the egg white and sugar for the glaze together in a bowl just until frothy, then brush over the risen buns very gently and carefully.

Add a little water to the plain flour for the crosses until it forms a paste with the consistency of thick cream, then pipe this over the glazed buns. Bake in the oven for 12–15 minutes until dark golden, glossy and simply delicious.

Remove from the oven and eat warm or cold. The next day they can be toasted without the fear of burning under the grill or in the toaster.

LET ME SHOW YOU . . .

My Hot Cross Buns Video

CHELSEA BUNS

Packed with flavour, these buns made with enriched dough are absolutely delicious. Give them a try – you will not be disappointed.

FOR THE FILLING

- 150g (5½oz) dried fruits – try cranberries, apricots, mixed peel, cherries
- 30ml (1fl oz) marsala (or sherry), for soaking the fruits
- 30g (1oz) chilled marzipan, grated
- 1 tsp mixed spice
- 8 green cardamom pods, split, seeds removed and crushed
- ¼ tsp ground mace
- 1 tsp ground cinnamon
- grated zest of 1 orange (reserve the fruit for the glaze)
- grated zest of 1 lemon (reserve the fruit for the glaze)

FOR THE DOUGH

- 125ml (4¼fl oz) warm milk
- 50g (1¾oz) caster sugar
- 10g (⅓oz) dried yeast
- 1 egg
- 50g (1¾oz) butter, at room temperature
- 500g (1lb 2oz) strong white bread flour, plus extra for dusting
- 10g (1⅓oz) salt
- 80–100ml (2¾–3½fl oz) warm water

FOR THE GLAZE
  juice of 1 orange
  juice of 1 lemon
  caster sugar, as needed

FOR THE DRIZZLE ICING
(OPTIONAL)
  3 tbsp icing sugar
  lemon juice, as needed

Equipment: tabletop (stand) mixer (optional), square 25 × 25cm
(10 × 10 inch) cake tin (5cm/2 inch deep) base and sides lined
with non-stick baking paper

Start the night before. Put the dried fruits in a bowl and pour
over the marsala. Leave to infuse at room temperature overnight. The next day, add all the other filling ingredients to the
bowl and mix well.

Make the dough in a tabletop (stand) mixer fitted with the dough
hook. Pour the warm milk into the bowl of the mixer and add the
sugar, yeast, egg and butter. Give everything a good stir with a fork
then add the flour and finally the salt. Start the machine and as the
mixture comes together gradually add the water (80ml/2¾fl oz to
start with) until you have a soft dough. Mix until the dough is
smooth, stretchy and glossy. (If you don't have a tabletop/stand mixer,
you can make the dough in a large mixing bowl by hand.) Then
transfer it to a greased bowl, cover with a shower cap and leave to
rise in a warm place for about 1 hour, until doubled in size.

Lightly dust a work surface with flour and turn out the risen
dough. Flatten it with your hands then roll it out with a rolling
pin until you have a rectangle about 35 × 25cm (14 × 10 inches).

Spread the filling mix over the rectangle then, starting at the
widest edge, roll the rectangle towards you, encasing the filling.
You will end up with a sausage – make sure the join is underneath.

Divide the sausage into 9 equal pieces then place cut side down in the cake tin lined with a piece of non-stick baking paper. Allow each bun space to expand.

Leave to prove in a warm place for about 40 minutes and preheat the oven to 220°C/200°C (fan)/425°F/gas 7.

When the buns have risen and are touching each other in the tin, transfer to the oven and bake for 25–30 minutes until golden.

While the buns are in the oven, mix the squeezed juices from the two fruits you zested for the filling with half their weight in sugar (i.e. if you have 100ml/3½fl oz juice, use 50g/1¾oz sugar). Place in a small pan, dissolve the sugar over a low heat and when the liquid is clear bring to the boil and reduce for about 5 minutes until you have a syrup.

When the buns are baked, remove them from the oven and remove from the tin using the paper as an aid. Place on a cooling rack and while they are still warm, paint them with the warm syrup glaze.

If you want to enhance the appearance of your buns, mix 3 tablespoons of icing sugar with enough lemon juice to form a runny icing. Place in a piping bag and drizzle over the buns when cooled.

LET ME SHOW YOU . . .

My Chelsea Buns Video

SOURDOUGH

The bread-baking enthusiast at some point will probably want to try their hand at making sourdough. I used to believe that only dedicated bread bakers had the time, commitment and inclination to embark on creating the absolute wonder of nature that is natural leaven (aka the sourdough 'starter'). But don't be scared off: the process is not difficult, it just takes a little time and attention to detail. I remember when I made my first sourdough starter . . . rather than leave it in the fridge while I went on holiday I took it with me so that I could continue to feed and nurture it while I was away!

If you feel inspired to have a go, it is very rewarding to create live yeast from what appears to be nothing. Before you start, make sure you have about a week to ten days when you can be available each day for a few minutes to 'feed' your newborn. After that, once it has established a life of its own, you can go on holiday, leave it in the fridge for a fortnight, then feed it when you get back home and it comes to life again. Mine is now part of the family – I couldn't bear to let it die.

You might think it is not worth making a starter because you will only occasionally make sourdough bread, but it is not just for special occasions, it is for everyday use too. I use a couple of tablespoons of my homemade leaven when I am making any bread, even my daily white loaf. Oh my word, it makes such a difference to the rise!

FIRST, MAKE YOUR STARTER

1. Combine 125g (4¼oz) wholemeal bread flour, 125g (4¼oz) strong white bread flour and 300ml (10fl oz) bottled still (or tap) water in a large 500g (16oz) mason jar and mix with a fork or spoon to make sure there are no lumps. Add a couple of slices of peeled apple (about a quarter of a small apple, no pips) and bury them in the mixture. Cover with a clean cloth and leave at room temperature for 2 days.

2. After 2 days bubbles will have started to appear on top of the mixture. This is now your 'baby leaven'. Remove the lid, take out the apple slices with a spoon and discard them.

3. Add 2 tablespoons of strong white bread flour and about 2 tablespoons of bottled or tap water (room temperature) to the jar – you want enough water to make a fairly thick batter-like consistency. Cover with a cloth and leave at room temperature for 24 hours before repeating the feeding process.

4. Repeat step 3 every 24 hours until you get to a stage where your leaven smells aromatic and quite pleasant rather than pungent and stinging to the nose. I think it smells like emulsion paint! You will also discover that it gets itself moving quicker and doubles in volume within 6–8 hours after feeding. It took mine about 9 days to get to this stage. After this time, store in the fridge or you can start to bake with it.

5. Once your starter is established, it needs to be refreshed or 'fed' about once a week, or a few hours before you want to use it. To do this simply either remove about a third of your starter and discard it if your jar is getting too full, otherwise simply keep feeding. Add a couple of tablespoons of white bread flour and sufficient room-temperature tap or bottled water to the jar and stir until it has a thick batter-like consistency and all the flour is well incorporated. Leave at room temperature until bubbles start to form – a really active leaven will start to bubble within three or four hours. It is now ready to use or pop into the fridge to store for a week.

MY SOURDOUGH BREAD

If you want to make a sourdough loaf, you will love this recipe. Once you have thought about making it you will need 24 hours for it to materialize! It is worth the effort, I promise.

Let us say you want your loaf for Saturday evening . . .

FRIDAY AFTERNOON ABOUT 2PM

Refresh your starter or natural leaven. It should get bubbling after 3–4 hours at room temperature.

FRIDAY EVENING ABOUT 8PM

Make the sponge:

In the bowl of a tabletop (stand) mixer place 150g (5½oz) strong white bread flour, 50g (1¾oz) light or dark rye flour, 100g (3½oz) of your natural leaven and 200ml (7fl oz) warm water. Mix well, making sure there are no lumps, then cover the bowl with a shower cap and leave in the kitchen overnight.

SATURDAY

Just look at the bubbles!

10am: Fit the dough hook to your mixer then add 150g (5½oz) strong white bread flour and 7g (¼oz) salt to your bubbling sponge. Mix for 3–4 minutes until everything is well combined then increase the mixer speed and knead on slow speed for 8–10 minutes until the dough is stretchy and silky.

Turn the dough out onto a floured surface and start to knead. It is quite sticky to begin with, so you may find it easier to oil your hands. Transfer to a clean greased bowl and leave in a warm place for about 1 hour to rise until doubled in size: I pop mine into the microwave with the door closed then I don't have to cover it, or cover the dough with an upturned large bowl, shower cap or large bag.

11.30am: Turn the dough out again onto a floured surface, knead, shape into a ball and place in the greased bowl.

12.30pm: 2nd kneading – repeat the 11.30am knead

2.00pm: 3rd kneading – repeat the 11.30am knead

3.30pm: 4th and final kneading. Now shape the dough – handling the dough gently and bringing the edges into the centre until a ball is formed – then place in a well-floured proving basket, seam side up. Leave to prove in a warm place for 1 hour.

Preheat your oven to its highest setting.

5.00pm: Baking

Turning dough out of a proving basket can be tricky, so I use a sheet of reusable baking parchment as an aid. You will need two baking sheets – one preheating in the oven and a cold one, the cold one lined with a piece of reusable baking parchment. Place the baking parchment over the top of the risen dough, swiftly flip the dough out using the parchment as an aid and lay the parchment onto the baking sheet. Carefully lift off the proving basket and release the dough. Take the preheated baking sheet from the oven and lay it alongside the cold sheet, then use the baking parchment as an aid to slide the dough from the cold sheet onto the hot sheet then immediately pop into the oven. Bread enjoys a steamy baking environment so dropping an ice cube into the oven into a preheated small tin or container at the same time as the bread goes in will help make a lighter loaf.

Bake for 30 minutes, turning the oven down to 220°C/200°C (fan)/425°F/gas 7 after 20 minutes. Remove from the oven and leave to cool on a cooling rack.

6.00pm: Eat!

LET ME SHOW YOU . . .

My Sourdough Bread Video

STROMBOLI

Stromboli is great for snacks, lunch, barbecues, with soup, salads, you name it. I use all kinds of fillings – bacon, egg and sausage are real favourites – but this one is quite traditional and uses typical Italian ingredients. The recipe makes enough dough for two stromboli but you will need to double the filling ingredients. I tend to make a stromboli with half the dough and a small loaf with the other half.

FOR THE DOUGH

500g (1lb 2oz) strong white bread flour, plus extra for dusting
7g (¼oz) dried yeast
1 tbsp rapeseed oil or olive oil
300–320ml (10–11fl oz) tepid water
7g (¼oz) table salt

FOR THE FILLING

1 tbsp mixed dried herbs
100g (3½oz) Parma ham (about 8 slices)
a good handful of fresh basil leaves, stalks removed
6 sundried tomatoes, chopped
125g (4¼oz) mozzarella cheese
50g (1¾oz) grated Cheddar cheese
1–2 tbsp rapeseed oil or olive oil
freshly ground black pepper
sprinkling of sea salt flakes and some oil, to serve

Equipment: tabletop (stand) mixer (optional), baking sheet lined with reusable baking parchment

Put the flour, yeast and oil in the bowl of a tabletop (stand) mixer fitted with a dough hook then add about 280ml (9½fl oz) of the water and mix until dough is formed. Add more water as necessary, then add the salt.

Knead for about 10 minutes on low speed until the dough is smooth and stretchy. Place in a greased bowl, cover with a shower cap and leave to rise for 1–1½ hours (depending on the room temperature) until doubled in size. (You can make the dough by hand if you don't have a tabletop/stand mixer: using a large bowl and a wooden spoon or spatula to combine the ingredients then kneading on a clean work surface for 10–15 minutes.)

In the meantime, prepare the filling ingredients and have everything in front of you ready to use.

When the dough has risen, remove it from the bowl, divide it in half and use one half for the stromboli and the other half you can make a loaf (or more Stromboli if you double the filling ingredients). Roll one half out on a floured tea towel to a rectangle about 25 × 35cm (10 × 14 inches). Sprinkle the dried herbs over the dough then layer over the filling ingredients. I start with the ham then the basil leaves followed by the sundried tomatoes, mozzarella cheese, grated cheese, a grinding of pepper then a drizzle of oil.

Starting at the wide end, and using the tea towel as an aid, roll up the Stromboli, finishing with the seam underneath. Tuck the ends under then transfer to a lined baking sheet.

Leave to prove for 30–40 minutes somewhere warm, loosely covered with a damp, clean cloth, and preheat the oven to 220°C/200°C (fan)/425°F/gas 7.

Before baking, use a metal skewer to make 5 or 6 air holes in the Stromboli. Bake in the oven for 30–35 minutes until golden brown.

Remove from the oven, brush with a little oil and sprinkle with sea salt flakes while hot to give the Stromboli a yummy finish. Serve hot or cold.

LET ME SHOW YOU . . .

My Stromboli Video

Enjoy raw onion without the unwanted side-effects
I love using raw onion as a garnish on salads but find
the strong aftertaste unpleasant and then I wish I
hadn't eaten it! These two tips will ensure you can
enjoy it with no side-effects.

1. Place thinly sliced onion rings in a small shallow bowl
then sprinkle over ½ tsp sugar and 2–3 tbsp vinegar
(any vinegar is fine, but cider vinegar or white wine
vinegar give a lovely flavour). Leave for about
30 minutes. Your onion will still be crunchy
but will have been sweetened and the harshness
taken away by the vinegar.

2. Save a jar of pickled beetroot vinegar then drop
in a few onion rings. Not only does the vinegar
sweeten the onion, it also takes on a dark red colour.
Great for salads.

GARLIC AND CORIANDER
NO-KNEAD BREAD

For those new to bread baking or without a tabletop (stand) mixer, this is a great crowd-pleaser. Easy to make, there's no kneading required but you do need to plan ahead: the super-tasty dough needs to mature for 24 hours in the fridge before being baked.

  400g (14oz) strong white bread flour
  5g (⅕oz) dried yeast
  340ml (11½fl oz) lukewarm water
  30ml (1fl oz) rapeseed oil or olive oil
  7g (¼oz) salt
  50g (1¾oz) butter
  3 garlic cloves, peeled and crushed
  3 tbsp fresh finely chopped coriander

Equipment: shallow rectangular baking tray about 26 × 36cm (10½ × 14 inches)

Start the day before you want to bake and serve the bread. Put the flour, yeast, water and oil in a roomy mixing bowl. Mix well with a spatula or wooden spoon until the dough is rough and shaggy but well combined, then cover the bowl with a shower cap and leave in a warm place for 10 minutes. The salt is not added yet as we want to give the yeast a chance to get working and salt impedes the rising of the yeast.

After 10 minutes, remove the shower cap and add the salt, stir well, replace the shower cap and leave in a warm place for 20 minutes.

Remove the cap, rub your right hand with oil and give the very soft, wet dough ten turns: hold the bowl with the left hand and, using the oiled hand (so that the dough doesn't stick), imagine your hand is a large spoon and bring the dough from the outside edge to the inside of the bowl, turning the bowl 45 degrees as you go. Do this ten times then get the cap back on the bowl and leave in a warm place for 20 minutes.

Repeat the turning of the dough, but this time place the dough in a well-oiled plastic box – I have a square box with a lid (23 × 25cm, 15cm deep/9 × 10 inches and 6 inches deep), but you can use anything with similar dimensions, such as a baking dish. Push the dough into the corners of the box/container/dish, pop the lid on and chill overnight in the fridge (or for up to 24 hours).

The next day, oil a shallow rectangular baking tray about 26 × 36cm (10½ × 14 inches) or brush it with lining paste. Take the dough from the fridge, invert it onto the baking tray and use oiled hands to push it around the tin so that it covers the tray in an even layer. Allow to prove in a warm place for 1½ hours: the dough will rise and at the end of the proving time you can push down any large bubbles. Preheat the oven to 240°C/220°C (fan)/475°F/gas 9.

Bake the proved dough for 20 minutes.

While it is baking, melt the butter with the garlic in a saucepan or the microwave, then stir in the coriander.

Take the bread from the oven and brush over the garlic butter and coriander. Pop it back into the oven and bake for a further 10 minutes, then remove from the oven, slice into squares and serve warm or cold. This bread freezes well too.

LET ME SHOW YOU . . .

My Garlic and Coriander Bread Video

BRIOCHE

Brioche is special. Truly beautiful, soft, rich and so tasty, it's delicious on its own, toasted, served with bacon or pâté and makes a great base for many desserts. Brioche is so much easier to make if you have a tabletop (stand) mixer fitted with a dough hook but it can also be mixed by hand. To make excellent brioche, you'll need to start making the dough the day before you want to bake the loaf.

7g (¼oz) dried yeast
40ml (1¼fl oz) whole milk
30g (1oz) caster sugar
250g (9oz) strong white bread flour, plus extra for dusting
1 tsp salt
3 eggs
175g (6oz) butter, diced, at room temperature

Equipment: tabletop (stand) mixer, 900g (2lb) loaf tin or 2 × 450g (1lb) loaf tins, generously greased with butter or brushed with lining paste

||||||||||||||||||||||||||||||||||||||||||||||||||||||||||||||||||||||||||||||||||||||||||||||||||||||||||||||||||||||||||

Leftover brioche makes the most beautiful bread and butter pudding – use it in place of the bread in the recipe on page 312.

||||||||||||||||||||||||||||||||||||||||||||||||||||||||||||||||||||||||||||||||||||||||||||||||||||||||||||||||||||||||||

The day before you plan to bake the dough, put the yeast, milk and sugar in the bowl of your tabletop (stand) mixer, give it a quick stir then add the flour and salt followed by the 3 eggs. Mix on a low setting for 5 minutes or so until the ingredients are well combined, then lift the dough hook from the mix – it should be stretchy though raggy in appearance.

With the machine still on a low speed, add the soft butter little by little until well combined. Increase the speed setting slightly and knead for 5 minutes or so until the mix becomes smooth, very stretchy and glossy in appearance.

Using a spatula, scrape the sticky dough into a greased bowl then cover with a shower cap and leave in a warm place to rise for up to 2 hours or until doubled in size.

Sprinkle a little flour on the work surface then tip out the risen dough and knock it back – I find it easier to use a bench scraper than my hands to do this. Form into a rough ball and place back in the bowl, cover again with the cap and place in the fridge overnight to rest.

The next day, transfer the chilled dough onto a lightly floured surface. It will now be so easy to work with. Knead it gently then divide it into four even-sized balls. I place four into my tin if I'm making one large loaf (900g/2lb loaf tin) – if you are using 2 × 450g (1lb) tins then put two balls in each. Cover again and leave to prove in a warm place for 1½ –2 hours until doubled in size and almost reaching the top of the tin. Towards the end of the proving time, preheat the oven to 220°C/200°C (fan)/425°F/gas 7.

When ready to bake, uncover the dough and carefully place the tin(s) into the preheated oven. You can also brush the top with some of my non-sticky bread glaze (see page 114) before you put it into the oven. Immediately turn the oven temperature down to 200°C/180°C (fan)/400°F/gas 6 and bake for 25 minutes (for small loaves) or 40 minutes (for a larger loaf) until the loaf is/loaves are risen, golden and smelling amazing.

Remove from the tin(s) and leave on a cooling rack.

The bread will keep for up to 2–3 days.

LET ME SHOW YOU . . .

My Brioche Video

YORKSHIRE TEACAKES

MAKES: 12 TEACAKES OR 6 TEACAKES
AND A 450G (1LB) TEA LOAF

A traditional Yorkshire teacake is totally moreish. It has a dark, well-baked crust and is best eaten fresh on the day it's baked, but is still delicious toasted the next day and served warm with lashings of butter.

7g (¼oz) dried yeast

450g (1lb) strong white bread flour, plus extra for dusting

240ml (8fl oz) whole milk

1 egg

5g (⅕oz) salt

40g (1½oz) caster sugar

40g (1½oz) lard or butter, melted and cooled

100g (3½oz) dried fruit (I use chopped apricots and cherries but currants, sultanas, etc. are fine), roughly chopped

¼ tsp ground cinnamon

½ tsp freshly grated nutmeg

grated zest and juice of 1 lemon

Equipment: tabletop (stand) mixer (optional), 450g (1lb) loaf tin, 1 or 2 baking sheets lined with reusable baking parchment

Freezing a tea loaf

If you are making a tea loaf with the mix, to enjoy another time, it can be frozen as a raw dough or baked then cooled and frozen. To thaw frozen dough, remove from the freezer bag and thaw in the oven with just the light on for 5–6 hours (or at room temperature) until the dough is well risen and proved, then bake for 25 minutes.

Non-sticky glaze for bread

Beat 1 egg white with 1 teaspoon of caster sugar just until frothy for a shiny, dark and non-sticky glaze for your teacakes. Brush just a little of it over the proved cakes just before they go into the oven. If you like to toast your teacakes, this glaze will not burn.

Put the yeast then the flour in the bowl of a tabletop (stand) mixer fitted with the dough hook then add the rest of the ingredients (except the lemon juice). With the machine on its lowest setting bring the mixture together to a rough shaggy mix, then turn up the speed and mix for about 10 minutes. The dough will look very sticky and wet – if it doesn't and has instead formed a large ball then add the lemon juice. Continue to knead until the dough firms up and comes together, is smooth and leave the sides of the bowl. (If you don't have a tabletop/stand mixer, you can make the dough by hand: bring the ingredients together in a mixing bowl using a spatula or wooden spoon then transfer to a clean work surface and knead by hand for 10–15 minutes until smooth and stretchy.)

Transfer the dough to a greased bowl, cover with a shower cap and leave to rise in a warm place for 1½ –2 hours until doubled in size.

Remove the dough from the bowl and halve it on a lightly floured surface. If you are making a tea loaf and 6 teacakes, shape one half and place into a well-greased 450g (1lb) loaf tin and pop straight into the freezer in a freezer bag. Divide the remaining dough into 6 equal-sized pieces. Alternatively, if making 12 teacakes and skipping the loaf, divide the dough into 12 equal pieces (you may want to use the scales). Shape into balls, pop onto two baking sheets and leave to prove for 50 minutes in a warm place until doubled in size.

A Yorkshire teacake is flat rather than round, so after shaping and proving, roll it to a thickness of 2cm (¾ inch) with a rolling pin and place onto a baking sheet. Preheat the oven to 220°C/200°C (fan)/425°F/gas 7.

Bake the loaf for 25 minutes until golden, and the teacakes for 15–18 minutes until golden. They are delicious buttered on the day of baking, then toasted the next day.

LET ME SHOW YOU . . .

My Yorkshire Teacakes Video

CAKES

E veryone loves cake.

A child's birthday cake is a delight to make and it's cheaper if you make your own. Although the decorating bit can seem daunting, I'd encourage you to just do it. When your child has grown up, I promise you the cake that will be remembered will not be the bought, themed unicorn cake with all the bells and whistles, it'll be the chocolate cake covered in runny chocolate that didn't quite set which was covered in Smarties. The candles were stuck into the runny chocolate and everyone had to sing 'Happy Birthday' really quickly before the wax ran onto the cake. The thing is, you made it. And the next one you make will be better. The chocolate will set, and you will put the candles in little holders.

Don't worry, there is a time for spinning sugar, tempering chocolate and obtaining the perfect mirror glaze – this book is aimed at taking you to a level where all the basics have been mastered and you have the confidence and desire to move on to bigger things.

There are several cake-making methods that fit different types of cake. A Victoria sponge cake, probably the most popular, is made differently to a Swiss roll, for example, or a rich fruit cake. This chapter covers a number of cake-making methods and throws in a few relevant popular recipes too.

MAKING A SPONGE USING
THE CREAMING METHOD

If you want to make the perfect Sponge Cake – anything from a simple Lemon Drizzle Cake, a three-tier sponge Wedding Cake, Christmas Cake or Fondant Fancies – this is how you will get started.

Most recipes give scant instructions and assume the baker knows exactly what the perfect sponge should be. For me, the perfect sponge cake is soft, springy, not dry, not cracked or overbaked and, of course, tastes delicious. An overbaked sponge will have a dark crust on its sides, bottom and maybe even the top. The perfect sponge should be the same colour all over.

Cake ingredients should all be at the same temperature, so take the margarine out of the fridge about an hour before you need it (unless the weather is really hot). I often use margarine – I believe it makes a lighter sponge. Use room temperature butter if you prefer. Eggs should never be kept in the fridge. The perfect temperature for the ingredients is about 20°C/70°F (room temperature). If your ingredients are too cold, they will be more difficult to emulsify and may curdle.

I try to give exact baking times as I find it unhelpful when recipes give windows of baking times (i.e. bake for 30–45 minutes) Ovens do vary though, so if after a quoted baking time in a recipe your cake isn't right then adjust your oven by 15 °C / 30 °F one way or another. For example: if after the quoted baking time, your cake is risen, brown at the sides and cracked in the middle, then your oven is too fierce and temperature needs to be adjusted down next time. On the other hand, if your cake seems risen but the centre does not spring back when touched, then the cake is probably under done and the oven temperature needs to be increased or the cake baked for longer next time.

SIMPLE VICTORIA SANDWICH CAKE

MAKES: 1 SMALL SANDWICH CAKE

This simple recipe makes a small Victoria Sandwich Cake. The recipe can be scaled up to different round or square cake tins using the cake tin converter on pages 116–119. It's light, moist and always delicious.

125g (4¼oz) margarine or butter, at room temperature
125g (4¼oz) caster sugar
2 eggs, at room temperature
125g (4¼oz) self-raising flour
1 tsp vanilla extract

Equipment: hand-held electric whisk, 2 × 15cm (6 inch) round loose-bottom sandwich tins – use lining paste at the edges and a circle of greaseproof paper cut exactly to fit the base

Preheat the oven to 210°C/190°C (fan)/425°F/gas 7. Cream the margarine (or butter) and sugar in a medium mixing bowl with a hand-held electric whisk until light and fluffy. Do not rush this step: I whisk for about 2 minutes then stop while I collect and weigh out all the other ingredients. This allows time for the sugar to dissolve slightly into the margarine (or butter). Then whisk again until the mixture is pale, light and mousse-like.

This next stage is where you apply my unique creaming technique. Lift the whisks out of the mix and in the hole that is left drop in one of the eggs. Place the whisk back into the bowl, switch it on at low speed and do not move it at all. Keep that whisk attachment in exactly the same place, increasing the speed as you go. You will see the mixture turn from a curdled state (a bit like scrambled eggs) to a smooth, creamy consistency. At this point, move the whisk around the bowl to incorporate the rest of the butter and sugar. Repeat with the second egg, scraping down the sides of the bowl with the spatula before restarting the whisk. Your finished batter will be smooth, light, thick and gorgeous – I always think it has the look and colour of melted ice cream. Following this method will ensure you get the perfect mix, with no curdling, no need to add flour to bind during mixing, and no need to incorporate additional raising agent to help your cake rise.

You now need to incorporate the flour and any flavourings into the light, mousse-like mixture which is full of air. I always sift the flour (even though we are told that modern flours do not require it) – this ensures no lumps of flour and by sifting the flour, more air is introduced into the mixture. Once the flour is added, add any flavours – for this cake, I add the vanilla.

||||||||||||||||||||||||||||||||||||||||||||||||||||||||||||||||||||||||||||||||||||||||||||||||||||||||||||||||||||||||||||||||

Flavours that can make your mixture curdle
I have been asked many times why I add some flavours (including fruit, nuts, citrus, coffee, etc.) at the end. The reason is that some flavours can cause a cake mix to curdle, but once the flour is added to the batter these flavours can be added with confidence, knowing that the mixture is stable.

||||||||||||||||||||||||||||||||||||||||||||||||||||||||||||||||||||||||||||||||||||||||||||||||||||||||||||||||||||||||||||||||

Using a large metal spoon, slowly and carefully fold in the flour. Imagine the bowl of mix is a clock face. The spoon is the big hand! Take the spoon from 12 o'clock to 6 o'clock then from 6 o'clock back up to 12 o'clock. Make a quarter turn with the bowl then repeat. I find it easiest to move the bowl a quarter turn at a time, maintaining the same movement with the spoon into the mixture.

When everything is fully combined, place the empty sandwich tin onto your digital scales. Spoon 3 large spoonfuls into the tin then do the same into the other sandwich tin. Carefully equal out the remainder of the mix between the two tins. This is important as you want your cakes to be uniform in size, but also they will bake together so you want to make sure one is not more baked than the other.

Bake the cakes in the oven for 18–20 minutes only. After 18 minutes have a look at your cakes. The perfectly baked sponge will be a sunny golden colour and will be starting to brown. It will have risen evenly, and the centre of the sponge will be firm to the touch.

Remove your perfect cakes from the oven and place onto cooling racks. As soon as you can handle the cake tins without burning your hands, carefully slide a knife around the outside edge then turn out onto the cooling rack. I try to do this immediately, as I do not want my cake to continue baking in the tin, not even for a minute. Allow the cakes to cool completely before filling and decorating.

Not all ovens are the same — foil trick

Some ovens, particularly older electric ovens (like mine), can be quite fierce and can burn the sides of the cake which are nearest the sides of the oven. In addition, if your cake tins are of a thin gauge and perhaps quite old, this can cause cakes to bake too quickly, which will make your cake rise up in the middle, form a dome, then a crack. Your perfect sponge should be almost flat on the top, with no crack and no burnt sides. If you have issues with your cakes baking too quickly, make a simple heat diffuser by wrapping a collar of kitchen foil around the outside of the tin(s). I take a strip of foil, fold it into four lengthways then secure this around the tin once it's filled with batter. The cake will then bake evenly. And you can use your foil collars again and again.

Avoid cooling your cakes upside down

The cooling rack will leave marks in the sponge which will affect the presentation of your cake. Decide which cake sponge will be the top then lay a clean tea towel over the top and quickly flip it over so that the presentation sponge turns out briefly onto the tea towel. Remove the tin then flip over and place the cake presentation side up on the cooling rack. No cooling ridges.

Cakes soon dry out, so once cool, if you don't intend to fill and decorate straight away, cover the cake with a piece of greaseproof paper and secure with elastic bands, then place in a tin and keep in a cool place.

MAKING LARGE CAKES USING THE CREAMING METHOD

For mixing large celebration cakes, I use a tabletop (stand) mixer. To avoid curdling with a large quantity of ingredients, first cream together the butter and sugar using the whisk attachment and mix on high speed until light and fluffy, then place the eggs for the recipe in a jug and blitz with a stick blender or beat well. With the motor of the mixer on high speed, add the egg in the thinnest, slowest, yet continuous, stream. Even if your arm is aching, do not be tempted to rush the adding of the egg. Once incorporated, change the attachment to the paddle and – on very low speed – fold in the flour and flavourings. If the mixture does start to curdle while you are adding the egg, add a spoonful of flour and mix on a high speed until the mixture has emulsified and looks smooth again before adding further egg.

MAKING WHISKED SPONGES

Whisked sponges are used for Swiss rolls, certain dessert recipes and top-end cakes and patisserie. A light and lovely Swiss roll can fit the bill for so many occasions, from a simple dessert to a celebration such as Easter and Christmas, it's also a beauty for afternoon tea and with a little bit of thought when it comes to fillings it can be a very low-fat cake option. Whisked sponges are quick to make and to bake – a Swiss roll, for example, will take only about 8 minutes to bake. A whisked sponge is a great choice for people with a gluten intolerance – gluten-free flour works a treat in a whisked sponge. Because they contain little or no fat, whisked sponges dry out easily, so they need to be eaten within a day or two and the filling needs to be moist and wholesome. A Swiss roll is beautiful in that with every bite there is both cream and sponge. A whisked sponge is super easy to make and once mastered you will show it off again and again.

For other cake baking methods, see page 159.

CHOCOLATE FUDGE CAKE

SERVES: 6–8

A cake for any occasion, this moist chocolate cake with a fudge filling and frosting is easy to make and is a favourite with the whole family.

FOR THE CAKE

125g (4¼oz) margarine or butter, at room temperature

120g (4¼oz) caster sugar

2 eggs

1 tbsp golden syrup or black treacle

130g (4½oz) self-raising flour

1 tsp vanilla extract

30g (1oz) cocoa powder mixed to a paste with 100ml (3½fl oz) milk

50g (1¾oz) dark chocolate, melted and cooled (optional – if you want an extra-chocolatey cake)

FOR THE FUDGE FILLING AND FROSTING

100ml (3½fl oz) evaporated milk

100g (3½oz) caster sugar

125g (4¼oz) dark chocolate, broken into pieces, or chocolate chips

½ tsp vanilla extract

20g (¾oz) butter

Equipment: hand-held electric whisk, 2 × 15cm (6 inch) loose-bottom sandwich tins, greased and bases lined with greaseproof paper or reusable baking parchment

How do I measure 1 tbsp syrup?

Syrup, treacle, malt extract and honey are difficult to measure accurately, as they stick to the spoon. Take a small heatproof jug and fill it with boiling water then pop a metal spoon in and leave it a few minutes. Open the tin or jar of sticky syrup, honey or malt extract then take the spoon from the water, give it a shake to remove surplus water then take your spoon of syrup. The heat from the spoon will prevent the syrup sticking – the spoon will leave the tin cleanly and then will just fall off the spoon into your mix. If you need more than one spoonful, pop the spoon back into the water to clean it and reheat.

Preheat the oven to 190°C/170°C (fan)/375°F/gas 5.

Cream together the margarine (or butter) and sugar in a roomy mixing bowl with a hand-held electric whisk until light, pale and fluffy. Whisk in the eggs one at a time, whisking well after each addition, then whisk in the golden syrup (or black treacle). Sift in the flour and fold it in with a metal spoon, then add the vanilla extract and cocoa paste. Mix well then stir in the cooled melted chocolate (if using). Divide the mixture evenly between the two tins (I prefer to weigh the mixture – see page 123 for tip on using scales for this) and bake for 20–25 minutes or until the sponges are risen and springy to the touch.

Remove from the tins when cool enough to handle and leave on a cooling rack while you make the fudge filling.

Put the evaporated milk and sugar in a small saucepan, place over a low heat and stir until the sugar dissolves. Once the mixture is smooth, turn up the heat and bring to the boil, then reduce the heat and allow the mixture to bubble busily for 5 minutes exactly.

Put the chocolate in a small heatproof bowl then pour over the hot milk/sugar mix. Stir until the chocolate melts then add the vanilla and butter and mix well until you have a shiny thick fudge mixture. Allow to cool then use one third to sandwich the cakes together and the rest to coat the top and sides. I use an angled palette knife to apply the cream and a bench scraper to smooth and finish.

My fudge separated

I have made this fudge filling many times and it only separated once. If it happens to you, whisk 1–2 tablespoons of evaporated milk into the fudge and it will return to a smooth, silky state.

LET ME SHOW YOU . . .

My Chocolate Fudge Cake Video

LEMON DRIZZLE CAKE

MAKES: 2 CAKES (1 FOR NOW AND
1 FOR A FRIEND OR THE FREEZER)

This cake is probably one of the most popular, the easiest and certainly one of the cheapest to make: it has a light sponge, just enough tang from the lemon and a crunchy glaze on top.

FOR THE CAKE
165g (5¾oz) margarine or butter, at room temperature
165g (5¾oz) caster sugar
3 eggs
165g (5¾oz) self-raising flour
finely grated zest of 1 large lemon and ½ the juice

FOR THE CRUSTY TOPPING
juice of the other ½ lemon
50g (1¾oz) granulated sugar

Equipment: hand-held electric whisk, 2 × 450g (1lb) loaf tins, greased and brushed with lining paste

Preheat the oven to 200°C/180°C (fan)/400°F/gas 6.

Cream together the margarine (or butter) and sugar in a roomy mixing bowl with a hand-held electric whisk until light and fluffy, then add the eggs one at a time, whisking well after each addition. Sift in the flour then add the grated lemon zest and juice (just the juice from half the lemon) and fold in with a metal spoon. Divide evenly between two prepared loaf tins (you can use digital scales for this – see page 123) then bake for 25–30 minutes until the cakes are risen, firm to the touch and golden in colour.

Remove the cakes from the oven and place the tins on a cooling rack. Leave for just 5 minutes while you mix the granulated sugar and lemon juice together for the topping. Brush the mix over the tops of the hot cakes then leave the cakes in the tins to cool completely. The sugar will cool to a crunchy crust then you can easily remove the cakes from the tins. Time for a delicious slice – put the kettle on!

Ring the changes

Orange Drizzle Cake: use 1 large orange in place of the lemon and make the cake in exactly the same way.

What if I don't have the right size tin?

This recipe will also make a 20cm (8 inch) round cake or 18cm (7 inch) square cake which can then be finished off with the crunchy glaze. The Cake Tin Converter on pages 13–19 gives many options for adapting recipes to fit the size of tin you possess.

LET ME SHOW YOU . . .

My Lemon Drizzle Cake Video

BARBADOS BANANA BREAD

SERVES: 8

Inspired by a holiday on the beautiful island of Barbados, this is my take on the tasty moist banana bread which we were served at breakfast! It is delicious and a great recipe for using up overripe bananas. The lime water icing and crunchy banana chip topping are optional. This cake freezes well, so double the quantities and make one for now and one for later.

60ml (2fl oz) vegetable oil

1 egg

50g (1¾oz) brown sugar (light or dark)

1 ripe banana, peeled

¼ tsp freshly grated nutmeg

½ tsp mixed spice

1 piece stem ginger in syrup, finely chopped

2 tbsp ginger syrup (from the stem ginger jar)

90g (3oz) self-raising flour

FOR THE CRUNCHY TOP

2 tbsp icing sugar

lime juice (as needed)

6–8 dried banana slices, crunched to a crumb

Equipment: stick blender (optional), 450g (1lb) loaf tin, greased with butter or brushed with lining paste

Preheat the oven to 190°C/170°C (fan)/375°F/gas 5.

Put the oil, egg, brown sugar, banana, dried spices, chopped ginger and the ginger syrup in a medium bowl and mash everything together with a fork or blitz with a stick blender if you have one. Fold the flour into the thick mixture then transfer to a greased or lined loaf tin and bake in the oven for 30–40 minutes until risen and firm to the touch.

To make the topping, combine the icing sugar with enough lime juice to make a runny icing.

Remove the cake from the oven and, while still warm, apply a coating of runny icing using either a spoon or piping bag. Before it sets, sprinkle over the banana chips. Leave to cool completely.

I have over ripe bananas but don't have the time to bake today

Peel your bananas, pop them into a bag and freeze. When you have the time to bake you can thaw them in the bowl in which they will be mixed and use once softened. They won't thaw into the same form in which they were frozen – they'll look mushy and unappetising – but will taste the same.

LET ME SHOW YOU . . .

My Barbados Banana Bread Video

CHERRY ALMOND TRAYBAKE

MAKES: 12 SLICES

This easy bake is fit enough for any occasion – children love making these. The slices are moist, great for afternoon tea, and simply divine.

FOR THE CAKE

- 60g (2¼oz) morello glacé cherries
- 185g (6½oz) margarine or butter, at room temperature
- 185g (6½oz) caster sugar
- 3 eggs
- 100g (3½oz) self-raising flour
- 100g (3½oz) almond flour or ground almonds
- 1 tsp almond extract

FOR THE DECORATION

- 180g (6¼oz) fondant icing sugar
- ½ tsp almond extract
- 2–3 tbsp boiling water
- green food colour gel
- marzipan or red-coloured fondant (about 20g/¾oz)

Equipment: hand-held electric whisk, 20cm (8 inch) square tin, lined with greaseproof paper

Preheat the oven to 190°C/170°C (fan)/375°F/gas 5.

Start by prepping the cherries. Wash the cherries then cut each one into eighths. Dry them on kitchen paper then dust in flour by placing them in a small bowl and adding 1 teaspoon of the flour. Stir them to coat. This will prevent your cherries sinking to the bottom of the cake during baking.

Cream the margarine (or butter) and sugar in a large roomy mixing bowl with a hand-held electric whisk until light, pale and fluffy. Add the eggs one at a time, whisking well after each addition, then sift in the rest of the flour and fold in with the ground almonds or almond flour and almond extract using a metal spoon. When everything is well combined stir through the flour-dusted cherries. Transfer the mixture to the prepared tin and bake in the oven for 30 minutes until slightly risen, pale golden in colour and firm to the touch.

Remove from the oven and leave to cool, then turn out onto a rack to cool completely, making sure it's upside down so that the base of the cake is uppermost and completely flat.

To make the decoration, sift the icing sugar into a bowl then add the almond extract, followed by the boiling water, 1 tablespoon at a time, stirring well until you have a thick yet runny smooth icing. Take 2 tablespoons of the icing and colour it green – set aside and cover the bowl or place in an icing bag so that the icing doesn't form a skin. Pour the remaining the icing over the cake and smooth it out to the edges. Leave to set.

Decorate the cake with green-coloured icing for stalks and tiny red-coloured marzipan or fondant formed into tiny balls for the cherries.

*How do I cut neat slices when
the cake is so soft and fresh?*

To cut your fresh cake cleanly, just pop it into the
freezer for about 20 minutes. Take it out of the freezer
and see how firm it is. It is now possible to cut the
finest neat slices or squares - tidy!

LET ME SHOW YOU . . .

My Cherry Almond Traybake Video

COCONUT AND LIME TRAYBAKE

MAKES: 12 SLICES

Coconut and lime are a wonderful combo but so often coconut cake can be dry. To ensure a lovely moist cake I pre-soak the desiccated coconut before baking. This cake will keep well in a tin and is great when the weather is hot as the frosting is not heat sensitive.

FOR THE CAKE

50g (1¾oz) desiccated coconut

grated zest and juice of 1 lime

3 tbsp lime cordial

120g (4¼oz) margarine or butter, at room temperature

110g (4oz) caster sugar

2 large eggs or 3 medium

145g (5oz) self-raising flour

1 tbsp plain thick full-fat yoghurt

FOR THE DECORATION

finely grated zest of 1 lime

1 tsp caster sugar

2 tbsp desiccated coconut

FOR THE FROSTING

1 lime

½ tsp lime cordial

1 tbsp cold water

120g (4¼oz) icing sugar, sifted

Equipment: hand-held electric whisk, 20cm (8 inch) loose-bottom square cake tin, greased and base-lined with greaseproof paper

Preheat the oven to 190°C/170°C (fan)/375°F/gas 5.

Put the coconut for the cake in a small bowl with the lime zest and juice and the lime cordial. Stir well and set aside.

Cream the margarine (or butter) and caster sugar in a roomy mixing bowl with a hand-held electric whisk until light, pale and fluffy. Add the eggs one at a time, whisking well after each addition, then fold in the self-raising flour and finally add the soaked coconut and yoghurt. Transfer the batter to the prepared cake tin and bake in the oven for 20–25 minutes until pale golden.

Remove from the oven and leave to cool in the tin.

To make the decoration, finely grate the zest from the lime (you will use the segments in the frosting) into a small bowl and scatter over the teaspoon of caster sugar. Stir well then leave in a warm place for about 1 hour. The zests will dry and become crunchy and sweet – they will absorb some of the sugar.

Toast the desiccated coconut for the decoration in a dry frying pan for a few minutes over medium heat, keeping the coconut moving around in the pan so it doesn't catch and burn. As soon as it is pale golden, turn it out onto a cold plate – don't leave it in the hot pan.

After zesting the lime for the decoration, segment the lime: cut off the top and base of the lime then carefully remove the layer of pith. Now it should be easy to remove the fruit segments, leaving behind the membrane that separates the little segments. Break these segments into small pieces and place into a bowl with any lime juice, the lime cordial and the cold water. Add the sifted icing sugar a few tablespoons at a time until you have a thick icing about the consistency of whipped double cream.

When the cake has cooled, remove it from the tin and peel off the paper. Spread the icing over the top then decorate with the sugared lime zest and toasted coconut.

LET ME SHOW YOU . . .

My Coconut and Lime Traybake Video

LEMON SWISS ROLL

SERVES: 8

This Swiss roll is one of the best recipes for a whisked fatless sponge. It can be baked and filled simply or dressed up for any occasion, and freezes well, too.

FOR THE SPONGE
 3 eggs
 75g (2½oz) caster sugar, plus extra for sprinkling
 75g (2½oz) plain flour
 1 tsp lemon extract

FOR THE FILLING
 150ml (5fl oz) double cream
 150g (5½oz) lemon curd (see page 193 for my Quick Curd
  recipe if you want to make your own)

Equipment: hand-held electric whisk, 1 rectangular baking tray
26 × 36 × 2cm deep (10½ × 14 × ¾ inch deep) lined with
non-stick baking parchment

Preheat the oven to 200°C/180°C (fan)/400°F/gas 6.

Whisk the eggs and caster sugar in a large roomy bowl with a hand-held electric whisk for 5–8 minutes until the mix is thick and mousse-like. It should be pale and leave a trail for a number of seconds when you take the whisk out of the mix. Placing your mixing bowl over a pan of simmering water will speed up the mixing.

Sift the flour over the top and add the lemon extract then, using a large metal spoon, gently fold in the flour. This takes a few minutes to get right – don't rush it. You need to retain the air. Mix slowly and in large stirs. Don't be tempted to speed things up as you see unmixed flour regularly appear in the batter. With slow, regular stirs you will see that the batter has thickened, is smooth and no flour remains.

Turn the mixture out onto the lined baking tray and, using an angled palette knife or the back of a spoon, gently push the mixture into a large rectangle, leaving just a tiny margin around the side of the parchment. This batter is not runny, so it is important that you smooth it out evenly across the tray so that it is an even thickness all over. Make sure the batter is as thick at the edges as it is in the middle. It will not find its own level while baking – it will stay put! The mixture will not run in the oven so don't be afraid to go close to the edge.

Pop the tray straight into the oven and bake for 8–10 minutes, keeping a close eye on your precious sponge. Remove it from the oven when it is golden and slightly risen.

Transfer the sponge (still in the tin) to a cooling rack and leave for 5 minutes. When the tray is cool enough to handle, but before the sponge has cooled, sprinkle the baked surface of the sponge with caster sugar. Lay a piece of non-stick baking parchment or a piece of cotton cloth/a tea towel over the top, then a baking sheet, and quickly flip the whole thing over. Peel off the original baking parchment. Carefully and loosely roll up the sponge using the new piece of parchment or the cloth as an aid then leave and allow to cool completely in the rolled-up position. This prevents the roll cracking later.

When ready to fill the sponge, whisk the double cream to soft peaks with a hand-held electric whisk then stir in the lemon curd. I like to mix the cream and curd quite loosely so that there are streaks of lemon.

Gently unroll the cooled sponge. Leave it on the paper or cloth for now but just make sure it hasn't stuck to the paper anywhere. Your good sprinkling of caster sugar should have prevented this.

Spread the creamy lemon mix over the sponge in an even layer then use the paper or cloth again to help re-roll and bring together your Swiss roll. For perfect presentation, trim the ends with a sharp serrated knife and enjoy them as a snack reward for your good work.

Dust with a sprinkle of caster sugar then transfer to a serving plate, making sure the seam is perfectly hidden underneath.

Rolling a Swiss roll
It is important to remove the backing paper from the sponge and then roll it up while still warm. This prevents the sponge from cracking. Your finished Swiss roll will amaze your friends – it will be swirly, smooth and beautiful.

LET ME SHOW YOU . . .

My Lemon Swiss Roll Video

PISTACHIO AND RASPBERRY RIPPLE SWISS ROLL

SERVES: 6–8

This delightful bake can be served with afternoon tea or as a dessert. I use frozen raspberries for this Swiss roll which makes it a year-round favourite in our house.

FOR THE CAKE

3 eggs
75g (2½oz) icing sugar, sifted
75g (2½oz) plain flour
30g (1oz) pistachio paste (see page 144 for recipe)
caster sugar, for dusting

FOR THE FILLING

100g (3½oz) frozen raspberries
150ml (5fl oz) double cream
250g (9oz) mascarpone cheese
70g (2½oz) icing sugar

Equipment: hand-held electric whisk, 1 rectangular baking tray 26 × 36 × 2cm deep (10½ × 14 × ¾ inch deep) lined with non-stick baking parchment

Preheat the oven to 200°C/180°C (fan)/400°F/gas 6.

Whisk the eggs and icing sugar in a large roomy bowl with a hand-held electric for 5–8 minutes until thick and mousse-like

– the whisk should leave a trail on the top of the mixture for a number of seconds when lifted. Placing your mixing bowl over a pan of simmering water will speed up the mixing. Sift the flour over the mixture and fold it in. Loosen the pistachio paste with a little of the cake batter, then fold it all in. Transfer to the prepared tray, smooth out and bake for 8–10 minutes. The baked sponge will be evenly pale golden in colour, firm to the touch and slightly risen.

Transfer the sponge (still in the tray) to a cooling rack and leave for 5 minutes. When the tray is cool enough to handle, but before the sponge has cooled, sprinkle the baked surface of the sponge with caster sugar. Lay a piece of non-stick baking parchment or a piece of cotton cloth/a tea towel over the top, then a baking sheet, and quickly flip the whole thing over. Peel off the original baking parchment. Carefully and loosely roll up the sponge using the new piece of parchment or the cloth as an aid then leave and allow to cool completely in the rolled-up position. This prevents the roll cracking later.

How to make pistachio paste
If you want to make your own, let me show you how! Blitz 40g (1½oz) unsalted pistachios, 15g (½oz) ground almonds, 2 tsp almond extract, 2 tsp Amaretto, 1 tsp vegetable oil and 1 tsp green food colour gel together in a food processor until they form a dark green paste (makes 60g/2¼oz).

Make the raspberry coulis filling by blitzing 100g (3½oz) frozen raspberries in a food processor then passing through a sieve. You should have about 3 tablespoons of coulis.

The coulis should be very thick so if it is a bit runny reduce it down by boiling for a few minutes in a pan then allow to cool. Alternatively, you could use raspberry jam thinned with a little water but the coulis is better as I don't add any sugar. The tartness of the fruit is just divine amongst the filling.

Whisk the cream to soft peaks in one bowl and in the other bowl whisk together the mascarpone cheese and icing sugar. Fold the two together and then lastly ripple through the raspberry coulis or jam. Do not over mix – you need a strong ripple effect.

Unroll the cooled Swiss roll and spread the cream inside then re-roll.

For decoration a few chopped pistachio nuts and a dusting of freeze-dried raspberry powder, but you can use a dusting of icing sugar along with fresh raspberries and chopped pistachios.

LET ME SHOW YOU . . .

My Pistachio and Raspberry
Swiss Roll Video

CHERRY CHOCOLATE ROULADE

SERVES: 6–8

A delicious moist, non-cracking, truly chocolatey roulade filled with black cherry jam and fresh whipped cream then topped off with fresh chocolate-dipped cherries.

Fit for any occasion.

FOR THE SPONGE

- 75g (2½oz) plain flour
- 30g (1oz) cocoa powder
- 3 eggs
- 75g (2½oz) caster sugar
- 1 tsp instant coffee powder or granules dissolved in 2 tbsp hot water
- 1 tsp vanilla extract

FOR DUSTING

- 2 tbsp caster sugar
- 1 tsp cocoa powder

FOR THE FILLING

- 300ml (10fl oz) double cream
- 1 tbsp icing sugar
- 1 tbsp amaretto (optional)
- 3 tbsp black cherry jam
- ½ tsp almond extract
- 30g (1oz) white chocolate
- 10–12 fresh cherries

Equipment: hand-held electric whisk, 1 shallow baking tin – mine measures 26 × 36 × 2cm deep (10½ × 14 × ¾ inch deep) lined with non-stick baking parchment

Preheat the oven to 200°C/180°C (fan)/400°F/gas 6.

Sift the plain flour and cocoa powder together.

Whisk the 3 eggs and caster sugar in a roomy mixing bowl with a hand-held electric whisk until light, mousse-like and when the whisks are lifted from the mixture they leave a trail for a number of seconds. Add half of the flour and cocoa mix, sifting it a second time as you do so, then add the coffee and vanilla. Fold together slowly and carefully with a metal spoon to ensure as much of the air is retained as possible. Fold in the rest of the flour and cocoa mix until well combined then transfer to the prepared tin.

Use the back of a spoon or an angled palette knife to even the mixture and push to the sides and corners of the tin. This mixture will not find its own level in the oven. Bake for just 8 minutes, then check to make sure your sponge has risen slightly and is springy to the touch.

Transfer the sponge (still in the tin) to a cooling rack and leave for 5 minutes. When the tin is cool enough to handle, combine the caster sugar and cocoa powder for sprinkling, then sprinkle over the surface of the still-warm sponge. Lay a piece of non-stick baking parchment or a piece of cotton cloth/a tea towel over the top, then a baking sheet, and quickly flip the whole thing over. Peel off the original baking parchment. Carefully and loosely roll up the sponge using the new piece of parchment or the cloth as an aid then leave and allow to cool completely in the rolled-up position. This prevents the roll cracking later.

Mix the cherry jam and almond extract together.

Melt the white chocolate in a non-metal bowl in 15-second bursts in the microwave, stirring well between each burst. Overheating will cause your chocolate to seize but we can rescue it (see Tip).

Stone the fresh cherries then, holding the stalks, dip them into the melted chocolate and leave to set on a piece of baking parchment.

To prepare the filling, whisk the double cream with the icing sugar and amaretto (if using) in a bowl with a hand-held electric whisk until soft peaks form. Set aside.

When ready to assemble, unroll the roulade, spread over the jam, cover with the whipped cream and carefully re-roll. Trim the ends to neaten the roulade, transfer to a serving plate then decorate with a dusting of sugar/cocoa mix, a drizzle of the melted white chocolate and the chocolate-dipped cherries.

||||||||||||||||||||||||||||||||||||||||||||||||||||||||||||||||||||||||||||||||||||||||||||||||||||||||||||||||||||||||||||||||

Seized chocolate will clump, or be crumbly and set hard in the bowl. There's no need to throw it away and start again, just boil the kettle then add a teaspoon of boiled water at a time and stir well between each addition until the chocolate is smooth and silky.

||||||||||||||||||||||||||||||||||||||||||||||||||||||||||||||||||||||||||||||||||||||||||||||||||||||||||||||||||||||||||||||||

LET ME SHOW YOU . . .

My Cherry Chocolate Roulade Video

RICH FRUIT CAKES

For many people a homemade fruit cake, especially the home-made Christmas cake, is a family tradition. A fond memory for me is spending the day with my grandmother busily prepping all the ingredients for Christmas bakes. Many of us have a tried and trusted recipe that's been in the family for years.

Rich fruit cakes have been around for centuries of course, well before we started making sponges – I remember reading that the Roman soldiers used to have a slice of fruit cake to sustain them in battle.

CHRISTMAS CAKE

SERVES: 8–10

For those who have never made their own Christmas cake, I urge you to try mine. It fits in nicely with today's busy routines in that the fruit can be left to soak in the morning before heading out to work (or even left for up to a week if you've got other things to do). The mixing is straight forward and then – best of all – the cake bakes during the night while you sleep, cooking in a very low oven for ten hours. You will come downstairs the next morning to that warm comforting aroma of Christmas spice. Then you take your cake out of the oven, leave it in the tin on a cooling rack then when you come home from work remove it from the tin (leaving the baking paper on as it helps to keep everything moist), wrap it in foil and pop into a tin until nearer to Christmas.

I usually make my Christmas cake in October and store it until two weeks before Christmas. My cake doesn't need feeding because the low, slow bake ensures it doesn't dry out and the cake is moist. If you have a tabletop (stand) mixer this cake is so easy to make you will never buy one again.

Finally – consider the cost saving! A 23cm (9 inch) Christmas cake will only cost about £9 to make. Christmas cakes, especially mini cakes, make great gifts.

Using my cake converter on pages 16–19 the recipe below can be scaled up or down, square to round. As a rough rule of thumb, I adjust the baking time as follows: for every 2.5cm (1 inch) reduction in size of cake tin, I reduce the baking time by 1 hour; for every 2.5cm (1 inch) increase in size, I increase the baking time by an hour. If you have a temperature probe, the internal baked temperature needs to read between 92–94°C.

100g (3½oz) morello or glacé cherries
1kg (2lb 4oz) mixed dried fruit and peel
4 tbsp Cointreau, brandy, sherry or juice from the orange
   (after zesting)
finely grated zest and juice of 1 orange
finely grated zest and juice of 1 lemon
250g (9oz) butter
250g (9oz) soft dark brown sugar
5 eggs, beaten in a jug
1 tbsp golden syrup or black treacle
250g (9oz) plain flour
1 tsp ground mace (or 1½ tsp ground nutmeg)
1 tsp mixed spice
1 tsp ground ginger
½ tsp ground cinnamon

Equipment: tabletop (stand) mixer, 23cm (9 inch) round cake tin, bottom and sides greased and lined with greaseproof paper or baking parchment

Mini Christmas cakes
This recipe will also make 9 × 7.5cm (3 inch) mini Christmas cakes which need to bake for 5 hours.

Do I need to buy special small tins for mini Christmas cakes?

Mini Christmas cakes can work out to be expensive. Instead, save small baked bean tins. Remove the top and the base with a can opener and you will be left with a metal sleeve. Remove the label of course, give it a good wash then line with a ribbon of baking parchment and place on a baking sheet lined with paper. Don't worry that there is no base to the tin – the mixture is very thick and will not leak out at the bottom.

||||||||||||||||||||||||||||||||||||||||||||||||||||||||||||||||||||||||||||||||||||||||||||||||||||||||||||||||||||||||||||||||||

First thing in the morning, rinse the cherries in cold water to remove the sticky glaze, dry them, then cut them into thirds, then put the mixed fruit and cut cherries in a large bowl and add the Cointreau or other liquid, fruit zests and juices. Stir, cover with a plate or lid, then leave until the evening. The fruit can be left in a cool place for a number of days and even up to a week.

Preheat the oven to 120°C/100°C (fan)/250°F/gas ½.

In the evening, when you are ready to mix the cake batter, cream the butter and brown sugar in the bowl of a tabletop (stand) mixer fitted with the whisk attachment until pale, light and fluffy. Blitz the beaten eggs in the jug with a stick blender, or beat well a hand whisk, to make sure the egg is well mixed, then, with the mixer on medium speed, pour the egg into the butter and sugar mix in a very thin and steady stream, increasing the speed of the whisk as the mixture becomes thinner. This method should avoid any curdling. If you see that the mixture is starting to split (curdle) then add a tablespoon of the measured flour, bring the mixture back to a smooth consistency then continue adding the rest of the egg and, finally, the syrup and treacle. Change the whisk to the paddle attachment and add the flour and spices. Fold in the soaked fruits.

Transfer the mix to the prepared tin and bake in the oven for 10 hours. I usually put the cake into the oven at 10pm and take it out at 8am the next day. Allow the cake to cool completely in the tin then remove, leave on the papers, wrap in foil and store in a tin until ready to decorate at Christmas.

ICING YOUR CHRISTMAS CAKE

MARZIPAN LAYER

    1.25kg (2lb 12oz) room-temperature marzipan
    1–2 tbsp brandy or other alcohol, for brushing

Roll out the marzipan larger than the surface area of the cake to be covered. To do this, take a length of string and allow 2.5cm (1 inch) at the bottom then use the length of string to take up the side of the cake, across the top, down the side opposite and allow an extra 2.5cm (1 inch) at the base. This length of string is the length and width of the circle you need to roll to. You can dust the work surface with icing sugar for rolling out the marzipan, but this can cause the marzipan to dry out and crack, so I prefer to roll the marzipan between two sheets of plastic.

Just before covering the cake with marzipan, brush it all over with brandy (or other alcohol) to give it a sticky surface. This will also destroy any bacteria that could start to grow. For an extra-smooth flat surface, I often turn my cake upside down and cover the base and transfer the bobbly top surface to the underneath, so the base of the cake is uppermost and the part that gets iced.

Once rolled out, peel the top piece of plastic off the marzipan and use the other piece as an aid to centre the marzipan over the cake. Use cake smoothers dipped in icing sugar to smooth out the marzipan and eliminate any air bubbles then leave uncovered in a cool place for a few days to dry out. This will avoid any oil seeping from the marzipan into the white icing when you ice it.

You can now choose to cover the marzipan layer with either fondant icing or royal icing.

FONDANT ICING
   1kg (2lb 4oz) fondant icing

Use the marzipan rolling-out method for the fondant icing, but use a brushing of water instead of alcohol to brush the marzipan before laying over the fondant. Use cake smoothers dipped in icing sugar to smooth out the icing and eliminate any air bubbles.

This recipe will cover a 23cm (9 inch) cake or 9 mini cakes.

MARZIPAN AND ROYAL ICING
   2 egg whites
   400g (14oz) icing sugar, sifted
   ½ tsp lemon juice
   ½ tsp glycerine

Equipment: hand-held electric whisk

Beat the egg whites in a clean, roomy mixing bowl with a hand-held electric whisk just to a frothy stage then stir in the icing sugar one large spoonful at a time. When mixed and smooth, stir through the lemon juice and glycerine then beat by hand or with a hand-held electric whisk for 5 minutes until very thick, glossy and smooth. (The addition of glycerine prevents the icing from setting like concrete.) Cover the bowl with a damp cloth when not in use as it will start to dry out if not using straight away, or keep in a sealed plastic box for up to 4 days. For a 'snow scene', you want it to have a thick consistency, with the icing standing in peaks. For a pipeable icing, add more lemon juice to thin it down.

This recipe will cover a 23cm (9 inch) cake or 9 mini cakes.

LET ME SHOW YOU . . .

My Christmas Cakes Video

SIMNEL CAKE

SERVES: 6–8

Prior to becoming an Easter bake, the Simnel cake used to be made by girls in service at the early part of the last century and taken home as a gift on Mothering Sunday. Now famously celebrated as a traditional Easter bake, it is decorated with a layer of marzipan in the middle of the cake and on top, and eleven balls of marzipan to represent Jesus' disciples, minus Judas. It is lighter in texture than a traditional Christmas cake.

75g (2½oz) ready-to-eat dried apricots, cut into small dice
   (about the size of a sultana)
200g (7oz) mixed dried fruit with peel
finely grated zest and juice of 1 large lemon
75g (2½oz) glacé cherries
125g (4¼oz) margarine or butter, at room temperature
60g (2¼oz) caster sugar
60g (2¼oz) soft light brown sugar
2 eggs
150g (5½oz) plain flour
½ tsp baking powder
pinch of salt
1 tsp mixed spice
300g (10½oz) golden marzipan
1–2 tsp apricot jam, for brushing

Equipment: hand-held electric whisk, 15–18cm (6–7 inch) round cake tin, lined with greaseproof paper

Start the night before (if you remember), but no worries if you can't. Put the dried fruit (except the glacé cherries) in a small bowl then add the lemon zest and juice. Give the whole lot a stir, cover and set aside until the morning. The fruit will plump up and absorb the liquid.

When ready to bake, rinse the cherries in cold water to remove the sticky glaze, dry them, then halve them. Preheat the oven to 140°C/120°C (fan)/275°F/gas 1.

Cream the margarine (or butter) and sugars (if you don't have both sugars, use all caster sugar instead) together in a roomy mixing bowl with a hand-held electric whisk until light and fluffy. If using brown sugar, make sure there are no lumps. Add the eggs one at a time, whisking well after each addition.

Put a spoonful of the measured flour in a small bowl with the cherries, and stir so that the cherries are separated and coated in flour.

Sift together the remaining flour, baking powder, salt and mixed spice and stir to combine, then fold into the cake batter. Add the soaked fruit and, lastly, the cherries.

Spoon 450g (1lb) (or half of the mixture) into the base of the prepared cake tin then smooth out with the back of a spoon.

Roll out 125g (4¼oz) of the marzipan between two sheets of plastic to a circle (keeping the rest in an airtight container to prevent it drying out) and use the base of the tin as a template to cut around – I use a pizza cutter to cut out a circle. Ideally the circle should be just slightly smaller than the cake tin so trim the circle once the tin has been removed. Place this circle of marzipan over the raw cake mix then top with the rest of the batter and smooth out.

This cake needs to bake evenly with no rise and no burnt or overbaked sides. A foil collar will do the trick here (see page 124).

Bake the cake in the oven for 1 hour then reduce the temperature to 120°C/100°C (fan)/250°F/gas ½ and bake for another 3 hours. The cake will be a dark golden colour, firm to the touch, with a flat top.

Remove the cake from the oven and allow to cool in the tin.

Remove from the tin when cold, remove the lining papers then transfer to a cake board or cake stand.

Roll out the remaining marzipan and use the tin again to cut out a second circle. Brush the top of the cake with apricot jam then secure the marzipan. Flute the edges and decorate with the marzipan trimmings.

The marzipan balls on the top I think are better if they are not large and clumsy. I use just 3g of marzipan per disciple. Toasting the balls with a blowtorch, as well as being traditional also gives the marzipan a lovely flavour.

LET ME SHOW YOU . . .

My Simnel Cake Video

OTHER CAKE-BAKING METHODS

There are a couple of other cake-making methods I want to mention that are not often used. I call them 'forgotten cakes'. Many of us now have labour-saving gadgets, mixers and blenders that benefit us enormously but it means these traditional methods, even though they are easy and make brilliant cakes, are not often used.

Boil and bake method

The great thing about cakes made using this method is that there is hardly any washing up! The recipe's fats and liquids are boiled together in a pan, cooled and then the eggs and flour are added. A quick stir and into the tin – job done.

Rubbing-in method

If you like making pastry you will adore my second 'forgotten' method. My grandmother made fantastic pastry, but rarely made cakes. When she did make a cake, she used this method, probably because the two methods are so similar. The mixing of the cake starts with the fat being rubbed into the flour, then the sugar, eggs and flavours are stirred through. If you are new to cake-making and maybe have very little equipment, then this method is for you. No creaming, no curdling, and no mixer required.

DATE AND ORANGE CAKE

SERVES: 6–8

This traditional cake is made using the boil and bake method. It has no additional sugar, only the natural sugars in the dried fruit and the sugar in the condensed milk. It's an easy can't-fail recipe and actually improves with keeping (it keeps for several weeks in a tin). I like it sliced into thin fingers and served alongside other cakes, scones and patisserie for Afternoon Tea.

120g (4¼oz) chopped pitted dates
180g (6¼oz) mixed dried fruit
140g (5oz) butter
finely grated zest of 2 oranges
150ml (5fl oz) juice from the 2 fruits (make it up with water
    or bottled juice if you don't have enough)
400g (14oz) tin condensed milk
2 eggs
150g (5½oz) self-raising flour
½ tsp salt
1½ tsp ground ginger or 1 tbsp freshly grated ginger

Equipment: 20cm (8 inch) square cake tin, base and sides lined with greaseproof paper

Preheat the oven to 170°C/150°C (fan)/325°F/gas 3.

Put the dried fruit, butter, orange zest and juice and condensed milk in a medium saucepan and stir regularly over a low heat until the butter has melted. Increase the heat and bring to the boil. Once bubbling, cook for 4 minutes then take off the heat and give it a really good stir. I like to blitz the mixture with a stick blender now, to break down the fruit a little, but this is entirely up to you. Place the lid on the saucepan and leave to cool completely.

Once the mixture is cold, stir in the eggs, making sure they are well incorporated and thus loosen the mixture. Sift the flour, salt and ginger (if using ground) then fold them into the wet mix (add the ginger separately to the mix if using fresh). Transfer the thick mixture into the prepared tin and smooth it out.

Bake in the oven for 1 hour, until the cake is slightly risen and firm to the touch.

Remove from the oven and allow to cool completely in the tin on a cooling rack then turn out and store in an airtight tin. The flavour of this cake improves if it is stored for at least a day or two.

LET ME SHOW YOU . . .

My Date and Orange Cake Video

My cake is overbrowning!

Your cake may look baked as it is brown on the top but there is still 10 minutes' baking time left according to your recipe. What should you do? Do not be tempted to take the cake out of the oven. Instead, change your oven from 'fan' to 'conventional' cooking and take a piece of foil larger than the cake, fold it into four and tear out a hole that will be in the centre of the foil. Carefully open your oven door and lay the foil over the cake. The cake can then continue to bake and cook through without further browning.

ORANGE AND GINGER CAKE

SERVES: 4–6

This cake is utterly delicious, keeps well in a tin for at least a week, and in fact improves in flavour after sitting in a tin for a couple of days after baking. It is made using the rubbing in method which is not seen often these days – a handy bake if you have little equipment.

80g (2¾oz) stem ginger (from a jar of stem ginger in syrup)
200g (7oz) self-raising flour
pinch of salt
40g (1½oz) butter, diced, at room temperature
40g (1½oz) lard, diced, at room temperature (or use all butter if you prefer)
1 tsp ground ginger
100g (3½oz) caster sugar
1 heaped tbsp marmalade
finely grated zest and juice of 1 large orange
1 egg
100ml (3½fl oz) whole milk
1 tbsp demerara sugar or sugar nibs, to sprinkle over

Equipment: 18cm (7 inch) round cake tin, sides brushed with lining paste or greased and base lined with reusable baking parchment or greaseproof paper

Preheat the oven to 200°C/180°C (fan)/400°F/gas 6.

Wash the stem ginger pieces under a cold tap, dry on kitchen paper, then cut into small dice. Place in a small bowl with 1 tablespoon of the weighed self-raising flour and dust the ginger to coat. Set aside.

Put the self-raising flour, salt, butter and lard in a medium bowl and rub together just as you would for pastry, with your fingertips, until the mixture resembles breadcrumbs. Add the ground ginger, caster sugar, marmalade, orange zest and juice and give it all a stir, then add the egg followed by the milk, adding the milk a little at a time until you achieve a soft dropping consistency. You will probably need all the milk but add it gradually just in case. Finally, fold in the chopped ginger.

Transfer the batter to the prepared tin and sprinkle over the demerara sugar or sugar nibs. Bake in the oven for 35–40 minutes until the cake is golden, risen and springy to the touch.

Remove from the oven and leave to cool in the tin on a cooling rack for about 20 minutes before turning out onto a cooling rack to cool completely. Wrap in foil and store in an airtight tin for a couple of days before eating, but if you just cannot wait to eat it – enjoy!

LET ME SHOW YOU . . .

My Orange and Ginger Cake Video

RASPBERRY RIPPLE CUPCAKES

MAKES: 12 CUPCAKES

This easy bake is fit enough for any occasion – children love to make these. I use frozen raspberries for the cakes then top them with a fresh one.

FOR THE CAKES
- 130g (4½oz) margarine or butter, at room temperature
- 1 tsp vanilla extract
- 130g (4½oz) caster sugar
- 2 eggs
- 130g (4½oz) self-raising flour
- 70g (2½oz) frozen raspberries, broken up

FOR THE BUTTERCREAM AND DECORATION
- 150g (5½oz) butter, at room temperature
- 1 tsp vanilla extract
- 270g (9½oz) icing sugar, sifted
- 2 large tbsp thick full-fat plain yoghurt
- pink food colour gel
- 12 fresh raspberries

Equipment: hand-held electric whisk, 12-hole muffin tin lined with paper cases, piping bag fitted with a star nozzle

Preheat the oven to 200°C/180°C (fan)/400°F/gas 6.

Cream the margarine (or butter), vanilla and caster sugar in a roomy mixing bowl with a hand-held electric whisk until light and fluffy, then add the eggs one at a time, whisking well after each addition. Fold in the flour then finally stir through the frozen broken-up raspberries.

Divide the mixture evenly among 12 paper cases – a large dessert spoonful each is just about right. Bake in the oven for 20–25 minutes until risen, pale golden and springy to the touch.

Remove from the oven and leave to cool on a cooling rack. When cool enough to handle remove from the tin.

To make the cream, whisk the butter and vanilla extract with a hand-held electric whisk until pale and soft, then add the sifted icing sugar in three parts, whisking well after each addition. Finally, whisk in the yoghurt. You should have a light, smooth fluffy buttercream for icing your cupcakes.

Take a piping bag fitted with a star nozzle and using a long-handled paintbrush paint a line of pink food colour gel down the inside of the bag. Fill the bag with the buttercream and when the cakes have cooled completely pipe the buttercream over the cakes and top with a fresh raspberry. You will be delighted with the ripple effect when piping!

LET ME SHOW YOU . . .

My Raspberry Ripple Cupcakes Video

CARROT AND ORANGE CAKE

SERVES: 8–12

This deliciously moist carrot and orange cake is filled and frosted with a smooth cream cheese icing then decorated with glazed carrot chips and rosemary leaves.

FOR THE CAKE

110g (4oz) soft light brown sugar
120ml (4fl oz) vegetable oil
2 eggs
150g (5½oz) self-raising flour
1 tsp baking powder
1 tsp ground cinnamon
1 tsp mixed spice
finely grated zest and juice of 1 orange
125g (4¼oz) carrot, peeled and finely grated

FOR THE FILLING AND FROSTING

100g (3½oz) butter, at room temperature
100g (3½oz) icing sugar, sifted
½ tsp vanilla extract
125g (4¼oz) full-fat cream cheese
2–3 tbsp marmalade

FOR THE CARROT DECORATION (OPTIONAL)

50g (1¾oz) granulated sugar
30ml (1fl oz) water
1 carrot, peeled
fresh rosemary needles

Equipment: hand-held electric whisk, 2 ×18cm (7 inch) round loose-bottom sandwich tins, greased and base lined with non-stick baking parchment

Preheat the oven to 200°C/180°C (fan)/400°F/gas 6.

Put the light brown sugar in a roomy mixing bowl and make sure there are no lumps. Add the oil and eggs and whisk with a hand-held electric whisk until the mixture has thickened slightly and increased in volume. Sift together the flour, baking powder and dried spices, fold this into the mix, then stir in the orange zest and juice, and the grated carrot.

Divide the cake batter evenly between the two prepared tins (I prefer to weigh the mixture – see page 123) and bake in the oven for 20–25 minutes, until the cakes are golden and firm to the touch. Turn out onto cooling racks, turning them the right way up, and leave to go completely cold.

For the filling and frosting mix, simply whisk the butter in a bowl with a hand-held electric whisk until creamy, then add the sifted icing sugar a spoonful at a time, whisking after each addition. Mix in the vanilla and finally the cream cheese, adding a quarter of the cheese at a time and beating well after each addition.

If you are making carrot chips, first dissolve the sugar in a small saucepan with the water. Cut the carrot lengthways into thin slices about the thickness of a £1 coin. Cut each slice into mini carrot-shaped chips (I usually cut about 12 then use the best 8 for the cake). Add the carrot chips to the syrup and boil for 3–4 minutes until soft. Remove from the syrup and leave to cool on a piece of kitchen foil or parchment.

When ready to assemble the cake, spread the marmalade over the bottom cake then sandwich the two sponges together with a layer of one third of the cream then cover the top and sides with the remaining cream frosting. Top with the carrot chips, each topped with a few needles of fresh rosemary.

LET ME SHOW YOU . . .

My Carrot and Orange Cake Video

COCONUT AND PASSION FRUIT
ANGEL CAKES

MAKES: 12 CAKES

These cakes have only egg white in the sponge and are beautifully light. Traditionally a cake made with egg whites is called an angel cake – so there you go.

FOR THE CAKES

3 egg whites
125g (4¼oz) margarine or butter, at room temperature
180g (6¼oz) caster sugar
150ml (5fl oz) whole milk
½ tsp vanilla extract
150g (5½oz) plain flour
½ tsp baking powder
50g (1¾oz) desiccated coconut

FOR THE PASSION FRUIT CURD CREAM

4 passion fruit
2 eggs
75g (2½oz) granulated sugar
50g (1¾oz) butter
a few drops of passion fruit flavouring (optional)
200ml (7fl oz) double cream
10g (⅓oz) icing sugar

Equipment: hand-held electric whisk, 12-hole muffin tin lined with paper cases, piping bag (optional)

Start by making the passion fruit curd. Extract the juice from the passion fruit: cut the fruits in half then use a teaspoon to scrape out the seeds into a metal sieve set over a small bowl. Rub the fruit juice and pulp from the seeds and set aside. Keep the seeds for decoration later.

Put the eggs in a medium saucepan, beat well, then add the sugar, butter, reserved passion fruit juice and pulp and passion fruit flavouring (if using) and stir constantly over a low heat until the butter has melted. Increase the heat slightly and stir constantly for 3–4 minutes until the curd thickens. Transfer to a heatproof jug or bowl and allow to cool completely.

Preheat the oven to 200°C/180°C (fan)/400°F/gas 6.

To make the sponge, start by whisking the egg whites in a clean bowl with a hand-held electric whisk until they form soft peaks. In a separate bowl, with clean whisks, whisk the margarine and sugar until light and fluffy. Add about a quarter of the milk plus the vanilla extract and about a quarter of the flour (sifted into the bowl with the baking powder) to the margarine and sugar mix and keep mixing until everything is incorporated. Repeat until all the flour and milk have been incorporated and the mixture is smooth. Finally, fold in the coconut and the whisked egg whites with a metal spoon until combined.

Divide the mixture evenly among the paper cases and bake in the oven for 18–20 minutes until the cakes are risen, golden and firm to the touch. The sponges are quite pale because of the absence of egg yolk.

Remove from the oven and leave to cool completely on a cooling rack, taking the cakes out of the tin in their cases once cool enough to handle.

To make the cream, simply whisk the double cream and icing sugar in a bowl with a hand-held electric whisk until just thickened, but not too much! Fold in the cooled passion fruit curd. Pipe or spoon the cream over the cakes and top off with a few passion fruit seeds.

LET ME SHOW YOU . . .

My Coconut and Passionfruit Cakes Video

LEMON AND ELDERFLOWER CAKE

SERVES: 6–8

This is a wonderful cake for the summertime and a few edible flowers on top look simple yet stunning. If you like cake but the thought of sweet sickly buttercream puts your teeth on edge, then this is the frosting for you. The amount in the recipe is enough to fill and coat the cake – if you just want to fill it, not coat it, halve the quantities. Light, smooth and not overly sweet, this cake is a delight.

FOR THE CAKE
125g (4¼oz) margarine or butter, at room temperature
125g (4¼oz) caster sugar
2 eggs
125g (4¼oz) self-raising flour
finely grated zest of ½ lemon and all of the juice
½ tsp lemon extract

FOR THE 'NOT TOO SWEET BUTTERCREAM'
250ml (8fl oz) whole milk
3 tbsp cornflour
180g (6¼oz) butter, at room temperature
170g (6oz) icing sugar
4 tbsp elderflower cordial
grated zest of ½ lemon

Equipment: hand-held electric whisk, 2 × 15cm (6 inch) round loose-bottom sandwich tins, greased and bases lined with reusable baking parchment

Preheat the oven to 200°C/180°C (fan)/400°F/gas 6.

Cream the margarine (or butter) and sugar in a medium bowl with a hand-held electric whisk until light and fluffy, then add the eggs one at a time, whisking well after each addition. Sift in the flour then add the lemon zest, extract and juice and fold in.

Divide the cake batter evenly between the prepared tins (I prefer to weigh the mixture – see page 123) and bake in the oven for 18–20 minutes until the cakes are pale golden, risen and firm to the touch.

Remove from the oven then remove from the tins when cool enough to handle and leave to go completely cold right side up on a cooling rack.

To make the buttercream, first put the milk and cornflour in a small saucepan and heat gently, stirring constantly, until the mixture thickens. Transfer to a heatproof bowl, cover and leave to go completely cold.

In a separate bowl, whisk the butter with a hand-held electric whisk until creamy, then sift in the icing sugar in three parts, whisking really well after each addition. This is important for a smooth cream. Whisk the cold paste into the buttercream one spoonful at a time, whisking really well after each addition, then finally whisk in the elderflower cordial and lemon zest.

Use half of the cream to sandwich the cakes together and apply a thin 'crumb coat' to the top and sides. A crumb coat is a first, thin coating of icing or frosting that give a firm surface for the finished icing layer. I use a palette knife to apply the icing to the cake then a plastic bench scraper to spread it and smooth it out.

Chill the cake for at least 1 hour then spread over the rest of the buttercream and decorate as you wish.

LET ME SHOW YOU . . .

My Lemon and Elderflower Cake Video

CHOCOLATE AND AMARETTO
FESTIVE CUPCAKES

MAKES: 12 CUPCAKES

I do recommend you try these simple little festive treats. The chocolate sponge is light and the lovely amaretto flavour really comes through. If, like me, you are put off by frostings that are too sweet then this one is for you. Decorate them as you wish – I pipe a little ropework on the top then finish them off with marzipan holly leaves and berries: they are a good way to use any leftover marzipan offcuts if you make your own Christmas Cake (page 150).

FOR THE CAKES

100g (3½oz) dark chocolate (75% cocoa solids will give the best flavour), broken into small pieces

150ml (5fl oz) whole milk

125g (4¼oz) caster sugar

60g (2¼oz) butter or margarine, at room temperature

25ml (¾fl oz) amaretto

½ tsp almond extract

2 eggs

150g (5½oz) self-raising flour

FOR THE FROSTING AND DECORATION

100ml (3½fl oz) whole milk

2 tbsp cornflour

100g (3½oz) butter, at room temperature

100g (3½oz) icing sugar
½ tsp vanilla extract

Equipment: hand-held electric whisk, 1 large, deep 12-hole muffin tin lined with paper cases, piping bag (optional)

Preheat the oven to 190°C/170°C (fan)/375°F/gas 5.

Put the chocolate pieces in a heatproof bowl. Pour the milk into a small saucepan and add 40g (1½oz) of the caster sugar. Bring to a simmer then pour into the bowl of chocolate and stir until the chocolate has fully melted. Set to one side.

Cream the remaining sugar and butter in a bowl with a hand-held electric whisk until light and fluffy then add the amaretto and almond extract. Add the eggs one at a time, whisking well after each addition, then sift in the flour and fold it in with the chocolate mix. As the batter is very runny, I pour mine into a jug before transferring into the cupcake cases.

Fill each case about two-thirds full, transfer to the oven and bake for 18–20 minutes until risen and springy to the touch.

Remove from the oven, transfer the cakes from the tin to a cooling rack and leave to cool.

To make the frosting, put the milk and cornflour in a small saucepan over a medium heat and, whisking all the time, allow the mixture to thicken. Transfer to a heatproof bowl and leave to go completely cold.

Whisk the butter and icing sugar in a medium bowl, incorporating the icing sugar a little at a time and whisking well after each addition, then add the vanilla extract and whisk for about 4 minutes until the frosting is pale and fluffy. Add the milk paste a spoonful at a time, whisking after each addition, transfer to a piping bag (if using) and pipe (or spoon) the frosting onto the cakes. Top with marzipan holly leaves and berries if using.

LET ME SHOW YOU . . .

My Chocolate and Amaretto
Festive Cupcakes

CHOCOLATE, VANILLA AND STRAWBERRY DRIP CAKE

SERVES: 10–12

A celebration cake loved by children! I have made this cake many times and it really is a kids' showstopper, especially when decorated with chocolate drips and coloured sprinkles.

FOR THE SPONGES

500g (1lb 2oz) margarine or butter, at room temperature
500g (1lb 2oz) caster sugar
9 eggs
1½ tbsp vanilla extract
50ml (1¾fl oz) vegetable oil
650g (1lb 7oz) self-raising flour
40ml (1¼fl oz) milk

FOR A SIMPLE BUTTERCREAM

250g (9oz) butter, at room temperature
450g (1lb) icing sugar
4 tbsp freeze-dried strawberry powder
50g (1¾oz) full-fat cream cheese
3 tbsp whole milk

FOR THE CHOCOLATE DRIP AND DECORATION

200g (7oz) dark chocolate, broken into small pieces
200g (7oz) double cream (weigh it in a jug on digital scales)
coloured sprinkles or decoration of choice

Equipment: tabletop (stand) mixer or hand-held electric whisk, 2 × 23cm (9 inch) deep cake tins, greased and lined

Preheat the oven to 150°C/130°C (fan)/300°F/gas 2.

First, make the sponges. Cream together the margarine (or butter) and sugar in a large bowl with a hand-held electric whisk (or use a tabletop/stand mixer fitted with the creamer attachment) until light and fluffy. Beat the eggs with the vanilla and oil, then gradually add the egg mix to the creamed butter and sugar, whisking well after each addition. If the mixture starts to curdle, add 1 tablespoon of the weighed-out flour. When all the eggs have been incorporated, sift in the flour and fold it in with a metal spoon until you have a smooth mixture, then finally add the milk.

Divide the cake batter evenly between the two tins (I like to use digital scales for this – see page 123) then bake in the oven for 1¼ hours, until golden brown.

Remove from the oven and leave to cool in the tins for 15 minutes, then remove and leave to cool completely – right side up – on cooling racks. You may want to level the tops of your cakes with a knife or cake wire if they have risen up in the middle slightly during baking.

To make the buttercream, cream the butter well in a bowl with a hand-held electric whisk then add the icing sugar in three parts, beating really well after each addition. Add the strawberry powder, cream cheese and the milk and whisk well until the cream is light, smooth and fluffy. Use the buttercream to sandwich together the two cakes then apply a crumb coating to the top and sides using a palette knife and plastic bench scraper. Pop into the fridge for at least 2 hours to firm up.

To make the chocolate drip, put the chocolate pieces into a heatproof jug or bowl. Heat the double cream in a small saucepan and when it starts to form bubbles take it off the heat and pour it over the chocolate in the jug. Stir well until the chocolate has melted and you have a smooth and shiny ganache. Allow the chocolate to cool and thicken to the consistency of single cream then pour it over your chilled cake and, using the back of a spoon or a small angled palette knife, work at steering the drips so that they are fairly uniform around your cake.

Pop back into the fridge to firm up for about 15 minutes then finish the decoration with sweets, sprinkles, macaron . . . the possibilities are endless.

Piping lettering
Try piping onto a piece of baking parchment or greaseproof paper first. Have as many tries as you need, then pipe your perfect lettering on the paper. (You know it will fit because you measured it beforehand.) Pop the whole thing into the fridge and – once set – carefully remove it with an angled palette knife and transfer it to where you want it on the cake.

LET ME SHOW YOU . . .

My Chocolate, Vanilla and Strawberry Cake Video

PECAN AND APPLE CAKE

SERVES: 8

This cake is a real delight. It is light yet moist and has a delicious cinnamon frosting but, best of all I think, is the little apple surprise inside every slice.

FOR THE CAKE

    175g (6oz) margarine or butter, at room temperature

    175g (6oz) caster sugar

    3 eggs, plus 1 egg yolk

    175g (6oz) self-raising flour

    pinch of salt

    1 tsp ground cinnamon

    30g (1oz) pecan nuts, toasted and finely chopped (or just use mixed toasted chopped nuts)

    2 small dessert apples

    8 toasted pecan nuts, to decorate

FOR THE SWISS MERINGUE BUTTERCREAM FROSTING

    1 egg white

    30g (1oz) soft light brown sugar

    40g (1½oz) caster sugar

    125g (4¼oz) butter, diced, at room temperature

    1 tsp vanilla extract

    ½ tsp ground cinnamon

Equipment: hand-held electric whisk, deep 22cm (9 inch) round springform cake tin, greased and base lined with non-stick baking parchment

Preheat the oven to 190°C/170°C (fan)/375°F/gas 5.

Cream the margarine (or butter) and caster sugar in a medium bowl with a hand-held electric whisk until light and fluffy, then add the eggs one by one, plus the egg yolk (saving the white for the frosting), whisking well after each addition. Sift the flour, salt and cinnamon onto the bowl and fold in gently. Finally, add the toasted nuts and fold in until evenly dispersed throughout the batter.

Transfer the cake batter to the prepared cake tin and level it.

Peel, core and quarter the two apples (you want to do this now rather than ahead of time, so that they don't go brown). Make small cuts into the apple quarters, starting at the outside and towards the core but not all the way through, to aid the cooking process. Starting at the join of the tin (or a recognisable place), place the apples, cut side up into the mix, at 12 o'clock, 6 o'clock, 9 and 3 o'clock – with the top edge of each quarter (where the stalk would have been) by the edge of the tin – then space the other 4 apple quarters between, so they're arranged in a ring. Push them into the mix, so that you can still see about half of the apple.

Bake in the oven for 35–40 minutes, until the centre of the cake is springy to the touch and the sponge is golden brown. The apples should almost disappear and be covered by the cooked cake.

Remove the cake from the oven, remove from the tin and place on a cooling rack, but before you do, insert a wooden toothpick as a marker in the position where you placed the first piece of apple and where the tin seam was. Allow to cool thoroughly before frosting.

To make the Swiss meringue frosting, first put the egg white and both the sugars in a heatproof bowl over a pan of barely simmering water and keep stirring until the sugar has dissolved. Using a hand-held electric whisk, whisk the mixture for about 6 minutes until you have a thick pale caramel-coloured mix. Remove the bowl from the pan and continue to whisk until cool.

Whisk the room-temperature butter in a separate bowl with a hand-held electric whisk until soft then add the whisked egg white a large spoonful at a time, whisking after each addition until you have a deliciously smooth frosting. Finally, whisk in the vanilla extract and cinnamon.

When ready to decorate, cover the top of the cooled cake with the frosting, then the sides, making special note of where you inserted the wooden skewer. I think the frosting looks better if it's not too perfect. Place one pecan nut above where you have inserted your skewer then it is easy to determine where the other seven need to go. This means each serving will contain a hidden piece of apple.

LET ME SHOW YOU . . .

My Pecan and Apple Cake Video

CAKE FILLINGS AND FROSTINGS

I considered this section heading and immediately felt over-whelmed before I even start to write. There are so many fillings and frostings to choose from and so many flavours. I decided that maybe the most straight forward way to approach it was to start with the easiest and progress through to the more complex recipes.

The thing is, once you have mastered the art of making the smoothest fillings and frostings, you will be totally put off by very sweet, gritty type that puts your teeth on edge. By the end of this section, you will be well equipped to take on the lot!

With all of my recipes, I try to consciously work on reducing sugar and fat where appropriate. I like to decorate cakes simply, without resorting to piles of sugary sweets and chocolates – for me, such cakes are 'heartstoppers' not 'show stoppers'.

A slice of cake is not prohibitive – I can think of nothing more delicious just now than a piece of my Carrot and Orange Cake with cream cheese frosting, decorated just with a sliver of fresh glazed carrot (see page 167).

BUTTERCREAM

MAKES: ENOUGH TO SANDWICH AND DECORATE
A 20CM (8 INCH) CHOCOLATE CAKE OR
DECORATE 12 MINI CAKES OR CUPCAKES

This buttercream is smooth and rich yet uses less butter than typical buttercreams. It pipes well and will keep up to a week in the fridge. Allow to return to room temperature before using, as it sets quite firm. Alter the flavourings to suit your cake. (You can substitute the alcohol with extra milk if making the chocolate buttercream for kids.)

FOR A CHOCOLATE BUTTERCREAM FILLING
    150g (5½oz) butter, at room temperature
    450g (1lb) icing sugar
    30g (1oz) cocoa powder
    30ml (1fl oz) whole milk
    30ml (1fl oz) brandy (optional)

Equipment: hand-held electric whisk

Cream the butter in a bowl with a hand-held electric whisk until really soft and fluffy.

Sift the cocoa and icing sugar together so there are no streaks in your finished cream. Add the icing sugar mix little by little, whisking after each addition, until eventually the mixture has a crumbly consistency. Pour in the milk and brandy slowly and whisk again until light and fluffy.

FOR COFFEE BUTTERCREAM FILLING

150g (5½oz) butter, at room temperature

450g (1lb) icing sugar

2 tbsp instant coffee powder or granules
dissolved in 2 tbsp hot water

1 tsp vanilla extract

FOR LEMON BUTTERCREAM FILLING

150g (5½oz) butter, at room temperature

450g (1lb) icing sugar

finely grated zest of 1 large lemon

50ml (1¾fl oz) lemon juice

1 tsp lemon extract

LET ME SHOW YOU . . .

My Buttercream Video

ITALIAN MERINGUE BUTTERCREAM

MAKES: ENOUGH TO FILL AND DECORATE
A 15–20CM (6–8 INCH) CAKE

For me, this is the queen of cake frostings. It's light, not too sweet, smooth, pipes well and is utterly gorgeous. When I make wedding cakes, I always use this beautiful frosting. However, this recipe can have issues – the cream can be lumpy, it can curdle and can literally turn to soup!

I have encountered every disaster when making this frosting, but I promise you, if you follow my straightforward, simple instructions you will produce a perfect 'IMBC' every time. Why? Because I have decided to do things a little differently . . . here's how!

125g (4¼oz) caster sugar
3 tbsp water
1 egg white
110g (4oz) butter, at room temperature

Equipment: sugar thermometer, hand-held electric whisk, tabletop (stand) mixer (optional)

Put the caster sugar and water in a small saucepan and place over a low heat to dissolve the sugar. Do not stir but simply swirl the liquid in the pan. When fully dissolved bring to the boil then pop the thermometer into the pan.

You will need two large mixing bowls, one for the egg white

and one for the butter. Make sure the bowl and your whisks are absolutely clean, with no grease, otherwise your egg white will not whisk up to its full potential.

When the temperature reaches 105°C, start to whisk the egg white in a clean large mixing bowl with a hand-held electric whisk. When the whites form soft peaks, the sugar solution should have reached a temperature of 119°C. Take the pan off the heat and, while whisking, pour the sugar syrup in a slow, steady stream into the egg white. (I find it easier to warm a Pyrex jug then transfer my sugar syrup into it so that I have better control when pouring the hot liquid onto the meringue.) Whisk continuously, scraping down the sides of the bowl as you go, until the meringue finally cools to body temperature. If you pop your finger into the mix it should feel neither warm nor cold. This will take about 8 minutes. When cool set aside.

Using the same whisk, cream the butter in the other large mixing bowl until smooth, then add the meringue, a little at a time, until fully incorporated. Finally, whisk in your chosen flavouring (see page 190). The result will be unbelievably delicious cream which will keep in the fridge for up to 1 week. It will firm up in the fridge, so before using allow it to return to room temperature then give a whisk to return it to its former glory.

When making large amounts of this cream you will find it easier to use a tabletop (stand) mixer. The machine can be left running for about 10 minutes until the meringue has cooled. I bring the IMBC together by hand – whisking the butter up in a separate bowl with a hand-held electric whisk then adding the meringue one spoonful at a time.

DIFFERENT FLAVOURS FOR THE CREAM QUANTITY ABOVE

Lemon: grated zest and juice of 2 lemons

Coffee: dissolve 2 tbsp coffee powder in 1 tbsp hot water

Chocolate: mix 2 tbsp cocoa powder with 4 tbsp milk

Dried fruit powders: these are really good as they are intense in flavour. 1 tbsp added as it is, or mixed with water to bring to a paste, will flavour this cream too.

How to avoid curdling when making Italian meringue buttercream

The secret to success is to ensure that the butter and meringue are both at the same temperature before mixing them together. I have found that creaming the butter rather than adding it in chunks avoids any problems. If, however, your cream curdles during the mixing process do not stress. Take a large spoonful of your curdled mix and pop it into a non-metallic bowl then microwave for a few seconds just until you see the mixture turn to liquid. Take a hand-held electric whisk and blitz the liquid into the curdled cream. Miraculously you will see the cream return to its former glory.

LET ME SHOW YOU . . .

My Italian Meringue Buttercream Video

CHOCOLATE SWISS MERINGUE BUTTERCREAM

MAKES: ENOUGH TO TOP 18 CUPCAKES OR FILL
AND COAT A 20CM (8 INCH) SANDWICH CAKE

Standard buttercreams can be gritty, lacking in flavour and certainly too sweet. A Swiss meringue buttercream is less sweet than most buttercreams, easy to make, smooth, silky, full of flavour and the best news – no thermometer or special kit is required.

    120g (4¼oz) dark chocolate, broken into small pieces, or
        chocolate chips
    140g (5oz) soft light brown sugar
    2 egg whites
    250g (9oz) butter, at room temperature
    1 tsp vanilla extract
    2 tbsp cocoa powder mixed to a paste with 2–3 tbsp milk

Equipment: hand-held electric whisk

Put the chocolate in a small non-metal bowl and melt it in the microwave in three 20-second bursts, stirring after each burst, or until it's fully melted. Stir and set aside.

Put the sugar in a roomy heatproof bowl and press out any lumps with the back of a spoon. Add the egg whites and give everything a good stir. Place the bowl over a pan of recently boiled water and stir for about 5 minutes. The mixture will be dark and gritty to begin with but then, as the sugar dissolves, the mix will become paler, about the colour of caramel.

Once there is no gritty feel to the mixture (rub a little of the mixture between a thumb and forefinger and it should feel smooth) whisk it with a hand-held electric whisk, still over the hot water, for about 10 minutes until the mixture thickens, turns pale in colour and doubles in size. Once you have a cool meringue mix, set it aside.

In another bowl whisk the soft butter with a hand-held electric whisk until creamy then add the cooled meringue one large spoonful at a time, whisking well after each addition. Finally, add any flavours you are using (see page 190), the cooled melted chocolate, the vanilla and the cocoa paste.

This silky buttercream cream is will keep up to 1 week in the fridge. It pipes well and will not disappoint.

LET ME SHOW YOU . . .

My Chocolate Swiss Meringue
Buttercream Video

QUICK CURD

Curd is a massive favourite of mine and the extra few minutes it takes to make will make such a difference to your finished cake and its filling. When adding a lemon, lime or passion fruit cake filling I often make a lovely zingy, fresh, quick curd. The curd can be used on its own, but I prefer it whisked into fresh cream for a Swiss roll or to top a trifle, whisked into mascarpone cheese for a gorgeous less-sweet filling, or added to an Italian meringue or Swiss meringue buttercream.

The method is simple: everything just goes into the pan together.

LEMON CURD

    2 eggs
    75g (2½oz) caster sugar
    50g (1¾oz) butter, diced, at room temperature
    finely grated zest and juice of 1 large lemon

LIME CURD

    2 eggs
    75g (2½oz) caster sugar
    50g (1¾oz) butter, diced, at room temperature
    finely grated zest and juice of 2 limes

PASSION FRUIT CURD

    2 eggs
    75g (2½oz) caster sugar

50g (1¾oz) butter, diced, at room temperature

4 passion fruit (extract the juice – reserve seeds for decoration)

a few drops of passion fruit flavouring (optional)

Put the measured ingredients in a small saucepan and stir well off the heat, then heat gently, whisking all the time. When the butter melts, keep stirring and within a minute or so the curd will thicken. It is important to keep whisking briskly to avoid tiny white flecks of egg white being present in the finished curd. The recipe can also be made using 3 egg yolks rather than 2 whole eggs.

Transfer to a cold bowl or jar, cover and leave to cool to room temperature before chilling.

The curd will keep for at least 4 weeks in the fridge.

||||||||||||||||||||||||||||||||||||||||||||||||||||||||||||||||||||||||||||||||||||||||||||||||||||||||||||||||||||||||||||||

Choose wrinkled passion fruits

Wrinkled passion fruits are ripe and have more juice than smooth ones. To extract the most juice, cut it in half over a sieve set over a bowl. Scoop out the seeds, then push with a spoon until the juice and pulp leave the seeds.

Alternatively, cut the fruit and then blitz the seeds and flesh in a food processor for a minute or two and pour it through a sieve. This method is quicker!

||||||||||||||||||||||||||||||||||||||||||||||||||||||||||||||||||||||||||||||||||||||||||||||||||||||||||||||||||||||||||||||

CRÈME PÂTISSIÈRE

MAKES: 400ML (14FL OZ) – ENOUGH FOR
1 LARGE OR 12 SMALL OPEN FRUIT TARTS

This delicious thick and creamy custard has so many uses and, made using my simple one-stage method, will have you filling and topping your éclairs, fruit tarts, cakes, trifles and meringues effortlessly. Use as it is in open fruit tarts and éclairs or fold into 300ml (10fl oz) whipped double cream for a gorgeous filling or topping for your trifle, pavlova or cake.

3 egg yolks
1 tsp vanilla extract
50g (1¾oz) caster sugar
25g (1oz) cornflour
250ml (8fl oz) whole milk
15g (½oz) butter, at room temperature

Put the egg yolks in a small saucepan (off the heat) and beat with a small whisk. Add the vanilla extract, sugar and cornflour and mix to a smooth paste. Gradually add the milk, a little at a time, and when well combined add the butter. Place over a low heat and stir constantly until the butter melts. Increase the heat slightly and, still stirring, allow the custard to thicken – this will take 4–5 minutes. When it thickens, remove the pan from the heat, beating all the time, transfer to a cold heatproof bowl, cover with a sheet of crumpled greaseproof paper (this will avoid a skin forming on the crème) and then allow to cool.

Alternatively, if you are using the crème pâtissière in open fruit tarts, the warm custard can be poured directly into the baked pastry shell and left to cool.

LET ME SHOW YOU . . .

My Crème Pâtissière Video

FREE FROM

DIGESTIVE BISCUITS

MAKES: 8–12 BISCUITS

For those wanting a gluten-free digestive biscuit either to eat as it is, to have with cheese or use as a base for a cheesecake, you'll not go wrong with these. I may even go so far as to say they are my digestive biscuit of choice – never mind that I can eat gluten!

50g (1¾oz) rice flour
25g (1oz) ground almonds
25g (1oz) fine polenta
pinch of salt
½ tsp baking powder
20g (¾oz) soft brown sugar (dark or light)
¼ tsp Chinese five spice or ground star anise
25g (1oz) butter, diced, at room temperature
1 tbsp maple syrup or golden syrup
milk, to bind (about 1 tbsp)

Equipment: 6cm (2½ inch) pastry cutter, baking sheet lined with reusable baking parchment

Mix all the dry ingredients together in a mixing bowl then rub in the butter with your fingertips as you would for pastry, until the mixture resembles breadcrumbs. Add the maple syrup (or golden syrup) and enough milk to form a stiff dough.

Roll out the dough between two sheets of plastic to a thickness of 3mm (⅛ inch). Place the rolled-out dough in the fridge to chill for about 10 minutes, still within the plastic sheets.

Remove the dough from the fridge, peel off the top layer of plastic then use a 6cm (2½ inch) cutter to cut out your biscuits, re-rolling the trimmings as necessary. If the dough gets sticky, simply pop it back into the fridge for 5 minutes to firm up.

Transfer your biscuits to the baking sheet lined with parchment. Prick the biscuits with a fork then place in the fridge until the oven heats up. They need to chill for about 15 minutes.

Heat the oven to 200°C/180°C (fan)/400°F/gas 6 then bake the biscuits for 8–10 minutes until just starting to colour. Use an angled palette knife to lift and transfer the biscuits to a cooling rack to cool.

The biscuits will keep in an airtight container for up to 7–10 days.

LET ME SHOW YOU . . .

My Digestive Biscuits Video

SUMMER CAKE

SERVES: 8–10

A generous slice of beautiful creamy cake doesn't have to be bad for you. This whole cake, including the cream, contains just 200g (7oz) refined sugar and 164g (5¾oz) fat. Treat yourselves!

FOR THE CAKE

4 eggs
1 tsp vanilla extract
150g (5½oz) caster sugar
75g (2½oz) plain flour
1 tsp baking powder
50g (1¾oz) butter, melted and cooled but still runny

FOR THE LOWER-FAT VANILLA CREAM

3 egg yolks
1 tsp vanilla extract
50g (1¾oz) caster sugar
25g (1oz) cornflour
250ml (8fl oz) whole milk
300ml (10fl oz) whipping cream (lower in fat than double cream)

FOR THE DECORATION

500g (1lb 2oz) fresh late-summer fruits (blackberries,
    raspberries, blueberries, strawberries, plums, kiwi)

Equipment: hand-held electric whisk, 1 deep 23cm (9 inch) loose-bottom round cake tin, greased and base lined with reusable baking parchment

Preheat the oven to 190°C/170°C (fan)/375°F/gas 5.

First, make the sponge. Whisk the eggs, vanilla and sugar in a large roomy mixing bowl with a hand-held electric whisk until light, mousse-like and doubled in size. Placing your mixing bowl over a pan of simmering water will speed up the mixing. When you lift the whisk out of the mix it will leave a trail. If that is not happening, continue whisking some more.

Sift over the flour, cornflour and baking powder and fold in gently with a metal spoon, taking care not to knock out that valuable air. Pour in the cooled melted butter and stir this briefly through the thick mix – a few stirs is all it needs.

Transfer to the prepared tin and bake in the oven for 30–35 minutes until the cake is well risen and golden brown. If the cake starts to darken after 15–20 minutes, lay over a piece of foil with a hole in the centre (see Tip on page 162). This will protect the cake from over-browning.

Remove the cake from the oven and leave on a cooling rack (still in the tin) for about 15 minutes. The cake will leave the sides of the tin. Run a knife around the edges and remove the tin, then leave to cool completely.

To make the cream, start by making the thick pastry cream. Place the egg yolks, vanilla, sugar and cornflour in a medium saucepan and mix to a thick paste. Gradually pour over the milk and stir well. Place over a medium heat and keep stirring all the time until the mixture heats and thickens. Remove from the heat, give the mix a good beating, then transfer to a heat-proof bowl, cover and leave to go completely cold.

When the pastry cream is cold, whisk the whipping cream in

a large bowl with a hand-held electric whisk until thick and standing in soft peaks then whisk it into the cold pastry cream, little by little, until you have a very thick, smooth vanilla-flavoured cream for frosting.

Transfer your cooled cake to a cake board and slice it in half horizontally so that you have two sponges.

Use a third of the cream to sandwich the two cakes together then use the remaining cream to cover the top and sides of the cake. Chill in the fridge for a couple of hours to firm up.

Decorate with as much fresh fruit as you can.

Get ahead and make the pastry cream in advance.
The pastry cream can be made up to three days in advance and kept in the fridge.

LET ME SHOW YOU . . .

My Summer Cake Video

MALT LOAF

Malt loaf is a classic and very easy to make. There's no need to feel guilty about wanting to spread butter on it, there is hardly any fat in this recipe. Malt loaf is best kept in a tin for 2–3 days before eating, to allow the flavours and the squidgy moistness to develop.

150g (5½oz) chopped pitted dates
150g (5½oz) sultanas
150ml (5fl oz) hot tea
190g (6¾oz) malt extract
½ tsp salt
70g (2½oz) dark muscovado sugar
1 tsp mixed spice
50g (1¾oz) butter or margarine, at room temperature
2 eggs
250g (9oz) self-raising flour, sifted

Equipment: stick blender, 2 × 450g (1lb) loaf tins, greased and lined with greaseproof paper or brushed with lining paste

Try adding the finely grated zest of 1 orange or lemon to enhance the flavour. Use the juice too, but reduce the amount of tea used for soaking the fruits.

Preheat the oven to 140°C/120°C (fan)/275°F/gas 1.

This recipe is so easy. Just place the dates and sultanas in a small bowl and pour over the hot tea. Leave to steep until cool then add the malt extract, salt, sugar, mixed spice, butter and eggs – everything except the flour. Use a stick blender to blitz everything together to a runny batter. Fold in the flour and mix well, then divide evenly between the two prepared tins. Bake in the oven for 1 hour 15 minutes, until the cakes are firm and springy to the touch.

Remove from the oven, place on cooling racks and leave to cool in the tins. Turn out of the tins and transfer to an airtight tin for 2–3 days to mature. Serve sliced, with butter.

LET ME SHOW YOU . . .

My Malt Loaf Video

COFFEE AND WALNUT CAKE

SERVES: 8

I have tried gluten-free cake in the past and I either find it dry and almost sawdust-like in texture, or heavy and lacking depth of flavour. I think you will enjoy this recipe – it is moist, full of flavour and my family didn't even realize that it was gluten free. I have included a choice of buttercreams – both are good!

FOR THE CAKE
- 125g (4¼oz) margarine or butter, at room temperature
- 125g (4¼oz) caster sugar
- 2 eggs, plus 1 egg yolk
- 1 tbsp mayonnaise
- 35g (1¼oz) walnuts, blitzed to a paste in a food processor or coffee grinder
- 50g (1¾oz) rice flour
- 50g (1¾oz) gluten-free plain flour
- 2 tsp baking powder
- ½ tsp salt
- ½ tsp xanthan gum
- 1½ tbsp instant espresso powder or instant coffee powder or granules dissolved in 1½ tbsp hot water
- 8 walnuts, to decorate

FOR ITALIAN MERINGUE BUTTERCREAM

- 1 egg white
- 1 tbsp instant expresso powder or instant coffee powder or granules dissolved in 1 tbsp hot water
- 125g (4¼oz) caster sugar
- 3 tbsp water
- 110g (4oz) butter, at room temperature

OR

FOR A SIMPLE BUTTERCREAM

- 100g (3½oz) butter, at room temperature
- 180g (6¼oz) icing sugar, sifted
- 2 tbsp full-fat cream cheese
- 2 tbsp instant espresso or instant coffee powder or granules dissolved in 2 tbsp hot water

Equipment: hand-held electric whisk, 2 × 15cm (6 inch) round loose-bottom sandwich cake tins, greased and bases lined with reusable baking parchment

Preheat the oven to 200°C/180°C (fan)/400°F/gas 6.

Whisk the margarine (or butter) and sugar in a roomy mixing bowl with a hand-held electric whisk until light and fluffy. Add the egg yolk then the eggs one at a time, whisking well after each addition. Mix the mayonnaise and the walnut paste together then whisk this into the egg/sugar mix.

In a separate bowl, sift together the rice flour, gluten-free flour, baking powder, salt and xanthan gum. Sift them a second time into the cake mix, then add the coffee and water and fold everything together. Divide evenly between the two prepared tins and bake in the oven for 18–20 minutes until well risen, soft and springy to the touch.

Remove from the oven, remove from the tins and leave to cool on cooling racks.

While the cakes are cooling, make the cream. See page 188 for the Italian meringue buttercream method.

For a quicker, simpler filling, make the simple buttercream

Whisk the soft butter in a roomy mixing bowl with a hand-held electric whisk until really creamy then add the icing sugar in three separate parts, whisking well after each addition. Finally, whisk in the cream cheese and coffee mix.

Dust the 8 walnut halves with icing sugar then toast them lightly in a dry frying pan over a low heat for 2–3 minutes until the sugar begins to colour the nuts, then remove from the pan so they don't burn. Use them to decorate the iced cake.

LET ME SHOW YOU . . .

My Coffee and Walnut Cake Video

CHOCO-FUDGE SLICES

I decided to include these deliciously moist slices in this chapter because they are quite different in that they contain lots of stewed apple, which means you can reduce the sugar content of a typical cake sponge. Whenever I make these slices, I ask family and friends to guess the 'secret ingredient'– no-one ever detects the apple!

I store apples over the winter. By February they are starting to look a bit tired, yet they are perfect for baking and cooking. If you have no stored apples, then dessert apples will be fine (even better are those eating apples from the fruit bowl that you would otherwise probably throw away).

It can easily be made gluten free by using gluten-free flour instead of the self-raising flour.

FOR THE CAKE

- 4 medium dessert apples
- 35g (1¼oz) cocoa powder
- 175ml (6fl oz) milk
- 100g (3½oz) margarine or butter, at room temperature
- 80g (2¾oz) caster sugar
- 2 eggs
- 1 tsp ground cinnamon or ½ tsp Chinese five spice
- 250g (9oz) self-raising flour (or gluten-free self-raising flour)

FOR THE FUDGE TOPPING
  100ml (3½fl oz) double cream
  100g (3½oz) dark chocolate (I use Bourneville), broken into
    small pieces

Equipment: hand-held electric whisk, 1 square 20cm (8 inch) cake tin, greased and base and sides lined with greaseproof paper

Preheat the oven to 200°C/180°C (fan)/400°F/gas 6.

Start by preparing the apples. Peel them then slice the flesh into a non-metallic bowl until you have about 250g (9oz). I use the microwave to cook them in 3-minute bursts – stirring after each burst – but you can cook them in a pan if you prefer. The riper the apples, the quicker they will cook. Mash them with a fork until you have a smooth pulp, then leave them to go completely cold.

Put the cocoa powder in a small bowl then gradually add a little milk and mix to a smooth paste then add the remaining milk. Set aside.

Cream the margarine (or butter) and sugar in a roomy mixing bowl with a hand-held electric whisk, then add the eggs one at a time, whisking well after each addition. Sift in the flour and spice and fold them in with a metal spoon.

Add the chocolate paste and apple puree and stir everything together until well combined.

Transfer to the prepared tin and bake in the oven for 30–35 minutes until the cake is springy to the touch and slightly risen in the middle. The cake may crack, but don't worry.

Remove from the oven and set on a cooling rack, then remove the cake from the tin as soon as it is cool enough to handle. Place it back on the rack to cool completely.

To make the fudge topping, pour the double cream into a small saucepan and bring to the boil. Put the chocolate in a heatproof bowl, then pour over the cream and stir continuously until the chocolate has melted and the mixture is smooth and shiny.

When the cake has cooled completely, take a second cooling rack and invert the cake so that the very smooth underside becomes the top. Pour over the cooling fudge topping and smooth it with a knife over the top and sides.

When completely cold, cut into 16 even slices. The cake will keep in an airtight tin for up to 1 week.

LET ME SHOW YOU . . .

My Choco-Fudge Slices Video

LEMON CAKE

I wrote this recipe when I received a message from a desperate mum with a little girl who was then 8 years old and had never had a birthday cake! The child had an egg allergy and was therefore unable to eat standard cakes. Many egg-free cake recipes result in a pale and heavy-textured bake, but I came up with this delightful sponge that was enjoyed by the whole family, and the birthday girl. This cake is also a good standby if you find yourself out of eggs! Fill with jam and vegan cream, or jazz it up for a celebration.

300g (10½oz) self-raising flour
30g (1oz) custard powder (this adds colour and
    depth of flavour)
1 tsp bicarbonate of soda
¼ tsp salt
110g (4oz) caster sugar
finely grated zest and juice of 1 lemon
200ml (7fl oz) unsweetened almond milk
140ml (4¾fl oz) vegetable oil (or oil of choice)
30g (1oz) golden syrup
1 tsp lemon extract

Equipment: 2 × 20cm (8 inch) loose-bottom sandwich tins, greased and bases lined with reusable baking parchment

Don't throw away those zested and juiced lemon halves just yet . . . lemon juice is a fantastic limescale remover. If your taps are cloudy due to limescale build-up simply cup your lemon halves around the base of the tap and leave overnight. The limescale will dissolve away.

Preheat the oven to 170°C/150°C (fan)/325°F/gas 3.

Sift the self-raising flour, custard powder, bicarbonate of soda and salt together into a roomy mixing bowl, then stir in the sugar and the lemon zest. Make a well in the centre of the mix.

Put the milk, oil, golden syrup, lemon juice and lemon extract in a mixing jug – the mixture will separate but don't worry. Mix with a large spoon and add the liquid to the dry ingredients in thirds, stirring well after each addition, until you have a thick yet smooth batter.

Divide the batter evenly between the two prepared tins (I prefer to weigh the mixture – see page 123) then bake in the oven for 20–25 minutes until the cakes are risen and golden.

Remove from the oven and leave to cool in the tins on cooling racks for about 20 minutes then turn out and cool completely.

The cake will keep in an airtight container for 2–3 days.

LET ME SHOW YOU . . .

My Lemon Cake Video

VEGETARIAN 'SAUSAGE' ROLLS

I love sausage rolls but had never contemplated making (or tried) a vegetarian version until I was asked to during my *Bake-Off* Challenge. I experimented with various flavours because the last thing a sausage roll should be is bland. These are absolutely perfect – packed with flavour and, of course, they are meat-free!

FOR THE FILLING
   2 tbsp olive oil
   1 small onion, peeled and finely chopped
   2 garlic cloves, peeled and chopped
   100g (3½oz) chestnut mushrooms, roughly chopped
   20g (¾oz) butter
   80g (2¾oz) fresh white breadcrumbs
   50g (1¾oz) Cheddar cheese (or favourite hard cheese), grated
   400g (14oz) tin red kidney beans, drained and rinsed
   1 tsp ground mace
   2 tsp dried sage
   12 juniper berries, crushed (if you can't get these, use 1-2tsp
      finely chopped fresh rosemary leaves)
   4 tbsp brown sauce or tomato sauce
   2 tbsp finely chopped fresh herbs (chives, parsley, sage,
      thyme, mint – a mixture of any of these)
1 egg
salt and pepper

    300g (10½oz) puff pastry (see recipe on p 286 or use
       shop-bought block)
    plain flour, for dusting
    1 egg yolk, mixed with 1 tbsp water, for glazing

Equipment: food processor, piping bag fitted with a wide nozzle

Heat the oil in a medium frying pan over a medium-low heat, then add the onion and fry gently for 10 minutes until the onion is softened. Add the garlic and mix well, then add the mushrooms to the pan and fry for about 10 minutes until they start to colour.

Transfer the mushroom mix to the bowl of a food processor.

Melt the butter in the same frying pan until foaming, then add the breadcrumbs and stir regularly until the breadcrumbs are nicely browned. Transfer these to the food processor too.

Add all the remaining ingredients to the food processor, season with salt and pepper, and blitz to a thick paste. Fill a piping bag with the paste (piping the filling makes constructing the sausage rolls much easier). Refrigerate until ready to use.

Dust a work surface lightly with flour then roll out the puff pastry into a rectangle measuring about 50 × 20cm (20 × 8 inches). Use a pizza cutter (or knife) to straighten the sides. Cut the pastry in half lengthways – you will now have two long strips of pastry. Brush the beaten egg yolk mix down one long side of each strip then pipe the filling down the centre of each piece of pastry. Fold the unglazed side of the pastry over the filling then roll the filled half of the pastry strip over so that it encloses the egg-washed side underneath, forming a seal. Repeat with the second strip. Cut each roll in half then transfer to a baking sheet and pop into the freezer for 20–30 minutes.

Preheat the oven to 220°C/200°C (fan)/425°F/gas 7.

Take the rolls out of the freezer and brush egg wash all over the four lengths of filled pastry then, with a sharp knife, cut them into sausage rolls. The part-freezing process makes them much easier to cut. Now either freeze for baking later or bake in the oven for 20–30 minutes until golden brown.

LET ME SHOW YOU . . .

My Vegetarian Sausage Rolls Video

How to dice an onion

Ever wondered how chefs makes those tiny dice of onion? You need a sharp knife.

Start at the root end of the onion and cut off any tiny dried-up roots but leave the root core on. Turn to the other end of the onion and slice off the top and peel off the skin. Cut the onion in half north to south. Lay one half cut side down on a chopping board with the core to your left (if you are right-handed), take the point of the knife and follow nature's little cutting lines and cut from the core end to the right of the onion. The thinner the lines, the smaller the dice will be, so be patient. The onion will hold together because everything is anchored by the core. Now hold the onion half in the left hand, still cut side down on the board, and make horizontal slices in the onion. If the onion is small you may only be able to make one, if it is larger then you can make two or three slices.

The final stage is the exciting bit. With your half onion still firmly intact, and holding it with your left hand, make vertical slices. Your onion will come away in the tiniest of dice, perfect for cooking. Repeat with the other onion half. Once you have mastered this skill you will never go back to thick, lumpy chunks of onion in your cooking.

SPINACH AND RICOTTA LASAGNE

SERVES: 8 (OR MAKES 2 SMALLER
LASAGNES TO EACH FEED 4)

The whole family will love this meat-free dinner and having one in the freezer is a perfect go to meal which can be popped into the oven and cooked from frozen. Making a white sauce can seem a bit long-winded but by making it all in the pan together we can take a few shortcuts making it quick and easy.

30g (1oz) butter
1 banana shallot or small onion, peeled and finely chopped
3 garlic cloves, peeled and finely chopped
1 tsp dried mixed herbs
500g (1lb 2oz) baby leaf spinach (if using large-leaf spinach, remove the stems)
250g (9oz) ricotta cheese
300g (10½oz) tomato passata seasoned with 1 tsp sugar, ½ tsp salt and ½ tsp dried mixed herbs
6–8 fresh lasagne sheets (about 300g/10½oz)
120g (4¼oz) grated mozzarella or mild Cheddar cheese
2–3 tbsp grated Parmesan
salt and pepper

FOR THE SAUCE

    50g (1¾oz) butter, diced

    50g (1¾oz) plain flour

    750ml (25fl oz) whole milk

    1 tsp freshly grated nutmeg

    1 tsp salt

    1 tsp white pepper

Equipment: large ovenproof dish (mine is 30 × 25 and 5cm deep/12 × 10 inches and 2 inches deep), or two smaller dishes (about 25 × 16 × 5cm/10 × 6 and 2 inches deep)

Melt the butter in your largest casserole dish (large enough to accommodate all the spinach leaves) over a low heat then add the chopped onion, garlic and dried herbs and fry for about 5 minutes. Add the spinach (if you have washed it, make sure it has drained and dried), cover with a lid and leave to wilt for 5 minutes.

Remove the lid, stir well, then cook without the lid for a few minutes so that any liquid in the dish evaporates. Remove from the heat and stir in the ricotta and some seasoning. Set aside.

Now for the sauce. Put the butter, flour, milk, nutmeg and salt and pepper in a medium saucepan and stir over a low heat until the butter melts, then increase the heat and stir continuously until the sauce thickens to the consistency of single cream or custard. Take off the heat and set aside.

Now is the time to assemble the large lasagne (or two smaller lasagnes). Start by spreading about two-thirds of the seasoned passata over the base of the dish (or divide between smaller dishes). Cover with lasagne sheets (or a single sheet if making smaller ones) then add half of the spinach and ricotta mix and two to three large spoonfuls of sauce (dividing these between two dishes if making smaller ones). Cover with another/more lasagne sheet(s) then the rest of the spinach mix, the rest of the tomato and a further few spoonfuls of white sauce. Add another lasagne layer then finish with a final white sauce layer followed by the grated mozzarella and a grating of Parmesan. Chill or freeze until required.

Bake in an oven heated to 220°C/200°C (fan)/425°F/gas 7 for 40 minutes, from chilled, until dark golden brown and bubbling (or for 50 minutes–1 hour if cooking from frozen). Remove from the oven and allow to stand for 10 minutes before serving.

LET ME SHOW YOU . . .

My Spinach and Ricotta Lasagne Video

MUESLI

If you have ever examined the ingredients on the back of your pack of muesli you may be astounded at the amount of added sugar and, believe it or not, dried milk powder! My sugar-free version is now a breakfast staple in our house. Once you've tried it, there will be no going back.

300g (10½oz) porridge oats
45g (1½oz) oat bran
½ tsp ground cinnamon
½ tsp ground nutmeg
45g (1½oz) flaked almonds, toasted
70g (2½oz) pecan nuts or walnuts, chopped
150g (5½oz) mixed seeds (pumpkin, sunflower, poppy, chia,
   sesame, and goji berries for colour)
40g (1½oz) desiccated coconut or coconut flakes
100g (3½oz) ready-to-eat dried apricots, chopped

A 60g (2¼oz) serving is just about right, and pre-soaking it in a little milk then topping it with yoghurt is delicious. Try soaking the muesli overnight in apple juice then topping it with a blob of yoghurt – yummy!

Mix everything in a large bowl together then transfer to a large container with a pourer. The muesli will keep in an airtight container for up to 6 weeks.

LET ME SHOW YOU . . .

My Muesli Video

SUMMER PUDDING TERRINE

SERVES: 4–6

If you like summer pudding I promise this will be the best you have ever tasted! Sometimes there is a sort of bitter after-taste to summer puddings, but with this recipe there is a depth of flavour and lusciousness and it's not too heavy on the sugar either! I used a mixture of berries from the garden, with frozen blackberries. Frozen fruit works well. It's really easy to make gluten free, and is suitable for vegans, too.

20g (¾oz) caster sugar
30ml (1fl oz) blackcurrant cordial
grated zest and juice of 1 orange
30ml (1fl oz) water
20g (¾oz) morello glacé cherries, chopped (with scissors)
1 tbsp fruit jam
600g (1lb 5oz) fresh and/or frozen summer berries
    (redcurrants, blackcurrants, strawberries, raspberries,
    blueberries, blackberries), including some fresh for
    decoration
4–5 large slices of sliced white bread, crusts removed (use
    gluten-free bread for a GF dessert)

Equipment: 2 × 450g (1lb) loaf tins, 1 of them oiled

Put the sugar, cordial, orange zest and juice and water in a medium saucepan and place over a low heat. When the sugar has dissolved, add the cherries, the jam and all the berries apart from any very soft fresh raspberries and soft strawberries. Bring to the boil, simmer for a couple of minutes until just soft, then take off the heat and add the soft strawberries and raspberries. Stir and leave to one side.

Line the oiled loaf tin with one large sheet of plastic. The plastic will stick to the tin and make it easier to line – allow it to overlap the edges.

Use a rolling pin to flatten the bread slices a little then line the tin with the bread, making sure there are no gaps. Pile the fruit mixture into the tin and pack it in really tightly. Reserve a little juice in the pan for serving and patching up any white bread showing later. Cover with more bread, fold over the plastic then place the second tin over the top and weigh it down with weights from kitchen scales (or another heavy item such as a tin of baked beans). Place in the fridge and leave for 12 hours or overnight.

When ready to serve, remove the weights etc. and upturn the pudding on an oblong plate. Remove the sheet of plastic. Brush or pour the reserved juice over any white bits and serve garnished with fresh berries, crème fraîche, ice cream or double cream.

LET ME SHOW YOU . . .

My Summer Pudding Terrine Video

PASTRY

When we examine cooking and baking skills, pastry-making seems to be the one that causes the most problems. I think this is because pastry is precise; there are rules, and this alone can make people nervous.

I often describe 'top end' pastry as a beautiful young woman who's a little aloof. She is dressed in all her finery and is perfect to look at, slim and absolutely stunning. She appears superior and unapproachable, totally out of your league. A friend introduces her to you and once you get to know her you find out that she is easy to work with and not in the least bit complicated. She just needs to be approached positively and once your nervousness has passed you have a friend for life.

I was taught how to make pastry by my grandmother and the first thing I learnt to make was a deep custard tart. I was probably 8–10 years old.

My childhood wasn't great. My mother left when I was 13, and I found myself looking after the house from that early age. Looking back, my grandmother tried to hold things together for us and I spent hours with her, days in fact. Her house was always warm, and smelled of food and there was always lots to do whereas the house I lived in with my father and brother seemed barren and only as homely as I could make it.

Back then, pastry was of course always made by hand. These days I mostly use my food processor, which mixes it in seconds, but the ingredients are the same whichever method is used.

SHORTCRUST PASTRY

A basic shortcrust pastry is simply flour, fat and liquid – that's it! But the quantities have to be exact. The right amount of liquid is key to successful pastry.

I have read so many pastry-making recipes and methods, but have yet to find a recipe that gives exact quantities when it comes to the amount of liquid to be added. A standard quote will be 'add sufficient liquid to bring everything together to make a dough'. A better recipe may say 'add between 2 tablespoons and 4 tablespoons . . .' – this is not exact – we need to be exact! Too much liquid and the dough will be sticky, meaning more flour will have to be added and before we have even started, those exact ingredient quantities have already changed. This dough will have been overworked, resulting in a tough crust. On the other hand, too little liquid and the dough will be crumbly, difficult to form into a dough, will break when rolling out and will have such a crumbly (short) texture that it will easily break and not hold a filling.

Shortcrust is the perfect pastry — it's the most versatile of all pastries and can be used to make pies, tarts and quiches. Once you have mastered it, the others will be easy to learn. We've all seen poor pies and quiches with thick overworked pastry, grey and raw underneath, with a pale anaemic crust. Here's how to achieve perfection: thin and crispy pastry, that's baked all the way through and utterly delicious.

FLOUR

I use plain flour for shortcrust pastry. Some use self-raising flour but the raising agent will encourage the dough to puff up during baking and become thicker even though it may have a softer texture. My pastry (and yours) will be paper thin.

SALT

I add just a tiny pinch of salt to the flour because I use salted butter.

FATS

When mixing pastry in a food processor, the fats need to be well chilled. When mixing by hand, the fats need to be at room temperature to make 'rubbing in' more convenient. The type of fat is really down to taste. For a sweet shortcrust pastry, I use all butter, whereas for a savoury pie I use half butter and half lard.

HOW TO MAKE SHORTCRUST PASTRY

There is no guesswork involved in this method. Before you weigh out your ingredients, switch the button on your digital scales from kg to lb (or get the old pounds and ounces weights from the back of your cupboard for your balance scales). The rule is now simple: use half fat to flour and, for every ounce of fat used, use 1 tablespoon liquid. That's it.

1. Place the flour and salt (let's say 8oz) in the bowl of a food processor fitted with the blade attachment. Add 4oz well-chilled fat, cut into small cubes, and blitz for

4–5 seconds, just long enough for the mixture to look crumbly. Remember, pastry likes to be cool and hates to be handled.

2. Turn off the machine then measure out 4 tablespoons of ice-cold water.

3. Turn the machine on again and pour the cold water in a thin, steady stream, keeping the blade turning for about 10 seconds until the dough comes together in a ball.

4. Remove the dough from the machine and pop it into the fridge, wrapped in greaseproof paper or a beeswax wrap (I don't use cling film) to cool off, firm up and relax for about 30 minutes. Leaving the pastry to rest allows the gluten to develop making it easier to roll out.

5. Once the dough is rested, it's time for rolling out. Lay one piece of plastic on the work surface, place your ball of dough in the centre then your second piece over the top, and start rolling. The beauty of this method is that you can lift the pastry up, turn it around, try it for size over your tin and all the time the plastic holds it in place. You can also lift it up to the light and see 'thick' bits that need to be smoothed out. When the weather or your kitchen are very warm, you can slide the whole lot into the fridge for 10 minutes to firm up. Even better – there is no work surface to wipe down.

6. When ready to line your tin, take your chilled pastry, peel off one side of the plastic, and using the other piece of plastic as an aid, lay the pastry down into the tin. You can then shape the dough into the tin with your fingers,

moulding the plastic right into the corners. There should be no holes in the pastry as the plastic is protecting it.

7. Chill for about 10 minutes before peeling off that second piece. Wipe or wash the plastic sheets and store ready for your next pie or tart.

||||||||||||||||||||||||||||||||||||||||||||||||||||||||||||||||||||||||||||||||||||||||||||||||||||||||||||||||||||||||||||||||||||||||||||

How big is an egg yolk?
When using an egg yolk for a richer pastry each egg yolk counts as 1 tablespoon. Beat your egg yolk with the rest of the measured water.

||||||||||||||||||||||||||||||||||||||||||||||||||||||||||||||||||||||||||||||||||||||||||||||||||||||||||||||||||||||||||||||||||||||||||||

LET ME SHOW YOU . . .

My Pastry Video

SCHOOL DINNERS MEAT PIE

SERVES: 12–16 (MAKES 2 PIES)

I love this pie – it can be made in advance and baked when family arrive. It is also very economical, yet everyone loves it, particularly children. It actually reminds me of school dinners, which I adored! (I'm talking about the school dinners of 50 years ago, by the way).

The pie can be frozen unbaked, if required, then defrosted in the fridge or even baked from frozen. I serve it with mashed potatoes and peas – you will also need some lovely gravy. (I freeze leftover gravy, which is ideal with this pie.) The secret is to cut the vegetables very small. I tend to make a pie for now and one for the freezer, so I've done so below.

Spend a little extra time and add a lattice top to give your pie the wow factor!

FOR THE FILLING
- 2 tbsp vegetable oil
- 2 onions, peeled and finely chopped
- 2 carrots, peeled and finely chopped
- 2 celery sticks, peeled and finely chopped
- 2 garlic cloves, peeled and finely chopped
- 2 large potatoes, peeled and cut into 1cm (½ inch) dice
- 125g (4¼oz) lardons or bacon (smoked or unsmoked), cut into small pieces
- 1kg (2lb 4oz) minced beef
- 2 tbsp soft dark brown sugar
- 2 tbsp plain flour

100ml (3½fl oz) red wine
400ml (14fl oz) chicken or beef stock
1 tsp dried thyme
3 tbsp HP sauce
3 tbsp chopped fresh parsley
100g (3½oz) grated Cheddar cheese
salt and pepper

FOR THE PASTRY
800g (1lb 12oz) plain flour
200g (7oz) butter, diced
200g (7oz) lard, diced
1 egg plus 13 tbsp cold water to make 14 tbsp liquid in total
½ tsp salt
1 egg yolk, mixed with 1 tsp water, for egg wash

Equipment: casserole dish or slow cooker, food processor,
2 × 20cm (8 inch) square loose-bottom cake tins generously
greased with butter or brushed with lining paste

||||||||||||||||||||||||||||||||||||||||||||||||||||||||||||||||||||||||||||||||||||||||||||||||||||||||||||||||||||||||||||||||

How to keep a bunch of soft herbs fresh
Fresh herbs sold in plastic packets are great, but if you
leave leftover herbs in the packet and pop them into
the fridge, the next time you see them they are black,
slimy and unfit for use. To help them keep for longer,
take the herbs out of the packet (after you've taken
what you need for a recipe) and wrap them in a
piece of kitchen paper sprayed with water and
replace them in the fridge.

||||||||||||||||||||||||||||||||||||||||||||||||||||||||||||||||||||||||||||||||||||||||||||||||||||||||||||||||||||||||||||||||

Preheat the oven to 120°C/100°C (fan)/250°F/gas ½.

Heat the oil in a large casserole dish over a low heat, add the onions and fry for 10–15 minutes until soft and translucent. Add the carrot, celery, garlic and potato, stir well and cook for a further 5–10 minutes, then remove from the heat. Meanwhile, heat a frying pan over a medium heat and fry the lardons until well browned and crisp. Transfer the lardons to the casserole dish, then dry-fry the mince in the same pan – in batches – until browned and add it to the casserole dish. You want the pan really hot, with no added fat: add about two handfuls of mince at a time – no more, or else it will boil and not fry. The mince needs to have a brown crust before transferring it to the casserole. Add the sugar to the dish then the flour and stir well, seasoning the mixture with salt and pepper.

Deglaze the frying pan with the red wine and add this to the casserole, then turn off the heat under the frying pan. Deglazing means pouring the wine into the hot pan so that it bubbles and fizzes and takes all the lovely meat particles from the bottom of the pan. Finally, add the stock, dried thyme and brown sauce and give everything a good stir. Bring to a gentle simmer then cover and transfer to the low oven (or a slow cooker) and cook for 5 hours. You can cook the meat quicker in a hotter oven if you wish, with the oven set at 190°C/170°C (fan)/375°F/gas 5 for 1½ hours.

After cooking, remove the lid: the meat filling should be thick and wholesome. If it's still a bit thin, stir well and pop into a 220°C/200°C (fan)/425°F/gas 7 oven for 1 hour, uncovered, to thicken up.

Stir well then add the fresh parsley and grated cheese. Allow the filling to cool completely before tasting and checking the seasoning and assembling the pies.

I use a food processor to make pastry. Put the flour and salt in the bowl of a food processor fitted with the blade attachment. Add the chilled fats and blitz for about 10 seconds until the mixture resembles breadcrumbs then, with the blade turning, pour the liquid into the machine a steady stream and allow the dough to form a ball. Remove from the machine, divide into four (or six if making a lattice top), pop into a reusable freezer bag or wrap in a beeswax wrap or greaseproof paper and chill for 30 minutes.

Roll out one piece of the pastry between two plastic sheets into a rough square shape, large enough to fit the bottom and sides of a tin (about 33cm/13 inches wide), then line one of the two tins – fill to the top with the cold meat filling then roll out a second piece to about 20cm (8 inches) and top the pie with a pastry lid, sealing the top and bottom together by wetting the edge with a damp finger. Crimp the edges and make a few air holes in the pastry lid. Brush with egg wash and chill until required. Repeat with the second pie. If you're making a lattice top, see the next page for method.

Preheat the oven to 220°C/200°C (fan)/425°F/gas 7. Egg-wash the pies once more, then bake for 35–45 minutes until golden brown on the top.

Leave to stand for 10 minutes before removing the pies from the tin, cutting into portions and serving.

Egg washing the pastry twice gives a deeper, richer glaze to the pastry.

How to make a lattice top to your pie
Roll out two 20cm (8 inch) pastry squares and cut into strips as shown on the video (see the QR code below). There is sufficient pastry in the recipe to make two latticed pies. You will have leftover pastry (freeze it) if you go for a plain lid.

Never fill a pie with a hot filling
When working with pastry every part of the process has to be cold. A hot or warm filling will warm the pastry and your finished pie will probably be undercooked at the base.

LET ME SHOW YOU . . .

My School Dinners Meat Pie Video

CHICKEN AND TARRAGON PIE

SERVES: 6

Chicken pies can be dry and lacking in flavour, but this is an absolutely delicious pie, ideal for mid-week family eating and equally good enough to serve in the evening to friends. I poach the chicken breasts briefly before making pie, which makes it moist and flavoursome.

FOR THE BASIC SHORTCRUST PASTRY
    450g (1lb) plain flour
    pinch of salt
    110g (4oz) cold butter, diced
    110g (4oz) cold lard, diced
    8 tbsp ice-cold water

FOR THE FILLING
    small handful of dried wild mushrooms (10g/⅓oz)
    200ml (7fl oz) white wine
    400ml (14fl oz) chicken stock
    4 skinless chicken breasts
    1 tbsp vegetable oil
    40g (1½oz) butter, at room temperature
    1 small onion, peeled and finely chopped
    150g (5½oz) button chestnut mushrooms, thinly sliced
    20g (¾oz) plain flour
    2 tsp dried mustard powder
    pinch of ground mace (or 1 tsp grated nutmeg)
    4 spring onions, trimmed and finely chopped

60g (2¼oz) frozen peas

small bunch of fresh tarragon (about 2 tbsp leaves torn from
    stalks), or 1 tbsp dried tarragon

80ml (2¾fl oz) double cream

1 egg, beaten, to glaze the pie

salt and pepper

Equipment: food processor, square 20cm (8 inch) loose-bottom
cake tin or 23cm (9 inch) pie dish or 2 × shallow 20cm (8 inch)
metal pie plates, greased well or brushed with lining paste (lining
paste is perfect for pastry as well as cakes)

How do I get rid of onion and garlic smells from my chopping board?

Rub the cut side of half a freshly cut lemon across the
chopping board 'to and fro'. The lemon will neutralize
any odour from your smelly veg!

Put the dried mushrooms in a heatproof bowl with 200ml
(7fl oz) just-boiled water and leave to rehydrate for 30 minutes,
then drain and chop (keep the mushroom soaking liquid).

While the mushrooms are rehydrating, make the pastry. Put
the flour, salt and fats in the bowl of a food processor fitted
with the blade attachment and blitz until the mixture resembles breadcrumbs, then gradually add the ice-cold water with
the blade turning until a ball of dough is formed. Divide in
two then wrap in greaseproof paper or beeswax wrap and chill
in the fridge for at least 30 minutes.

While the pastry chills, poach the chicken. Pour the white wine and stock into a saucepan and bring to a gentle simmer, then add the chicken breasts, cover with a lid and poach for 15 minutes over the lowest heat. Remove the breasts from the liquid, allow to cool slightly then chop into 2cm (¾ inch) chunks and set aside.

Heat the oil and half of the butter in a large frying pan over a medium-low heat, add the onion and fry gently for 10 minutes until golden and soft. Add the mushrooms and chopped wild mushrooms and fry for a few minutes to cook off the excess liquid that the mushrooms release, then add the rest of the butter, flour, mustard powder, mace and some salt and pepper. Stir for a minute or two to cook the flour then add liquid from the chicken stock pan, little by little, until you have a thick sauce (you will need 150–200ml/5–7fl oz stock).

Transfer this mixture to a large bowl then add the spring onions, peas, fresh tarragon leaves, 50ml (1¾fl oz) of the double cream, the mushroom soaking liquid and all the poached chopped chicken. Stir thoroughly and leave to go completely cold. The filling should be quite thick.

Use the frying pan to slightly reduce the remaining stock and wine then add the remaining cream, stir, season to taste, then serve with the pie. If the sauce needs thickening, simply mix 1 tbsp cornflour with cold water to a thin paste, then stir into the hot sauce.

To make the pie, roll out the pastry between two sheets of plastic to a circle larger than the plate or dish. Peel off the top layer of plastic, flip over and lay the pastry onto the greased plate or dish. Press down then peel off the second layer of plastic. If the pastry dough sticks to the plastic, simply pop it into the fridge or freezer for 5 minutes to firm up, then the plastic will easily peel off.

Put the cold filling inside with a pie blackbird if your pie tin is deep then roll out the pastry lid, dampen the edges then place the lid over, seal the edges and decorate. If you do not have a pie blackbird, you can make slits in the pastry lid. Brush the pie with egg wash then chill for 30 minutes. Preheat the oven to 220°C/200°C (fan)/425°F/gas 7.

Brush the pie with egg wash again then bake in the oven for 40–45 minutes until the pie is golden. Serve hot, on warmed plates.

'Season to taste'

I have read this so many times in recipes, but how do I know my food tastes the best it can be without over- or under-doing the salt and pepper? This applies to casseroles, pie fillings, soups . . . well in fact anything that needs to be well seasoned. Take a ladle of the sauce and place it in a separate bowl. Add more salt and pepper and taste. If this sample dish tastes better than your original, then you know to add more seasoning. If, on the other hand, it is too salty or too peppery then you know your original panful is seasoned well enough.

Too late – I have oversalted!

Do not worry – you can rescue it. Adding a tablespoon of jam will help counteract saltiness in food, so if you have oversalted your gravy, casserole or stew, stir through raspberry jam or redcurrant jelly and no one will ever know.

Quick plate warmer

Your meal is ready to plate up, but you have forgotten to warm the plates. Providing you have a microwave oven and your plates do not have any silver or gold trim, you can warm them instantly. Spray each plate with a little water then stack them on top of each other in the microwave for 30 seconds – that is sufficient for two plates. More plates need more time – 4 plates probably a minute. Remove and wipe with a clean dry tea towel before plating up your meal.

LET ME SHOW YOU . . .

My Chicken and Tarragon Pie Video

CHEESE AND ONION FLAN

SERVES: 8

Cheese and onion are perfect partners, and are delicious in this family bake. Thin, light crispy pastry is an essential and I have a few tips to ensure success.

FOR THE PASTRY
 170g (6oz) plain flour
 pinch of salt
 90g (3oz) cold lard (or butter), or half of each
 3 tbsp ice-cold water

FOR THE FILLING
 1 tbsp butter
 1 tbsp vegetable oil
 2 large onions, peeled and thinly sliced
 3 tbsp water
 1 tsp finely grated nutmeg
 4 eggs, lightly beaten
 200g (7oz) strong Cheddar cheese, grated
 150g (5½oz) cream cheese
 150ml (5fl oz) whole milk
 3 tbsp finely chopped chives
 salt and pepper

Equipment: food processor, 23cm (9 inch) loose-bottom flan tin, lightly greased, or for a really deep flan a 20cm (8 inch) tin that's 5cm (2 inches) deep, stick blender (optional)

When baking a quiche, flan, custard tart or lemon tart –
in fact anything with a very runny filling – I tend to fill
the pastry shell half full then transfer it to the oven on a
low shelf. Once in place, I then fill it to the very top
knowing there will be no spills.

To make the pastry, put the flour and salt in the bowl of a
food processor fitted with the blade attachment then add the
diced fat and blitz for a few seconds until the mixture resembles
breadcrumbs. With the blade turning, pour in the water
and allow the dough to come together in a ball then remove
from the machine, wrap in greaseproof paper and chill for at
least 30 minutes.

Now cook the onions for the filling. Place a large frying pan
over a medium-low heat, add the butter and oil then add the
onions. Stir and cook gently, uncovered, for 3–4 minutes. Add
the 3 tablespoons of water and the nutmeg, cover with a lid
and cook on the gentlest heat for 10 minutes. Remove the lid,
stir again to check that the onions are soft and tender, then
transfer the cooked onions to a large cold bowl and set aside.

Preheat the oven to 200°C/180°C (fan)/400°F/gas 6.

Roll out the chilled pastry thinly between two sheets of thin
reusable plastic and use it to line the prepared flan tin, allowing
surplus pastry to overhang the edges of the tin. Chill for 15
minutes, then prick the base of the pastry shell with a fork,
line with baking paper, fill with either dry rice, lentils or baking
beans and bake 'blind' for 15 minutes. Remove the tart from

the oven and carefully lift off the baking paper and beans. Your pastry base should be dry and pale golden. If it looks grey and waxy then pop it back in the oven for 2–3 minutes to completely dry out.

Once you are happy with your pastry shell, trim the overhanging edges of the pastry with a serrated knife. To make sure the pastry shell is completely waterproof, paint over the base with some beaten egg taken from the eggs to be used for the filling. Pop back into the oven and bake for a further 2 minutes.

To make the filling, put the eggs, cheese, cream cheese, milk and some seasoning in the bowl with the onions and mix well. I prefer a smooth filling, so I blitzed my filling with a stick blender, but that's up to you. Stir in the chopped chives.

Pour the filling into the trimmed pastry shell, slide the tart into the oven and bake for 35 minutes, until dark golden and set. If you bake a deep flan then allow about 50 minutes, turning the temperature of the oven down to 150°C/170°C (fan)/375°F/gas 5 for the final 20 minutes to avoid over browning.

Remove from the oven and leave to cool in the tin. This tart is easier to cut once cooled.

LET ME SHOW YOU . . .

My Cheese and Onion Flan Video

COURGETTE QUICHE

SERVES: 8–10

Growing courgettes is easy and once they get going you will have so many! They are best harvested while small and before the seeds form inside. Courgettes on their own are pretty tasteless, so I have bumped up the flavour with green pesto and finely grated cheese. It tastes (and looks) so good!

FOR THE PASTRY

170g (6oz) plain flour
pinch of salt
90g (3oz) cold butter, diced
1 egg yolk, mixed with 2 tbsp cold water

FOR THE FILLING

2 tbsp green pesto
50g (1¾oz) strong Cheddar cheese, finely grated
4–5 small courgettes
3 eggs
300ml (10fl oz) single cream
about 1 tsp freshly grated nutmeg
1–2 tsp finely chopped fresh mild red chilli
salt and white pepper

Equipment: food processor, loose-bottom 23cm (9 inch) flan tin that's 2.5cm (1 inch) deep, lightly greased

If you are afraid your liquid filling may overfill your quiche, fill it as full as you dare then bake for 10 minutes, by which time the filling will have settled. You can then open the oven door and pour in any you have left over from the jug.

Start by making the pastry. Put the flour and salt in a food processor fitted with the blade attachment, add the cold butter and blitz for a few seconds just until the mixture resembles breadcrumbs. With the blade turning, add the egg mix in a steady stream and allow the machine to run until the dough forms a ball. Wrap in greaseproof paper or beeswax wrap then chill for 30 minutes.

Place the chilled pastry between two sheets of plastic and roll it out large enough to comfortably fit the greased tin, then peel off one sheet of plastic, fit the pastry into the tin and chill again for 10–15 minutes.

Peel off the second sheet, prick the base all over with a fork then chill again (when making pastry dough I never allow it to warm up, so at any opportunity it goes into the fridge to keep cool). Preheat the oven to 210°C/190°C (fan)/425°F/gas 7.

When the oven has reached temperature, line the pastry with paper, fill with either dry rice, lentils or baking beans and bake 'blind' for 15 minutes then remove from the oven, trim the pastry overhang using a serrated knife while warm and then brush the inside with beaten egg (taken from the mixture for the filling) and pop back into the oven for 3 minutes to set.

Remove from the oven and set aside. When the pastry case has cooled a little, spread the pesto over the base of the tin then sprinkle over the cheese and a grind of white pepper and salt.

To prepare the courgettes, use a vegetable peeler to peel long ribbons from the courgettes and roll these – they don't need to be particularly uniform: have some rolled tightly and others rolled loosely, it just adds interest to your finished tart. Starting around the outside and finishing in the centre, arrange the little courgette rolls skin side down then grind over some white pepper.

Whisk together the eggs and cream in a jug, season with salt and pepper, add the nutmeg then carefully pour this over the filling. So that the courgettes are defined during baking it is important not to bury them with the egg and milk. I fill each hole carefully – it's time consuming I know, but it is worth it.

Sprinkle over the chopped chilli then place in the oven, turn down to 200°C/180°C (fan)/400°F/gas 6 and bake for 25–30 minutes until just starting to brown.

Remove from the oven and allow to cool completely before removing from the tin. The quiche is best served at room temperature but can be eaten hot or cold.

LET ME SHOW YOU . . .

My Courgette Quiche Video

SINGLE-SERVE WHOLE APPLE
AND BLACKBERRY PIES

SERVES: 6

These individual pies look amazing - a whole, cored, skinless apple filled with blackberries and covered in a sweet shortcrust pastry - sure to impress your friends and family. They can be served with cream, custard or ice cream and can be frozen unbaked (but apply egg wash before freezing!).

FOR THE FILLING

- 1 tbsp lemon juice
- 1 cinnamon stick
- 6 medium dessert apples (evenly sized)
- 18–20 frozen blackberries
- 2 tbsp white chocolate chips
- 1 egg, separated (yolk beaten with 1 tsp water for egg wash, egg white for glue)

FOR THE PASTRY

- 340g (12oz) plain flour
- 170g (6oz) cold butter, diced
- 1 tbsp icing sugar
- 2 egg yolks beaten with 4 tbsp cold water

Equipment: food processor (optional), a pan large enough to hold the apples in a single layer, baking sheet lined with reusable baking parchment or paper, small oval or round cutter, small paintbrush

Fill a large saucepan to just over halfway with water, add the lemon juice and the cinnamon stick and bring the water to the boil. While the water is heating, core the apples then gently score the skin of each apple all around the circumference, halfway up, with a sharp knife. Just score the skin, don't cut through to the apple flesh. As each apple is cored, pop it into the pan of water. The lemon juice in the water will prevent discolouration of the apple. Bring back to the boil and cook for 5 minutes. This is the tricky bit because it really depends how hard the apples are to start with, as to how long they need to cook. I have found 5 minutes is just right. Using a slotted spoon, take each apple from the water and leave to cool on kitchen paper.

When cool enough to handle, use a vegetable knife to carefully lift and peel off the skin. Leave your apples to go completely cold. Keep the cinnamon stick for later.

To make the pastry, rub together the flour and butter with your fingertips in a bowl until the mixture resembles breadcrumbs, stir through the icing sugar with a round-bladed metal knife then stir in the egg yolks and water. Bring the dough together with your hands, then form into a ball, wrap in greaseproof paper, beeswax wrap or place in a reusable plastic bag and leave to rest in the fridge for 30 minutes. Alternatively, if you have a food processor, place the flour, icing sugar and butter in the bowl with the blade attachment fitted. Blitz until the mixture resembles breadcrumbs then, with the blade turning, add the liquid.

Remove the dough from the fridge then divide the dough into six equal pieces.

When ready to assemble the apple pies, work on one apple at a time. Roll out a piece of the pastry between two sheets of plastic and cut out a circle large enough to sit the apple on comfortably with an overhang that can be pushed up and around the bottom of the apple. Using a small oval or round cutter, cut out a number of shapes from the pastry trimmings (you will need a lot!). Place a cold peeled apple on the pastry circle then force 2 or 3 frozen blackberries down the central core cavity, popping 5 or 6 white chocolate chips in there too. The white chocolate sweetens the fruit and also prevents the blackberries bleeding too much during baking.

Use a small paintbrush and egg white, and working from the bottom in a clockwise direction, patiently stick pastry pieces onto each other and around the apple, overlapping them as you go and not leaving any raw apple showing. When you get to the top of the apple, try using a shard from the cinnamon stick that was boiled earlier and cut out two pastry leaves to decorate the pie. Repeat with all the apples, pop them in the fridge to chill and firm up.

Preheat the oven to 210°C/190°C (fan)/425°F/gas 7. Brush the apples with egg yolk and bake for 25–30 minutes until the pastry is golden.

Serve warm.

LET ME SHOW YOU . . .

My Whole Apple and Blackberry
Pies Video

BLACKBERRY PIE

SERVES: 8

Blackberry pie baked well is one of Britain's classics. The most common problem is that the juice from the fruits runs from the pie, bubbles over the top or leaks so badly after the first slice is cut that the pastry is soggy and not pleasant. A slice of fruit pie should be full of fruit, not overly sweet, and cut well, with no wet or soggy bottom and no leaking juices. It's not as easy as it sounds, and blackberries are probably the most difficult fruit with which to accomplish the perfect pie. Here is my recipe – perfect in every way.

FOR THE PASTRY
    200g (7oz) plain flour
    pinch of salt
    30g (1oz) icing sugar
    110g (4oz) cold butter, diced
    1 egg and 1 egg yolk, beaten together

FOR THE FILLING
    2 tbsp semolina
    400g (14oz) fresh blackberries
    20g (¾oz) white chocolate, grated
    2 tsp caster sugar
    leftover egg white, for egg wash
    1–2 tsp vanilla sugar (or granulated sugar), for sprinkling

Equipment: food processor, 23cm (9 inch) pie tin, lightly greased

Put the flour, salt, sugar and cold butter in a food processor fitted with the blade attachment and blitz until mixture resembles breadcrumbs. With the blade turning, add the egg in a steady stream and allow the dough to form into a ball. Divide the ball in half, wrap in greaseproof paper, beeswax wrap or place in a reusable plastic bag and leave to rest in the fridge for 30 minutes.

Lay a sheet of plastic on the work surface, half of the pastry in the centre, place the other sheet over the top then roll out the pastry until it is large enough to fit in the tin with overhang. Chill for a couple of minutes then remove one sheet of plastic, line the pastry tin and with the other plastic sheet uppermost and mould the pastry into the tin. Chill again for a few minutes before peeling off the second sheet. Trim the edges then repeat the process with the second piece of pastry – keep it in the plastic and pop into the fridge while you prepare the filling.

Sprinkle the semolina over the pastry base, then add the blackberries followed by the grated white chocolate and sugar. Dampen the edges of the pastry with water then take the pastry top, peel the plastic off one side, then lay the pastry over the pie. Peel off the top layer of plastic. Secure the edges, trim the pastry, crimp and then chill until the oven reaches temperature.

Preheat the oven to 220°C/200°C (fan)/425°F/gas 7 with a baking sheet on the middle shelf. When the oven is at temperature, take your pie from the fridge and brush it with the leftover egg white then sprinkle with vanilla sugar or granulated sugar. Bake for 25 minutes until golden. The juices are prevented from leaking as they are soaked up by the semolina.

Leave the pie to cool before cutting, and when it is just warm slice and serve with vanilla ice-cream or fresh cream or custard.

LET ME SHOW YOU . . .

My Blackberry Pie Video

RICH CHOCOLATE TART

SERVES: 8–10

Totally delicious, rich and decadent. This tart can be decorated simply or lavishly depending on your mood, the occasion or the season.

FOR THE CHOCOLATE PASTRY

 110g (4oz) plain flour (00 flour is best)
 30g (1oz) cocoa powder
 30g (1oz) icing sugar
 pinch of salt
 ⅛ tsp ground star anise or Chinese five spice (optional)
 90g (3oz) cold butter, diced
 1 egg yolk and 2 tbsp egg white (beat the white up to frothy to make it easier to measure)

FOR THE CHOCOLATE FILLING

 300g (10½oz) dark chocolate, chopped
 2 tsp vanilla extract
 150ml (5fl oz) whole milk
 150ml (5fl oz) double cream
 2 eggs

Equipment: food processor, loose-bottom flan tin 23cm (9 inches) wide and 2.5cm (1 inch) deep, lightly greased

If you find chocolate pastry too difficult

Chocolate pastry can be tricky and needs to be rolled out very thinly. You can also make this tart with a sweet shortcrust pastry (same method, ingredients below).

140g (5oz) plain flour
30g (1oz) icing sugar
pinch of salt
90g (3oz) cold butter, diced
1 egg yolk mixed with 2 tbsp cold water
(instead of the egg white above)

To make the pastry, place all the dry ingredients in a food processor fitted with the blade attachment and blitz briefly until well combined. Add the butter and blitz for a few seconds until the mixture resembles breadcrumbs. With the blade turning, add the egg yolk and the 2 tablespoons egg white (no more) and allow the dough to form into a ball. Wrap in greaseproof paper, beeswax wrap or place in a reusable plastic bag and leave to rest in the fridge for 30 minutes.

Do not roll out the pastry using flour as this will streak and colour your dark chocolate pastry. Use two sheets of thin plastic instead. Place the pastry between the plastic sheets and roll it out until it is large enough to cover your flan tin with overhang. If the pastry is sticky between the plastic pop it back into the fridge for 10 minutes to firm up. Peel off one sheet of plastic and with the pastry adhered to the other piece, lay the pastry face down into the tin. Use your fingers along the plastic to mould the pastry into the edges of the tin. Chill for

10–15 minutes then peel off the second sheet of plastic. Preheat the oven to 210°C/190°C (fan)/425°F/gas 7.

After peeling off the second sheet of plastic, prick the base with a fork and line the chilled case with paper. The pastry can overlap the edges of the tin and be trimmed after 'blind' baking. Fill the lined case with either dry rice, lentils or baking beans and bake the pastry for 15 minutes then remove from the oven and carefully lift the paper and beans. Trim the edges with a serrated knife while warm then set aside while the filling is prepared. Reduce the oven temperature to 120°C/100°C (fan)/250°F/gas ½.

To make the filling: put the chocolate in a roomy heatproof bowl with the vanilla. Heat the milk and cream in a small saucepan over a gentle heat until at simmering point, then pour the warmed milk and cream over the chocolate and stir well until the chocolate is melted and the mixture is smooth and shiny. Allow to cool down slightly then stir in the eggs. Give everything a good mix then pour into the cooked, trimmed pastry case.

Make sure your oven has cooled right down then pop the tart into the very low oven and bake for 50 minutes. The tart filling should be just firm when gently touched with the finger.

Remove from the oven and leave to go completely cold, then decorate as you wish. Raspberries are fabulous.

LET ME SHOW YOU . . .

My Rich Chocolate Tart Video

CUSTARD TARTS

A classic bake like this can be difficult to get right, but my recipe ensures you end up with crisp and light sweet shortcrust pastry baked all the way through, filled with a smooth nutmeg and vanilla-flavoured creamy custard.

FOR THE PASTRY
250g (9oz) plain flour
pinch of salt
30g (1oz) icing sugar
140g (5oz) cold butter, cut into 1cm (½ inch) dice
2 egg yolks
3 tbsp ice-cold water

FOR THE CUSTARD FILLING
100ml (3½fl oz) double cream
150ml (5fl oz) whole milk
25g (1oz) caster sugar
knob of butter (15g/½oz)
½ tsp vanilla extract
2 eggs
½ grated nutmeg

Equipment: food processor, 10cm (4 inch) round pastry cutter, lightly greased 12-hole deep muffin tin, 9 paper muffin cases, baking sheet

To make the pastry, put the flour, salt and sugar in the bowl of a food processor fitted with the blade attachment. Add the diced butter and blitz for just a few seconds until the mixture resembles breadcrumbs. Mix the egg yolks with the water in a small jug then, with the blade turning, pour in the liquid in a steady stream and allow the dough to come together to form a ball. Wrap in greaseproof paper, beeswax wrap or place in a reusable plastic bag and leave to rest in the fridge for 30 minutes.

Remove the dough from the fridge and roll it out between two sheets of plastic to about the thickness of a £1 coin then use a 10cm (4 inch) cutter to cut out 9 circles. Re-use trimmings as necessary and place the circles in the greased tin holes. You may find it easier to mould the pastry circles around the end of your rolling pin and then lower them into the muffin tin. The pastry will then fit perfectly and there is no danger of it cracking, or splitting by putting your fingers through it. Pop the tray of pastry into the fridge to firm up while you preheat your oven to 210°C/190°C (fan)/425°F/gas 7.

Once the oven has reached temperature, line each of the pastry cups with a paper bun case (slightly smaller than a cupcake case) then fill with either dry rice, lentils or baking beans. Pop straight into the oven and bake 'blind' for 14 minutes.

Remove from the oven and have ready a baking sheet. Hold onto those little paper cases and lift the pastry shells from the muffin tin immediately – the pastry will adhere to the paper, but only while hot. Place the pastry shells on the baking sheet and then, once cooled slightly, you can remove the paper cases and lentils, rice or baking beans.

Pop the pastry shells back in the oven to bake through and dry out for just 2–3 minutes, then take them out of the oven and immediately reduce the oven temperature to 160°C/140°C (fan)/320°F/gas 2. I leave the oven door open for about 30 seconds to allow some heat to escape.

To make the filling, put the cream, milk, sugar, butter and vanilla in a small saucepan and heat gently, stirring all the time, just to the point where the sugar and butter dissolve. When there is no gritty feel to the bottom of the pan take it off the heat. Don't let it boil.

Beat the eggs in a 1-pint (570ml/16fl oz) heatproof jug then pour over the warm milk mixture in a thin, steady stream. Grate over about half of the nutmeg and mix this in too. Pour the mixture into the little pastry cases, filling them as full as you can. You may find it easier to fill the cases once the tray is in the oven then there is no chance of them spilling but be careful – don't burn yourself. Sprinkle over more grated nutmeg then bake for just 13–15 minutes.

Take the tarts from the oven when the centre of each tart still has a slight wobble when you move the baking sheet – the custard will firm up as it cools. An overbaked custard is rubbery and tough and may even crack. Allow to cool to room temperature. Delicious.

LET ME SHOW YOU . . .

My Custard Tarts Video

LUXURY MINCE PIES

MAKES: 12 DEEP-FILLED MINCE PIES

Even though they are mine, I have to say these mince pies are the best I have tasted. The mincemeat is easy to make and the pastry quick to make – it just needs a little careful handling. The addition of the chocolate chips and the fact that there is no suet in my mincemeat means they are less likely to bubble up during baking.

FOR THE MINCEMEAT –
MAKES 2 × 450G (1LB) JARS
(ENOUGH FOR 24 PIES)
  50g (1¾oz) butter
  200g (7oz) soft dark
    brown sugar
  8 tbsp orange/lemon juice
    from the zested fruits
  finely grated zest of 1
    orange
  finely grated zest of 1 lemon
  300g (10½oz) mixed
    dried fruit and peel
  100g (3½oz) ready-to-eat
    dried apricots, finely
    chopped
  100g (3½oz) dried
    cranberries
  ½ tsp ground mace

  1 tsp ground cinnamon
  2 tsp ground mixed spice
  4 tbsp Cointreau or
    brandy
  6 green cardamom pods,
    split and seeds
    crushed
  20g (¾oz) dark
    chocolate chips

FOR THE PASTRY
  250g (9oz) plain flour
  pinch of salt
  140g (5oz) cold butter,
    diced
  30g (1oz) icing sugar,
    plus extra for dusting
  1 egg yolk, beaten with 4
    tbsp cold water

Equipment: 2 x 450g (1lb) jars food processor, pastry cutters, lightly greased 12-hole deep muffin tin

Melt the butter with the sugar and fruit juices in a large saucepan over a low heat. When the sugar is no longer grainy, add all the other ingredients and mix well, making sure everything is well combined. Stir over a low heat for about 10 minutes then remove from the heat and place in warm sterilized jars (or cool if using straight away).

To make the pastry, put the flour and salt in a food processor fitted with the blade attachment then add the butter and blitz for a few seconds until the butter is completely dispersed. Add the icing sugar, repeat, then with the blade turning add the egg-and-water mix. Stop the machine when the pastry has formed a ball. Gently remove it from the food processor, halve it, form into two balls then wrap in greaseproof paper, beeswax wrap or place in a reusable plastic bag and leave to rest in the fridge for 30 minutes.

Roll out the chilled dough pieces between two sheets of plastic to about the thickness of a £1 coin. Cut out circles with the pastry cutter large enough to line the muffin tin and press them gently into the tin holes. I use a 9cm (3½ inch) cutter for the bases and a 7cm (2¾ inch) star or snowflake cutter for the tops.

Fill the pastry shells with the mincemeat about two-thirds full, dampening the edges of the pastry and gently laying the top pieces of pastry over – do not squash them down, there is no need. Do not egg-wash the mince pies as there is enough sugar in the pastry to colour them. Chill for 30 minutes before baking.

Preheat the oven to 220°C/200°C (fan)/425°F/gas 7.

Bake in the oven for 18–20 minutes until the mince pies are light golden. Allow to cool and firm up before attempting to remove them from the muffin tin.

Dust with icing sugar to serve.

Mincemeat can be made in advance and will keep in jars

How to get pastry into the bottom of a muffin tin
Mould the pastry circle around the base of your rolling pin to aid placing in the base of your deep muffin tin. You'll not then push your fingers through!

Get ahead: prepare and freeze unbaked pies
Assemble and freeze your pies in their tins, then remove from the tins and store in bags. When ready to bake, take from the freezer, pop back into the tin and bake from frozen for an extra 10 minutes, or until the pastry is golden brown.

Lining the muffin tin

If you are worried about your deep-filled pies sticking to the muffin tin, a strip of baking paper placed in the tin before the pastry shell will ensure they come out easily (I have found brushing the muffin tins with lining paste works even better). Allowing the mince pies to go completely cold in the tin ensures they will easily pop out.

If your pastry becomes difficult to handle, pop it in the fridge for 10 minutes to firm up. If you find your filling boils over your pastry, your cases are too full.

Leftover mincemeat

When Christmas has passed, and you have decided to clear out your pantry or cupboards and come across a half jar of mincemeat – you must try the fabulous little recipe below for Viennese Tart. Apples from the fruit bowl past their best are put to good use too!

LET ME SHOW YOU . . .

My Mince Pies Video

VIENNESE TART

Whenever I eat this tart (or tarts), I always think I must make it again very soon. Not overly sweet and certainly very delicious, the sweet mincemeat is paired with the acidity of apples, a light pastry crust, then the luxury Viennese topping – yummy. Dust with icing sugar and you will love these!

3 dessert apples
200g (7oz) sweet shortcrust pastry (see Chocolate Tart tip text on page 256)
200g (7oz) mincemeat

FOR THE VIENNESE TOPPING
150g (5½oz) butter, at room temperature
1 tsp vanilla extract
40g (1½oz) icing sugar
150g (5½oz) 00 plain flour (or pasta flour)

Equipment: 12-hole muffin tin or 18cm (7 inch) pastry ring placed on a baking sheet, hand-held electric whisk, piping bag fitted with a star nozzle

Start by cooking the apples as they need to be cooled before using. Peel and core the apples, then slice them into a non-metallic bowl, cover with a plate and microwave for 2–3 minutes until reduced to a pulp. Mash with a fork and leave to go cold

– there's no need to add sugar. If you don't have a microwave, you can cook the apples in a saucepan instead.

Place the dough between two sheets of plastic and roll out into a circle about the thickness of a £1 coin, then use it to line 9 holes in a 12-hole muffin tin, or a 18cm (7 inch) pastry ring placed on a baking sheet. Chill for at least 30 minutes.

Divide the mincemeat between the tartlets or place on the base of the chilled pastry ring. Top with the cold apple puree and pop the whole lot back into the fridge.

To make the Viennese topping, whisk the butter and vanilla in a bowl with a hand-held electric whisk until really smooth then whisk in the sugar. Incorporate the flour little by little, whisking after each addition, until you have a very thick yet smooth mixture. Load a piping bag fitted with a star nozzle with the topping mix and pipe it over the tart or tartlets. I like to pop the tart(s) back into the fridge while the oven reaches temperature. Preheat the oven to 210°C/190°C (fan)/425°F/gas 7 and bake for 16–18 minutes until the Viennese tops are light golden brown.

Remove from the oven, place on a cooling rack and allow the tart or tarts to cool in their tins.

Use leftover trimmings

My grandmother taught me never to throw away pastry trimmings. About 200g (7oz) leftover pastry will make the most gorgeous tartlets. Line a 12-hole muffin tin with the rolled-out trimmings, rolling them as thinly as you can. Chill while you make the apple filling.

LET ME SHOW YOU . . .

My Viennese Tart Video

TWO TARTS

I always save pastry trimmings. I pop them into a bag keep them in the freezer then when I have gathered 200g (7oz) I know I have enough dough to make 12 tarts. These two tarts are my favourite budget leftover pastry recipes: Coconut Tarts with a raspberry jam surprise in the base, and my Cheat Almond Tarts – my grandmother's recipe. She used economical ground rice and almond extract in place of ground almonds – I can't tell the difference!

200g (7oz) leftover pastry

COCONUT TARTS

50g (1¾oz) margarine or butter, at room temperature

50g (1¾oz) caster sugar

1 egg

50g (1¾oz) desiccated coconut

1 tbsp self-raising flour

6 tsp raspberry jam

icing sugar, for dusting

CHEAT ALMOND TARTS

50g (1¾oz) margarine or butter, at room temperature
50g (1¾oz) caster sugar
50g (1¾oz) ground rice
1 tbsp self-raising flour
1 tsp almond extract
1 egg
6 tsp apricot jam
a few flaked almonds
icing sugar, for dusting

Equipment: 12-hole tart tin well greased or brushed with lining paste, 8cm (3 inch) round pastry cutter, hand-held electric whisk

Roll out the pastry, cut out 12 circles using the 8cm (3 inch) pastry cutter and line the tart tin with the circles. Place in the fridge.

Mix the ingredients for your chosen tarts in a mixing bowl with a hand-held electric whisk or a wooden spoon (excluding the jam and icing sugar, and flaked almonds for the almond tarts). Pop ½ teaspoon of jam in the base of each tart shell, top with a heaped teaspoon of mixture and bake in the oven for 18–20 minutes at 200°C/180°C (fan)/400°F/gas 6 until golden brown. If making the almond tarts, scatter them with a few flaked almonds before baking. Remove from the oven and dust with icing sugar.

LET ME SHOW YOU . . .

My Coconut Tarts Video

You can make ground rice at home by blitzing dried rice in a strong blender or coffee grinder until very finely ground. Or you can use almond flour instead.

LET ME SHOW YOU . . .

My Cheats Almond Tarts Video

CHOCOLATE-CRUSTED
PASSION FRUIT TART

SERVES: 8–10

This tart takes a little time but is a great one if you want to impress – you may remember seeing something similar in the *Bake-Off* tent! I use a chocolate pastry which can be tricky to handle and can rise a little in the oven, so it is important that you roll it out really thinly. The passion fruit custard filling is delicious and is a non-bake custard which is set with gelatine. This is great because you can fill your tart right to the very brim. The filigree decoration is optional, but I think it gives a contemporary finish to this beautiful tart (a filigree icing pattern is a delicate form of piping work that looks a little bit like an organized scribble).

FOR THE PASTRY
- 125g (4¼oz) plain flour
- 20g (¾oz) cocoa powder
- 30g (1oz) icing sugar
- ½ tsp Chinese five spice (optional)
- 90g (3oz) cold butter, diced
- 2 tbsp beaten egg yolk
- 1 tsp vanilla extract

FOR THE FILLING
- 5 gelatine leaves
- 200g (7oz) caster sugar

200ml (7fl oz) passion fruit juice (about 8 fruits, strained of
  seeds, or 60g/2¼oz dried fruit powder reconstituted with
  water)
6 eggs
100g (3½oz) butter, at room temperature, diced

FOR THE FILIGREE
  1 egg white
  100g (3½oz) icing sugar, sifted

Equipment: food processor, 23cm (9 inch) loose-bottom tart tin, a
thermometer, hand-held electric whisk (optional), piping bag
fitted with a small writing nozzle (optional)

Start by making the pastry. Put the flour, cocoa, icing sugar
and spice (if using) in the bowl of a food processor fitted with
the blade attachment then add the butter and blitz for a few
seconds until everything is combined. With the blade turning,
add the yolk and vanilla extract and allow everything to come
together to form a ball. Wrap in greaseproof paper, beeswax
wrap or place in a reusable plastic bag and leave to rest in the
fridge for 30 minutes.

Preheat the oven to 220°C/200°C (fan)/425°F/gas 7.

Roll the pastry out very thinly between two sheets of plastic
until it is large enough to fit the tin, allowing for an overhang.
If the pastry becomes difficult to handle, pop it in the fridge
for 5 minutes to firm up. Line the tin with the pastry, prick
the base all over with a fork then line the pastry with baking
paper, fill with either dry rice, lentils or baking beans and bake
'blind' for 10 minutes. Remove the paper and baking beans

and pop it back into the oven to firm up for another 3 minutes. Trim the edges with a serrated knife while warm, then leave to go completely cold.

To make the filling, put the gelatine leaves in a bowl of cold water and allow to soak for at least 10 minutes.

Dissolve the sugar and passion fruit juice together in a small saucepan over a low heat.

Whisk the eggs in a separate small saucepan, and while whisking, carefully and slowly add the warm juice. Place the pan over a gentle heat and, stirring constantly, bring the mixture to a temperature of 85°C, testing it with a thermometer. This ensures the eggs are cooked. Remove from the heat once it reaches temperature and add the drained, softened gelatine leaves one by one, stirring after each addition.

Transfer the mixture into a heatproof jug, first passing it through a sieve – this makes sure your custard is ultra smooth and there are no pieces of cooked egg or undissolved gelatine going into your tart. Add all the diced butter and stir well until the butter is completely incorporated. Allow the custard to cool slightly then pour it into the pastry case, allowing it to come right to the top of the tart. You may want to do this when the case is first put into the fridge, then you don't have to move it at all. Place in the fridge for a few hours, to set.

When the tart is set, and about 2 hours before you are ready to serve, decorate with the filigree or with fresh fruits if you wish.

To make the filigree (if using), place 1 tbsp egg white into the bottom of a small basin then whisk in the icing sugar with a hand-held electric whisk for 4–5 minutes until you have a thick smooth paste. Spoon into a piping bag and decorate the tart.

Serve the tart at room temperature. If you serve it chilled, you don't get its full flavour.

LET ME SHOW YOU . . .

My Chocolate-Crusted
Passion Fruit Tart Video

HOT WATER CRUST PASTRY

Once you have mastered the art of shortcrust pastry, this method is so straightforward you'll wonder why you have never made pork pies before. In a nutshell it is what it says – the pastry is simply brought together by pouring hot water (with fat melted in it) over flour, then stirred with a wooden spoon until a dough is formed. Many recipes suggest working with the pastry while it is warm, but I prefer to wait for it to cool. It firms up and is easier to roll out to an even thickness.

HAND-RAISED PORK PIE

My pork pie recipe is a real winner and can be formed into picnic pies, small pies or one large celebration pie. I like to include a small quantity of diced lean pork with the minced pork: it gives the pies a proper meaty, home-made feel. You will feel quite accomplished because you are not making a pie using the support of a tin – this is a true hand-raised pie. Well done!

FOR THE PASTRY
    500g (1lb 2oz) strong plain flour
    1 egg yolk, plus an extra yolk mixed with 1 tsp water for egg
        wash
    300ml (10fl oz) water
    1 tsp salt
    150g (5½oz) lard

FOR THE FILLING
    350g (12½oz) minced pork
    130g (4½oz) lean pork (loin is a good choice), cut into
        1.5cm (½ inch) dice
    40g (1½oz) bacon (whatever type you prefer), finely
        chopped
    4g salt
    ½ tsp freshly ground white pepper
    ¼ tsp ground mace

1½ tsp dried sage
25g (1oz) anchovies in oil, drained and finely chopped
10 juniper berries, crushed
½ tsp smoked paprika
½ tsp freshly ground black pepper

Equipment: reusable non-stick baking parchment and string

||||||||||||||||||||||||||||||||||||||||||||||||||||||||||||||||||||||||||||||||||||||||||||||||||||||||

How to get pies out of a tin easily
If you decide to make the picnic pies and you don't
have a loose-bottom muffin tin, brushing with lining
paste and leaving the pies in the tin until completely
cold and firmed up will ensure they come out easily.

||||||||||||||||||||||||||||||||||||||||||||||||||||||||||||||||||||||||||||||||||||||||||||||||||||||||

Adding apricots to a pie filling
Ready-to-eat dried apricots make a great addition to
the meat filling. Try half-filling the pie with the meat
mix, then place a layer of apricots then top off with the
rest of the filling.

||||||||||||||||||||||||||||||||||||||||||||||||||||||||||||||||||||||||||||||||||||||||||||||||||||||||

How to add jelly to a pork pie
If you want to finish your pork pie with a jelly, you need
200ml (7fl oz) pork or chicken stock and 3 gelatine
leaves. Soak the gelatine in cold water then add to the
stock which has been heated to almost boiling.

||||||||||||||||||||||||||||||||||||||||||||||||||||||||||||||||||||||||||||||||||||||||||||||||||||||||

Allow to cool to body temperature then pour through the hole in the top through a little funnel (a metal icing nozzle works well) into your cool pork pie. Leave to set in the fridge completely before cutting.

First, make the pastry. Put the flour into a warm, heatproof mixing bowl then with a wooden spoon make a well all the way to the bottom of the bowl and drop in the egg yolk. Cover the yolk with flour.

Heat the water, salt and lard in a medium saucepan over a medium heat until the lard has melted, then bring to the boil and immediately pour into the bowl containing the flour. Mix with a wooden spoon until the mixture starts to come together and when it's cool enough to handle, tip out onto a work surface and knead into a smooth dough. When warm, this pastry is very soft and greasy. I prefer to wrap it in greaseproof paper, beeswax wrap or place in a reusable plastic bag and chill it for 30 minutes then use it cold when it's easier to handle.

Combine all the filling ingredients in a large mixing bowl and keep chilled in the fridge until ready to use.

TO MAKE 12 PICNIC PIES

If you are making picnic pies, roll out half of the dough on a lightly floured work surface and use a large 10cm (4 inch) pastry cutter to cut the pastry into 12 rounds and line a deep muffin tin, making sure you have enough pastry to provide an overhang that can be moulded over the pastry lid. Pack tightly with the chilled meat filling, dampen the edges of the pastry overhang then cut out and fit pastry lids using a 7cm (2½ inch) round cutter with the other half of the dough, making little holes in the pastry lids before placing them over the filling. Fold the dampened overhang over the lid and crimp together. Pop into the fridge to chill until ready to bake.

Preheat the oven to 200°C/180°C (fan)/400°F/gas 6 then brush the tops with the egg wash and bake for 45 minutes.

Remove from the oven and leave to cool in the tin.

LET ME SHOW YOU . . .

My Hot Water Crust Pastry Video

TO MAKE 4 SMALL HAND-RAISED PIES

I find small individual 175ml (6fl oz) metal pudding basins make excellent moulds. I use four to use as moulds for the filling. I grease them first and then line the inside with thin plastic, then pack the filling inside, forcing as much into the basin as I possibly can. Transfer to the fridge and leave to firm up for 1 hour or so. Take four more pudding basins and turn them upside down on the work surface. Dust each one with a little flour.

Divide the pastry into four pieces then take a quarter from each piece (this will be for your pie lids). Roll out your pieces of pastry large enough to cover the upside-down pudding basins which have been dusted with flour. Lay the pastry over and mould it around the outside of the tins. Give yourself a little extra pastry at the bottom as this will be needed to secure the lid. Try to avoid any creases. Transfer to a tray and pop into the fridge and chill for about 30 minutes.

To assemble the pies, take the pastry moulds and carefully remove the tins by twisting them slightly. The pastry shells will be able to stand unaided. Remove the plastic from the chilled fillings and place them upside down in the pastry shells (i.e., the wide part of the filling will go into the narrow part of the pastry shell). This will make a uniform pie rather than a pudding-shaped one. Roll out the pastry pieces reserved for the tops and use an 8cm (3½ inch) pastry cutter to form lids. Make an air hole in the centre (the wide end of a metal piping nozzle is handy for this) of each, then place over the filling, dampen the edges and fold the edges of the shells over the lids. Trim away any thick or uneven scraps of pastry then crimp in true pork-pie style.

In order to maintain straight sides and a neat shape, your hand-raised pies will need a paper sleeve to support them during the first 20 minutes of baking. Fold a 23cm (9 inch) length of baking parchment into three lengthways then wrap this around the pie and tie with string. Place on a baking sheet lined with non-stick baking parchment or baking paper. Brush the tops with egg wash and chill for 1 hour minimum.

Preheat the oven to 220°C/200°C (fan)/425°F/gas 7.

When ready to bake, pop the pies into the oven for 20 minutes then take from the oven and carefully remove the string and paper. Egg-wash the sides and give the top a second coat of egg wash. Pop them back into the oven immediately and bake for another 40 minutes – 1 hour total baking time.

Leave the pies to cool completely on the baking sheet before removing.

This same mix makes 1 large pork pie. Apply the method as for the small pies but mould the pastry and meat mixture using a 15cm (6 inch) solid-bottom deep cake tin. The cooking time will be 2 hours.

LET ME SHOW YOU . . .

My Pork Pies Video

CHOUX PASTRY

Choux pastry, a delicious light and crispy pastry used to make profiteroles and éclairs, may feel a bit 'top end' for some, but it is easy to make as long as the consistency of the choux mix is just right and not too much egg is added. Here are my favourite recipes using this pastry.

When mixing choux

Add the egg gradually as sometimes, depending on the size of the eggs less than the total amount is required. Check on the consistency – the paste should hang (in a 'v' shape) from the end of the whisk.

Encourage steam

Choux dough has a high water content which turns to steam in the oven, causing the dough to puff out. A steamy environment encourages a good rise too, so spray your baking sheet with a fine film of water before piping over your éclairs or spooning your profiteroles.

Piping the choux

I use a star-shaped nozzle for piping my choux paste. The shape of your finished baked éclairs and profiteroles will be more even as they are less likely to spread. You can also spoon your blobs of choux paste onto the baking sheet for rustic, beautiful puffs of crispy deliciousness that you can then fill with cream.

Can I make my choux buns in advance?

Choux pastry doesn't keep well, so freezing the uncooked dough is a great way to get ahead, then you can bake as you need. You can freeze the choux once piped or spooned on a baking sheet, or place the dough in bags and keep for up to 3 months. Once filled, choux buns go soggy after 2–3 hours so are best eaten fresh.

ÉCLAIRS AND PROFITEROLES

MAKES: 12–16 ÉCLAIRS OR 20–25 PROFITEROLES

Once you have made your own profiteroles you will find that mass-produced versions just don't hit the spot. I have chosen a light lemon cream filling, topped with dark chocolate, and they are absolutely delicious.

FOR THE CHOUX
150ml (5fl oz) water
100g (3½oz) butter
10g (⅓oz) caster sugar
1 tsp salt
150g (5½oz) plain flour, sifted
3 eggs, beaten

FOR THE LEMON CREAM FILLING
2 egg yolks
75g (2½oz) caster sugar
50g (1¾oz) cornflour
225ml (7½fl oz) whole milk
50g (1¾oz) butter, at room temperature
50ml (1¾fl oz) plain full-fat yoghurt
100ml (3½fl oz) double cream
finely grated zest of 1 large lemon

FOR A CHOCOLATE PASTE FOR PIPING ONTO THE ÉCLAIRS
100g (3½oz) dark chocolate, broken into pieces
20g (¾oz) butter
1 tbsp water

FOR THE DIPPING CHOCOLATE FOR PROFITEROLES

100g (3½oz) dark chocolate, broken into pieces

Equipment: hand-held electric whisk or tabletop (stand) mixer, 3 x piping bags (1 fitted with a large star-shaped nozzle, 1 fitted with a long nozzle, 1 fitted with a 1.5cm/½-inch-wide nozzle), baking sheet lightly greased or lined with baking parchment

Preheat the oven to 220°C/200°C (fan)/425°F/gas 7.

To make the choux pastry, heat the water, butter, sugar and salt in a medium saucepan over a low heat until the butter melts, then increase the heat and bring to a fast boil. Take off the heat, immediately tip in the sifted flour and stir briskly (I use a wooden fork for this) until the mixture comes together and forms a very thick paste which leaves the side of the pan. Turn the paste into a large mixing bowl and use a hand-held electric whisk mix on a low speed just to help cool it down a little (or do this using a tabletop/stand mixer). Don't be tempted to add the eggs straight away as they will cook. Once the paste has cooled a little, start to add the beaten egg, little by little. Keep an eye on the consistency of the paste – this is crucial to the success of your choux (you may not need all of the egg). When you lift your whisk, the paste should stick to the whisk yet hang off, so not stick rigidly neither drop off.

Load the paste into a piping bag fitted with a large star-shaped nozzle then spray the surface of the greased or lined baking sheet with water and use a bench scraper dipped in flour to mark out a regular 13cm (5 inch) length for the éclairs. Pipe the choux either in an éclair shape (or a large star for profiteroles) and flatten the point of your star peaks with a wet finger. Bake in the oven for 18–20 minutes until risen and golden brown, with a crispy finish. Remove to cooling racks and allow to go completely cold before filling.

To make the lemon cream filling, put all the ingredients except the yoghurt, cream and lemon zest in a medium saucepan over a low heat and allow to warm gradually, stirring constantly, for about 5 minutes until the cream thickens and leaves the side of the pan. Transfer to a cold heatproof bowl and cover to prevent a skin forming, then leave to cool completely. When the mixture has cooled, whisk the double cream in a bowl to soft peaks then whisk everything together including the yoghurt and lemon zest. The cream should be thick and delicious. Fill a piping bag fitted with a long metal or nozzle with the cream (if it's too thick, slacken it with a little lemon juice).

For profiteroles, use a metal skewer to make a hole in the side of each bun then inject enough lemon cream to fill the bun. I use my kitchen scales and 15–20g (¾oz) per bun is just about right. *For éclairs*, use a metal skewer to make three evenly spaced holes in the base of each éclair and inject lemon cream through each of the three holes to fill the éclair. 25g (1oz) per éclair is enough.

To make the chocolate piping paste for éclairs, melt all the ingredients in a heatproof bowl over a pan of hot water (not boiling), without stirring, or in the microwave in three 30-second bursts (stirring after each burst). When the mixture is shiny and thick, allow to cool slightly so that it holds its shape then fill a piping bag fitted with a 1.5cm (½-inch) wide nozzle. Pipe the chocolate paste over the presentation side of the éclairs then decorate with sprinkles, melted white chocolate or fruit crumb (optional).

To make the dipping chocolate for profiteroles, melt the chocolate in a heatproof bowl over a pan of hot water (not boiling) then the decorating is up to you. The consistency of the chocolate needs to be that of single cream (40°C if you have a thermometer). You can dip your profiteroles face down in the chocolate then carefully lift out and spin the final trail of chocolate back on itself. You will then have no drips running down. Alternatively, stack your profiteroles on a presentation plate and pour the melted chocolate over.

LET ME SHOW YOU . . .

My Éclairs Video

PUFF PASTRY

This pastry chapter wouldn't be complete without puff pastry. Traditional puff pastry recipes can seem complicated and time-intensive, involving folding, resting, more folding . . . This leads many of us to the chilled cabinet in the supermarket to buy it ready-made. Have you seen the number of ingredients contained in a pack of ready-made puff? On my last count there were 11, and many brands of puff pastry do not contain butter but are instead made using margarine and palm oil (all-butter puff pastry is expensive). This quick, 'all in one' home-made puff pastry has only four ingredients, is made with butter, and is cheaper and more tasty than anything you can buy. I urge you to try a batch.

250g (9oz) plain flour, plus extra for dusting
pinch of salt
250g (9oz) cold butter, cut into very small 1cm (½ inch) dice
125ml (4¼fl oz) ice-cold water, to bind

LET ME SHOW YOU . . .

My Puff Pastry Video

Put a roomy mixing bowl in the fridge for 10 minutes before you start making the pastry.

Put the flour and salt in the cold bowl, then rinse your hands in cold water, dry them, take the butter from the fridge and stir it into the flour with a knife. Once the butter is well distributed and coated in flour, then pour in the ice-cold water. Use the knife to stir everything around until the dough starts to clump together. Once you have a lump of scraggy dough, use your cold hands to briefly mould it into a ball. Turn the ball out onto a floured work surface and, using both a rolling pin and bench scraper, form the dough into a rectangle shape.

Roll this rectangle to roughly 40 × 15cm (16 × 6 inches) then carry out what is called a 'double fold': fold the two ends into the centre then fold the two ends into the centre once more. Turn the pastry 45 degrees and roll out again to the same size and repeat the double fold. Turn the pastry once more, roll out again, but this time carry out a single fold. Imagine the rectangle in thirds – fold an end third over the centre third and then the other end third over that.

Like shortcrust pastry, puff pastry needs to be kept cold otherwise the fat will start to turn oily and will be difficult and sticky to handle and roll out. If you start to get into a sticky mess, simply pop the whole lot into the fridge for 15 minutes and have a breather.

Once all the folds have been completed, wrap the pastry in a cloth or greaseproof paper and chill for 1 hour before using. Alternatively, freeze the pastry until required. When baking, some of the fat will run from your pastry so I find it better to bake using a lipped baking sheet.

PORK AND JUNIPER SAUSAGE ROLLS

MAKES: 20–30 SAUSAGE ROLLS OR 1 LARGE PLAIT

Sausage rolls are a huge crowd-pleaser and are absolutely delicious warm. This pork and juniper recipe is a family favourite. If you can't get hold of juniper berries, just use 1–2 tablespoons of fresh rosemary leaves, very finely chopped.

500g (1lb 2oz) puff pastry (see recipe on page 286 or use
   shop-bought block)
a little flour, for dusting
1 egg yolk, mixed with 1 tsp water, for the egg wash

FOR THE FILLING
500g (1lb 2oz) good-quality pork sausage meat
1 heaped tsp fennel seeds, crushed
½ tsp cayenne pepper
2 garlic cloves, peeled and crushed
3 large fresh sage leaves, finely chopped, or ½ tsp dried
10 juniper berries, crushed then chopped (if you can't get
   these, use 1-2tsp finely chopped fresh rosemary leaves)
4 spring onions, trimmed and finely chopped
grated zest of 1 lemon
salt and pepper

Equipment: piping bag (optional), baking sheet lined with reusable baking parchment

How do I get a really deep shiny glaze on my pastry?
For a fabulous glaze apply two coats! Apply one coat of
egg wash (just egg yolk mixed with 1 tablespoon of
water) then pop the pastry into the fridge. Apply a
second coat just before it goes into the oven to bake.
Your glaze will be deep golden, shiny and crisp.

Using your hands, mix together all the filling ingredients in a
bowl, seasoning with salt and pepper. I find it easiest to fill a
large piping bag and pipe the filling for both the sausage rolls
and the plait, so the meat is evenly distributed, though you can
make the rolls using a spoon or your hands for the meat mix.

TO MAKE INDIVIDUAL SAUSAGE ROLLS

Roll out the puff pastry on a lightly floured surface into a
30 × 20cm (12 × 8 inch) rectangle, neaten the edges with a
pizza cutter then cut in half lengthways. Place the pieces of
pastry on a lined baking sheet. Pipe a length of sausage meat
down the centre of each piece of pastry. Dampen the edges of
the pastry with water then roll up and keep the seam underneath. Brush egg wash along the two long sausages then transfer
to the freezer on the sheet for 15 minutes to firm up. Preheat
the oven to 220°C/200°C (fan)/425°F/gas 7.

Remove the long sausages from the freezer and cut each length
into 10–15 pieces, depending on your preferred size. Bake in
the oven for 25–35 minutes until golden brown.

These sausage rolls freeze very well uncooked. Open freeze the cut sausage rolls, then place into bags. The sausage rolls can then be baked from frozen until golden brown (add 5–10 minutes to the cooking time when baking from frozen). They already have their egg wash applied, so will brown nicely.

TO MAKE A SINGLE PLAIT

Roll out the puff pastry to a large 40 × 30cm (16 × 12 inch) rectangle, then neaten the edges with a pizza cutter. Transfer the rectangle to a sheet of baking paper or reusable baking parchment before shaping starts.

With the pastry positioned 'portrait style', place a score line at 10cm (4 inch) intervals so that the pastry is divided into three lengthways (don't cut through the pastry). Pipe the sausage meat filling onto the centre section of the pastry, leaving a margin of 2.5cm (1 inch) top and bottom. Using a pizza cutter, cut even-sized strips at the two sides. Dampen the pastry strips as you work and, starting at the top, fold over the top margin and the bottom margin then alternating left and right wrap the sausage meat in the pastry, forming a plait.

Chill the plait for at least 30 minutes then brush with egg wash and chill for a further 15 minutes. Preheat the oven to 220°C/200°C (fan)/425°F/gas 7. Place a baking sheet in the oven to preheat at the same time.

Just before placing the plait in the oven, give it a second egg wash – this ensures a lovely rich deep shiny brown finish to your bake. Using the paper or baking parchment as an aid, slide your chilled plait onto the preheated baking sheet – this ensures the underneath will bake thoroughly. Bake in the oven for 30 minutes.

The uncooked plait will freeze extremely well. Egg wash before freezing then bake from frozen for 40 minutes.

LET ME SHOW YOU . . .

My Pork and Juniper Sausage Rolls Video

MEAT PIE FOR ONE

MAKES: 4 INDIVIDUAL PIES

So many recipes are for families and large numbers, so I thought I'd create this single-serve meat pie. It needs no tin, it freezes well unbaked, and can be cooked from frozen. This is a hearty plateful – real comfort food! The oxtail and kidney are optional, but it's worth using them if you can, as they greatly enhance the flavour of the pie.

2–3 tbsp beef dripping or vegetable oil, plus extra for
   greasing
1 onion, peeled and finely diced
1 red pepper, deseeded and diced
3 garlic cloves, peeled and finely chopped
1 carrot, peeled and diced
100g (3½oz) chestnut mushrooms, halved
1 celery stick, thinly sliced
500g (1lb 2oz) beef skirt or braising steak, cut into
   2cm (¾ inch) cubes
1 × 5cm (2 inch) piece oxtail (optional)
1 lambs' kidney, membrane removed and kidney finely
   chopped (optional)
25g (1oz) plain flour, seasoned with salt and white pepper,
   plus extra for dusting
½ tsp mixed spice
200ml (7fl oz) beef stock
50ml (1¾fl oz) red wine
1 tbsp tomato puree

2 tbsp fresh thyme or 1 tbsp dried

1 beef stock cube

500g (1lb 2oz) puff pastry

1 egg yolk, mixed with 1 tsp water, for egg wash

Equipment: large casserole dish, slow cooker (optional) tea plate, 4 x large cups or soup bowls

---

Covering hot food

Lay a piece of kitchen paper over your bowl of hot pie filling then top off with a piece of foil, securing it around the rim of the bowl. When the filling has cooled, the paper will have absorbed all of the moisture which will have prevented the foil from tarnishing and getting wet. The foil can then be used again and again. The kitchen paper will be wet and can be discarded. No cling film in sight.

Preheat the oven to 210°C/190°C (fan)/425°F/gas 7.

Melt the fat (or heat the oil) in a large ovenproof casserole dish over a medium heat, add the onion and fry for about 10 minutes until softened but not browned. Add the pepper, garlic, carrot, mushrooms and celery, stir well, keep the heat low and cook for 5 minutes.

Put the beef, oxtail piece and chopped kidney (if using), along with the seasoned flour and spice, into a large bowl and give everything a good stir to coat all the meat in the flour. Drop the meat and residual flour into the casserole dish and stir over a high heat for a few minutes. Reduce the heat and add the beef stock, red wine, tomato puree and thyme. Give everything a good stir with a wooden spoon. If there are any stuck-on deposits at the base of the dish these will release as the liquid gets to work on them. Transfer to a slow cooker for 12 hours or put on the lid and cook in a low oven at 100°C/80°C (fan)/200°F/gas ¼ for 12 hours or conventional oven at 180°C/160°C (fan)/350°F/gas 4 for 1½–2 hours or until the meat is very tender.

When the meat is cooked, use a slotted spoon to remove the meat and vegetables, leaving behind a delicious gravy. Check the gravy for seasoning then transfer to a small saucepan to reheat later. Note: if you used oxtail, you need to find it and remove and discard the bone. The meat will just fall from it.

Once the filling is completely cold, crumble over the beef stock cube and stir this through the cold meat and vegetables. It darkens everything and adds a little more flavour.

Divide the puff pastry into four equal pieces then roll each one out on a lightly floured work surface to the size of a tea plate (about 18–20cm/7–8 inches in diameter) – I use a pizza cutter to neatly cut around the plate. Use these circles of pastry to line four large, greased cups or soup bowls. With the pastry trimmings roll out four smaller circles which will be used as a base for the pie.

Fill the cups or bowls with the cold meat filling then top with the small circle of pastry. Dampen the top circle then gently fold over the edges of the larger circle, sticking them down onto the pastry. Transfer the cup/bowl to the fridge to firm up for about 1 hour.

Tap the cup/bowl and the pie will pop out. Transfer it to a baking sheet lined with paper or baking parchment then make an air hole in the centre using the wide end of a metal piping nozzle. Brush with egg wash and pop back into the fridge while you preheat the oven to 220°C/200°C (fan)/425°F/gas 7.

Give the pies a second egg wash then pop them in the oven to bake for 30 minutes until dark golden brown. Serve hot on warmed plates, with the reserved gravy, mash and a green vegetable. If baking from frozen, bake for 40 minutes.

LET ME SHOW YOU . . .

My Meat Pie for One Video

TARTE TATIN

A classic bake using home-made or shop-bought puff pastry. I have seen so many tarte tatins with soggy pastry, and the apple sliding off an unset caramel which, for me, is not ideal. This recipe is a beauty and needs only a blob of vanilla ice cream to serve.

350g (12½oz) puff pastry
plain flour, for dusting
finely grated zest and juice of 1 lemon
13 or 14 small-medium dessert apples
125g (4¼oz) butter
200g (7oz) caster sugar

Equipment: 20cm (8 inch) heavy-based tarte tatin tin or ovenproof frying pan

Roll out the puff pastry on a lightly floured surface until it is slightly larger than the tarte tatin tin or ovenproof frying pan and about the thickness of a £1 coin. Turn the tarte tatin tin or pan upside down and make an impression on the pastry with the rim. Using this as a guide, cut a circle out of the pastry, 1cm (½ inch) larger than the pan, all the way round. Transfer the circle of pastry to a baking sheet and chill in the fridge until required.

Grate the zest from the lemon and put to one side.

Peel, core and halve the apples. While preparing the apples, have a large bowl of water to hand and squeeze in the lemon juice. Drop the apples into the water and then they will not turn brown.

Melt the butter in the tin or pan over a low heat and add the sugar, stirring until it has dissolved. Do not allow the mixture to colour at all at this stage. Remove from the heat and stir in the lemon zest.

Arrange the halved apples around the pan, standing them on their ends and forming an interlocking circle of fruit. Depending on the size of the apples, you may have room for a second circle of apples in the centre. Make sure your apples are very tightly packed as they will shrink during cooking.

Place the pan over a medium heat and, once all of the butter and sugar mixture is bubbling gently, turn down to a simmer. The juice will come out of the fruit and gradually evaporate. After a while, the apples will start to colour as the butter and sugar begins to caramelize. This will take about 45 minutes – don't be tempted to speed up the process otherwise your sugar will burn and your tarte tatin will be spoiled.

After this long cooking time, the apples will be tender and will still hold their shape. The caramel will be a golden colour. Take off the heat and leave to cool completely. I leave mine to cool to around room temperature. Preheat the oven to 210°C/190°C (fan)/425°F/gas 7.

Remove the pastry from the fridge and place it over the apples, tucking it down inside the rim of the pan.

Bake in the oven for about 45 minutes, until the pastry is crisp, well risen and dark golden in colour.

Remove from the oven and leave in the tin or pan until cooled enough to be able to handle the tin or pan easily (this usually takes about 15 minutes).

To turn out, briefly loosen the apples and caramel by running a knife around the edge of the pan. Place a serving plate upside down over the pan, then quickly turn the pan and plate over together. You will now have the pastry on the bottom and the apples on the top. Once turned out, the tart can be kept warm in a low oven. Best served warm with cream, crème fraîche or vanilla ice cream. It is good cold for a few days afterwards.

LET ME SHOW YOU . . .

My Tarte Tatin Video

VANILLA SLICES

Never discard puff pastry trimmings. Just 200g (7oz) leftover pastry can be easily transformed into 8 delicious vanilla slices.

Crème pâtissière is not difficult. How many recipes have you read that involve whisking eggs and sugar together, pouring over hot milk, washing the pan then returning the whole mixture to the pan and continuing to mix until it thickens, then transferring to a cold bowl? My method is much simpler, and everything is mixed together in one go.

200g (7oz) leftover puff pastry
icing sugar, for dusting (if not making water icing)

FOR THE CRÈME PATISSIERE
3 egg yolks
1 tsp vanilla extract
50g (1¾oz) caster sugar
25g (1oz) cornflour
15g (½oz) butter, at room temperature
250ml (8fl oz) whole milk

FOR THE WATER ICING (OPTIONAL)
110g (4oz) icing sugar, sifted
a little lemon juice

Equipment: 2 baking sheets, 2 sheets of reusable baking parchment, 18cm (7 inch) square loose-bottom cake tin

Preheat the oven to 220°C/200°C (fan)/425°F/gas 7. Divide the pastry trimmings in half then roll each one out slightly larger than the size of the tin. Do not cut the pastry to size at this stage – that can be done once the pastry is baked.

Lay one piece of pastry on a baking sheet lined with baking parchment then cover with another piece of baking parchment and another baking sheet. Bake for 15 minutes, then remove from the oven and trim to the size of the tin. Repeat with the second piece of pastry.

To make the easy crème pâtissière, whisk the egg yolks in a saucepan, then add the rest of the ingredients and heat slowly, stirring continuously, until the mixture thickens. Remove from the heat and beat well.

Line the square cake tin with foil then lay one sheet of baked pastry in the base. Pour the crème pâtissière over the pastry in the cake tin and spread it out, then top with the second square of pastry. Gently press the top layer of pastry onto the custard layer then leave in a cool place for 2–3 hours to firm up and set. Remove from the tin using the foil as an aid, peel back the foil then cut into 8 equal-sized pieces. Dust with icing sugar or drizzle with water icing: add enough lemon juice to the icing sugar to form a thick yet runny, smooth icing. Drizzle over the vanilla slices and leave to set.

PUDDINGS AND DESSERTS

We are continually warned about the need to reduce our sugar consumption but for me that doesn't mean we cannot enjoy pudding or dessert as part of our meal. Sweets, soft drinks and snacking are our enemies – not a portion of delicious home-made pudding.

I routinely reduce the sugar in my recipes, and many include fresh fruits. I know exactly what ingredients are included when I bake something myself, and I can control portion size.

Don't be afraid of eating pudding – remember though not to eat it as a snack!

I adore the way puddings and desserts particularly reflect the seasons. For example, I would not serve a steamed treacle sponge on a hot summer's day, nor would I offer a slice of summer pudding when there is snow on the ground, even though these days soft fruits are available all year round.

I have so many favourite recipes, from the traditional to the very contemporary. I have woven in tips as I go to ensure success every time.

HOT PUDDINGS

The British pudding is something to be celebrated yet it is sad to see that many restaurant menus fail to include a traditional pudding on their menu, and as a result some are in danger of becoming forgotten foods. Mention to anyone of my vintage the words Treacle Sponge (dates back to 1615), Jam Roly Poly (dates back to the 1800s), Queen of Puddings (first documented 1699), Eve's pudding (known from 1824) or Apple Charlotte (referenced in 1796) and eyes light up and a smile appears on a face as we remember our childhood and these treats that were part of our everyday lives.

I adore these hot puddings – they are comfort food at its best. They are economical to make, and while many of these creations involved 'steaming', I have a method that will allow you to steam your beloved pudding with no steamy windows, no pan boiling dry and no special equipment required.

Steaming without a steamer

The recipes that follow all include this method.
You will need a large casserole dish with a tight-fitting lid, and a trivet for the bottom of the pan so that your pudding basin is raised and doesn't sit directly on the base (otherwise it could crack and the sponge inside will not cook evenly). If you don't have a trivet, use an upturned metal plate, a metal pastry ring or cutters. (I have even used a metal teapot stand.)

Place your prepared pudding in its basin on the trivet and pour boiling water around it so that it comes about one-third up the sides of the basin. Place the lid on the dish, place on the hob and bring to the boil. Simmer for just 20 minutes. During this time, preheat the oven to 120°C/100°C (fan)/250°F/gas ½.

After the 20-minute simmer, don't be tempted to take the lid off the dish but transfer it straight away into the preheated oven and allow it to continue to 'steam' slowly and peacefully for the time given in the following recipes. No runny windows, no danger of the pan boiling dry and no need to go out and buy a steamer!

FRUIT PUDDING

SERVES: 4–6

I hate food waste and when I can create something out of leftovers I am very happy. This great little pudding is a cross between a sponge and a crumble and makes excellent use of day-old scones (see pages 56–65 for recipes).

2–3-day-old sweet scones, blitzed in a food processor
    (yielding 125g/4¼oz crumbs)
finely grated zest and juice of 1 lemon
1 egg
100g (3½oz) crème fraîche
20g (¾oz) caster sugar, plus 1–2 tsp for sprinkling
300g (10½oz) apples (or any fruit, including frozen
    fruit)

Equipment: food processor, hand-held electric whisk,
24 × 16 and 5cm deep (9 × 6 and 2 inches deep) ovenproof dish

Preheat the oven to 200°C/180°C (fan)/400°F/gas 6.

Put the scone crumbs in a roomy mixing bowl and add the lemon zest and juice.

Separate the egg and put the white in a separate clean bowl. Add the yolk to the crumbs then fold in the crème fraîche.

Whisk the egg white with a hand-held electric whisk in a clean bowl until it forms soft peaks, add the sugar and whisk until quite thick, then fold this meringue into the crumb mix until everything is well combined.

Peel and core the apples, then slice them into the base of the deep ovenproof dish (or use other fruit) and sprinkle over a little sugar. Spoon over the scone mix and cover all of the fruit with the back of a spoon then bake in the oven for 30 minutes until well risen and golden brown.

Serve warm with ice cream, custard or cream.

STEAMED TREACLE SPONGE

MAKES: 6 INDIVIDUAL PUDDINGS

I don't know anyone who doesn't love this delicious pudding: it's a real winter warmer. The recipe will also make one large 900g (2lb) pudding – the steaming time for one large sponge will need to increase to 3 hours.

125g (4¼oz) margarine or butter, at room temperature
125g (4¼oz) caster sugar
2 eggs
1 tsp vanilla extract
125g (4¼oz) self-raising flour
4 tbsp golden syrup, plus extra to heat for pouring (if desired)
custard, to serve

Equipment: hand-held electric whisk, 6 × 175ml (6fl oz) mini pudding basins generously greased with butter or brushed with lining paste, or for one large family pudding a 900g (2lb) pudding basin generously greased with butter or brushed with lining paste, baking parchment and kitchen string, trivet, large lidded casserole dish

Preheat the oven to 120°C/100°C (fan)/250°F/gas ½.

Cream the margarine or butter with the sugar in a roomy mixing bowl with a hand-held electric whisk until light and fluffy, then add the eggs one at a time, whisking after each addition, then add the vanilla and finally sift in the flour and fold it into the mix.

Place 1 dessertspoon of golden syrup into the bottom of each pudding basin. Divide the sponge batter evenly among the 6 prepared tins then cover each one with a piece of baking parchment, making a pleat in the centre of the parchment to allow for expansion. Tie to secure with a piece of string.

Place a trivet in the base of a large casserole dish then pop in the puddings. Add enough boiling water to come to about one-third up the sides of the tins. Cover with a lid then pop onto the hob, bring to the boil and simmer for 20 minutes. At the end of the simmering time immediately transfer the dish into the oven and cook for 1½ hours.

Remove the puddings from the dish, cut the string and remove the parchment. Invert each one into a dessert bowl and pour over more warmed golden syrup (if desired) plus custard.

These puddings also freeze well. I freeze them uncooked, then allow to defrost for about 6 hours in the fridge before cooking as above.

LET ME SHOW YOU . . .

My Steamed Treacle Sponge Video

JAM ROLY POLY

This beautiful winter warmer pudding is inexpensive to make, nostalgic and adored by children and adults: a great family pudding. Historically, this type of pudding was called a 'shirt sleeve' pudding as it was secured in a shirt sleeve for cooking. I add lemon for extra flavour – the taste of this pudding really is fabulous.

finely grated zest and juice of 1 lemon
140ml (4¾fl oz) whole milk
200g (7oz) self-raising flour
1 tbsp caster sugar
pinch of salt
100g (3½oz) vegetable suet
4 tbsp raspberry jam
desiccated coconut

Equipment: 'roly-poly tin' well greased or brushed with lining paste (optional), oblong roasting tin or casserole dish, trivet (or roasting drip tray)

Put the lemon zest in a roomy mixing bowl. Squeeze the juice from the lemon into a measuring jug then add the milk. As it stands, the milk will thicken and start to look curdled – that is absolutely fine.

Into the mixing bowl containing the zest add the self-raising flour, sugar, salt and suet. Stir with a knife then gradually add the thickened milk. You will probably need all of the liquid but keep a little back just in case. Bring the dough together with your hands. The consistency needs to be a little sticky but not so wet that it sticks all over your hands and certainly not hard and so dry that it is crumbly and falling apart.

Roll the dough between two sheets of plastic to a rectangle about 18 × 30cm (7 × 12 inches). The rectangle needs to be neat so don't be afraid, after peeling off the top sheet the plastic, to trim with a pizza cutter and use the trimmings to patch up where required. When you are satisfied with your finished rectangle, spread it with the raspberry jam, allowing a 5cm (2 inch) margin on all four sides. Using the bottom sheet of plastic as an aid, roll the dough from one short end to the other short end. Then, roll the pastry log in desiccated coconut.

Transfer the roll into a greased (use lining paste for this) 'roly poly' tin or enclose the roll loosely in non-stick baking parchment then wrap in foil, sealing securely at both ends (in the style of a Christmas cracker) – the parcel needs to be fairly roomy to allow for the dough to expand during cooking, yet securely fastened so that water droplets cannot penetrate. Seal the ends well and make sure the join of the foil is uppermost. At this point, you can chill the pudding parcel for a couple of hours if you wish.

When ready to cook, preheat the oven to 200°C/180°C (fan)/400°F/gas 6. Place the casserole dish or deep roasting tin in the oven to preheat at the same time. You will need a trivet or drip tray in the casserole dish or roasting tin. Have a full kettle of water which has just boiled. When the oven has reached temperature, take the roasting tin or casserole dish and trivet and place the pudding parcel or 'roly poly' tin on the trivet and add the boiling water so that it fills the roasting tray or casserole dish to about halfway. The pudding should be about one-third submerged in the water. Cover and cook in the oven for 1 hour then leave to stand for about 5 minutes before unwrapping or turning out of the tin.

Slice and serve hot with custard.

LET ME SHOW YOU . . .

My Jam Roly Poly Video

BREAD AND BUTTER PUDDING

SERVES: 6–8

Classic bread and butter pudding is super tasty, and I have been making it for years – my family always ask whether it is on the menu.

40g (1½oz) dried mixed fruit and peel

1 tsp mixed spice

50g (1¾oz) caster sugar

6 slices of thick white bread from a large loaf, crusts removed (slightly stale bread is best)

50g (1¾oz) butter

finely grated zest of 1 lemon

3 eggs

280ml (9½fl oz) whole milk

80ml (2¾fl oz) double cream

1 tbsp demerara sugar, for sprinkling

Equipment: pie dish that measures 26 × 20 and 2.5cm deep (10 × 8 and 1 inch deep) well greased or brushed with lining paste, roasting tin large enough to hold the pie dish

Put the mixed fruit and peel in a small bowl, sprinkle over the spice and sugar and stir.

Butter the bread slices on one side then cut the slices into neat squares.

Place a layer of bread, butter side down, into the pie dish. Sprinkle over a third of the fruit and sugar mix and a good grating of lemon zest. Layer over more buttered bread, fruit, sugar and lemon zest then finish with a final layer of bread, butter side down.

Beat the eggs in a large jug then add the milk and cream and stir well. Pour the mixture over the bread, allowing it to run down between cracks and crevices. Push the bread down into the liquid making sure the surface bread gets a coating.

Preheat the oven to 210°C/190°C (fan)/425°F/gas 7 and bring a kettle of water to the boil.

Place your pie dish in the roasting tin then carefully pour boiling water into the tin until it comes about halfway up the pudding dish. Sprinkle over the demerara sugar then bake in the oven for 30–35 minutes until risen and golden brown.

Remove from the water bath and serve warm with cream, ice cream or custard. The pudding will be deliciously light, tasty and wholesome, with a crunchy top!

This pudding works beautifully using my leftover brioche (see page 110). If you decide to use brioche, omit the butter in the recipe.

This pudding can be prepared ahead of time and kept in the fridge covered. In fact, it is much improved if the egg and milk mix soaks into the bread for at least 1 hour before baking.

Do use a bain marie (placing the pudding in the roasting tin with boiling water). Your pudding will be much better for it with no burning around the edges.

LET ME SHOW YOU . . .

My Bread and Butter Pudding Video

NANCY'S CHRISTMAS PUDDING

MAKES: 1 × 900G (2LB) PUDDING
OR 2 × 450G (1LB) PUDDINGS (SERVES 8)

This delicious traditional Christmas pudding can be made as one large pudding or 2 smaller puddings. I have also used small 300g (10½oz) foil pudding containers with lids and this recipe makes enough mix for three of those. I like to give them as presents. We make the pudding on Stir-up Sunday (the last Sunday before advent) and each family member gives the mix a stir, closes their eyes and makes a wish!

Once cooked, the pudding will keep for a very long time – in fact, if you make two or more, you can have one this Christmas and one next Christmas! I have added a bit of a twist and included morello glacé cherries and green cardamom for extra flavour.

FOR THE DRY MIX
    50g (1¾oz) self-raising flour
    100g (3½oz) vegetable or beef suet
    120g (4¼oz) fresh wholemeal breadcrumbs
    1 tsp mixed spice
    ¼ tsp ground mace
    ½ tsp ground cinnamon
    5 green cardamom pods, split and seeds crushed
    125g (4¼oz) dark muscovado sugar

FOR THE FRUIT AND NUT MIX
    100g (3½oz) morello glacé cherries
    500g (1lb 2oz) mixed dried fruit and peel

1 bramley apple

grated zest and juice of 1 orange

grated zest and juice of 1 lemon

25g (1oz) mixed chopped nuts, lightly toasted (see Tip)

FOR THE LIQUID MIX

2 eggs and 1 egg yolk, beaten

170ml (5¾fl oz) stout or real ale

2 tbsp Cointreau or brandy

EQUIPMENT LIST:

1 x 900g (2lb) pudding basin or 2 x 450g (1lb) pudding basins, casserole dish large enough to hold basin (s), trivet

||||||||||||||||||||||||||||||||||||||||||||||||||||||||||||||||||||||||||||||||||||||||||||||||||||||||||||||||||||||||||||||

Toasting nuts and seeds

Toasting or roasting nuts and seeds enhances their flavour but take care because they can burn easily. Use a dry frying pan and heat the nuts gently, swirling them around so they toast evenly. Once they have taken on a good pale, golden brown colour, transfer them to a cold plate.

||||||||||||||||||||||||||||||||||||||||||||||||||||||||||||||||||||||||||||||||||||||||||||||||||||||||||||||||||||||||||||||

Oven–steaming

The main drawback with making your own Christmas pudding is that it has to steam over a pan of boiling water for 6–8 hours!

||||||||||||||||||||||||||||||||||||||||||||||||||||||||||||||||||||||||||||||||||||||||||||||||||||||||||||||||||||||||||||||

I have a solution: steam the pudding overnight (or for 10 hours) in a covered pan of simmering water in a very low oven. It is clean, convenient and it looks after itself. Or, if you have a slow cooker, preheat it for 1 hour, pour in boiling water from the kettle, place your wrapped pudding inside, cover with the lid and slow cook for 10 hours.

Start the morning before you want to bake the pudding. Rinse the morello cherries in cold water to remove the sticky glaze, dry them, then quarter them. Mix all the dry ingredients together in a very large mixing bowl, then add the fruit and nuts. I don't peel the apple, just wash it then grate it straight into the bowl, peel and all, until I get down to the core. Discard the core. Mix everything well then incorporate the liquids. Give everything a good stir – the mixture will be quite sloppy and drop easily from a spoon. Cover the bowl and set aside at room temperature for at least 8 hours (or overnight).

Following a long soak, the mixture will be thick and wholesome. Now it is time to give a good stir and prepare for cooking.

Lightly grease a 900g (2lb) pudding basin (or two smaller basins) with butter or brush with lining paste, then invite everyone to have a stir the mix before spooning it into the basin(s) and smoothing with the back of a spoon. Cover the basin(s) with a sheet of greaseproof paper, making a centre pleat to allow for any expansion, then tie with string. Cover with a sheet of foil, securing it around the rim of the basin.

Place a trivet in the bottom of a large casserole dish (if you haven't a trivet use a metal plate turned upside down – I have even used a few even-thickness metal cutters as a trivet). Place the pudding on top then pour in boiling water so that it comes about one-third of the way up the basin. Cover the casserole dish with a lid, place on the hob and bring the water to the boil, then reduce the heat and simmer for 20 minutes before transferring to the oven preheated to 120°C/100°C (fan)/250°F/ gas ½. Steam in the oven for 10 hours or overnight. I usually put mine in the oven at 10pm and bring it out at 8am the next morning. Alternatively, if you have an electric slow cooker, preheat it for 1 hour on high then stand the pudding inside and pour in boiling water from the kettle until it comes one-third of the way up the basin. Cover and cook for 10 hours.

Leave to cool completely then remove the paper and foil. Place a clean piece of paper and string over the pudding, wrap in foil and leave in a cool, dark place until Christmas Day.

The pudding can be reheated by steaming it for 2 hours the same way, placed in a casserole dish with boiling water. Alternatively, reheat in the microwave (without the foil, just the paper): microwave on high power for 5 minutes, covered with a microwave-safe plate, leave for 10 minutes, then micro-wave again for 3 minutes. Remove the greaseproof paper, turn out onto a plate and serve with rum sauce or thick cream.

LET ME SHOW YOU . . .

My Christmas Pudding Video

LAST-MINUTE CHRISTMAS PUDDINGS

MAKES: 8 PUDDINGS

This is a lighter version of traditional Christmas pudding and I actually prefer it because there is so much rich food going on at Christmas – these puddings give me the Christmas spice without the Christmas overload! The individual puddings are superb in January for using up any leftover mincemeat, and can be made gluten free, too.

75g (2½oz) margarine or butter, at room temperature
75g (2½oz) caster sugar
2 eggs
100g (3½oz) self-raising flour (or gluten-free self-raising flour)
75g (2½oz) ground almonds
½ tsp mixed spice
½ tsp ground cardamom
300g (10½oz) mincemeat
1 tbsp black treacle
1 small dessert apple, washed
grated zest and juice of 1 orange
grated zest and juice of 1 lemon

Equipment: hand-held electric whisk, 8 × mini 175ml (6fl oz) pudding tins, generously greased or brushed with lining paste

Preheat the oven to 200°C/180°C (fan)/400°F/gas 6.

Cream the margarine or butter with the sugar in a bowl with a hand-held electric whisk until light and fluffy then add the eggs, one at a time, whisking well after each addition. Sift in the flour, sifted with the spices, then add all the other ingredients, grating in the apple, peel included (discard the core) and stir to combine.

Divide the mixture evenly among the prepared tins, place the tins on a baking tray or sheet and bake in the oven for 20–25 minutes until risen and dark golden.

Remove from the oven and serve with a brandy sauce or custard.

The puddings freeze very well and can be thawed and reheated in the microwave.

LET ME SHOW YOU . . .

My Last-Minute Christmas
Puddings Video

EVE'S PUDDING

SERVES: 4–6

Eve's pudding is a British classic made traditionally as a sponge over apples. My version has a few twists, is naturally gluten free, inexpensive, yet very tasty and delicious hot or cold.

450g (1lb) baking apples (or any apples you can get hold of
   – even a few wrinkled apples from the fruit bowl)
2–4 tbsp caster sugar, depending on the tartness of the apples
1 tbsp flaked almonds, for sprinkling

FOR THE GLUTEN-FREE SPONGE
50g (1¾oz) granulated sugar
125g (4¼oz) margarine or butter, at room temperature
125g (4¼oz) caster sugar
2 eggs
125g (4¼oz) ground almonds (or, for a more economical
   option, use ground rice)
½ tsp almond extract

Equipment: hand-held electric whisk, deep pudding tin or gratin dish – mine measures 23 × 15 and 5cm deep (9 × 5 and 2 inches deep), buttered or brushed with lining paste

Preheat the oven to 190°C/170°C (fan)/375°F/gas 5.

Start by making the gluten-free sponge. Put all the ingredients in a large mixing bowl and whisk with a hand-held electric whisk until well combined. The mixture needs to be fairly thick – a bit like mashed potato – not thin and runny.

Peel and core the apples, then slice them thinly into the prepared pudding tin or gratin dish. Sprinkle over the sugar – baking apples will need 4 tablespoons, dessert apples will need only 2 tablespoons – then immediately (before the apples start to go brown) spoon the sponge mixture on top. Spread the mix over the apples using a fork or the back of a spoon then sprinkle over the flaked almonds.

Bake in the oven for 50 minutes exactly.

Remove from the oven and serve warm with custard or cream. Any leftovers are delicious cold, and the pudding will keep for up to 4 days in the fridge.

My pudding is over-browning!
If your pudding starts to over-brown before the end of the cooking time, turn the oven from the fan to the conventional cooking setting and place a piece of foil with a hole in the centre (about the size of a cup) over the pudding. This will allow the centre to complete its baking and the edges will not brown any further.

LET ME SHOW YOU . . .

My Eve's Pudding Video

APPLE CHARLOTTE

SERVES: 4–6

This delightful, inexpensive, almost forgotten British pudding is great served warm with custard! A perfect way to use up leftover bread.

5–6 large slices of white bread, crusts removed
80g (2¾oz) butter, melted

FOR THE APPLE MIXTURE
25g (1oz) butter
grated zest and juice of 1 lemon
500g (1lb 2oz) cooking apples (peeled weight)
1 tbsp water
1 tbsp apricot jam
1 tsp sugar, plus more to taste
¼ freshly grated nutmeg
1 egg yolk

Equipment: 450g (1lb) pudding basin

Start by cooking the apples as they need to be cold before assembling the pudding. Melt the butter in a medium saucepan then add the lemon zest and juice. Peel the apples then simply cut thin slices from the apple down to the core. Add the thin apple slices to the melted butter and lemon, stirring well after each addition. The lemon juice will prevent any discoloration. Add the water then bring to a simmer, cover with a lid and cook for about 20 minutes until the apple is pulpy and very soft. Remove from the heat, stir well and add the apricot jam and sugar. When cool, stir in the nutmeg and egg yolk. Taste and check for sweetness – you may need no further sugar.

Roll the slices of bread gently with a rolling pin to flatten slightly then slice in two from corner to corner. You will have triangular slices of bread. Try the slices in the basin for size – use them to line the basin by fitting them with the pointed ends of the bread at the bottom of the basin. Once you are happy with the number you are going to need, take them from the basin and dip each one in the melted butter. Place back in the basin, butter side facing the basin, saving one slice of bread to be used for the top. Brush the inside of the bread with a little melted butter.

Pile the cooled apple filling into the bread-lined basin then cut the remaining piece of bread into a circle and place on the top of the filling, sealing the top securely by folding over any overhanging pieces of triangle bread. Place a heatproof saucer or loose bottom from a cake tin on the top then weigh down with a 1kg (2lb 4oz) heatproof weight. Pop into the fridge to chill for at least 1 hour.

When ready to bake, preheat the oven to 220°C/200°C (fan)/425°F/gas 7. Bake the pudding in the oven for 25 minutes. Keep the plate and the weight on the pudding during baking then after 25 minutes remove the plate and the weight and allow to bake for a further 10 minutes so that the top browns.

Remove from the oven and invert onto a plate, admire its beauty, then cut into slices and serve warm with custard, cream or ice cream.

LET ME SHOW YOU . . .

My Apple Charlotte Video

QUEEN OF PUDDINGS

SERVES: 6–8

This is my take on the classic Queen of Puddings, a dessert that dates back to 1699. For me, the pudding in its original form is a little too sweet so I have toned it down with a quick jam which is lower in sugar. This fabulous low-cost family pudding can be made using any seasonal fruit.

FOR THE JAM LAYER
- 300g (10½oz) fresh fruit (I used chopped apple and blackberries)
- 25g (1oz) caster sugar

FOR THE BOTTOM LAYER
- 300ml (10fl oz) whole milk
- 300ml (10fl oz) single cream
- grated zest and juice of 1 lemon
- 1 tsp vanilla extract
- 25g (1oz) caster sugar
- 15g (½oz) butter
- 130g (4½oz) fresh white breadcrumbs
- 2 egg yolks

FOR THE MERINGUE TOPPING
- 2 egg whites
- 125g (4¼oz) caster sugar
- ½ tsp cream of tartar

Equipment: pie dish – my Pyrex one is 25cm (10 inches) in diameter and about 4cm (2 inches) deep, generously greased or brushed with lining paste, hand-held electric whisk

Start by making the jam layer. Put the fruit and sugar in a medium saucepan and stir over a medium heat until all the sugar has dissolved. Turn up the heat and boil for 15–20 minutes until thick. Remove from the heat and leave to cool completely.

Preheat the oven to 200°C/180°C (fan)/400°F/gas 6.

For the bottom layer, bring the milk and cream to the boil in a medium saucepan then remove from the heat, add the lemon zest and juice, vanilla, caster sugar, butter and breadcrumbs and stir thoroughly. (I sometimes blitz my mixture with a stick blender if there are any lumpy bread pieces.) Leave to stand and cool for about 15 minutes, then whisk in the egg yolks. Transfer to the prepared pie dish then bake in the oven for 25 minutes until set. Reduce the oven temperature to 170°C/150°C (fan)/325°F/gas 3.

Remove the pie dish from the oven and allow to cool. Once the jam is cooled and the custard is cooled then you can start to assemble the pudding.

To make the meringue, whisk the egg whites in a roomy, spotlessly clean bowl with hand-held electric whisk until the whites are white and frothy. Add the sugar a tablespoon at a time, whisking well after each addition, and incorporate the cream of tartar during this process, whisking until the meringue is shiny and standing in stiff peaks.

Spread the jam over the set custard then pile the meringue over the jam, making sure you cover it right up to the edges of the dish. Swirl the top then pop into the cooler oven and bake for 45 minutes until the meringue is crispy and pale golden on the top.

Eat hot or cold.

||||||||||||||||||||||||||||||||||||||||||||||||||||||||||||||||||||||||||||||||||||||||||||||||||||||||||||||||||||||||||||||||||

Rhubarb and ginger work beautifully as a fresh jam
Use 300g (10½oz) fresh rhubarb cut into chunks,
1 piece of stem ginger in syrup, cut into tiny dice, and
1 tablespoon of syrup from the jar of ginger. Pile the lot
into a foil parcel and cook for 20–30 minutes in the
oven until tender, then mash with a fork. Alternatively,
cook on the hob over a low heat, covered with a lid,
stirring regularly, for about 15 minutes until tender –
taking care not to let it burn.

||||||||||||||||||||||||||||||||||||||||||||||||||||||||||||||||||||||||||||||||||||||||||||||||||||||||||||||||||||||||||||||||||

LET ME SHOW YOU . . .

My Queen of Puddings Video

FRUIT CRUMBLE

SERVES: 6

I have included my crumble recipe because it is one of those fantastic 'go to' puddings. Freeze crumble mix then scatter it over your choice of fruit (frozen or fresh) and you have a quick wholesome pudding – great with custard. I like my crumble to have proper crunchiness and bite and have found that adding a little milk to the mix creates little chunks of crunch. This crumble is easy, delicious and inexpensive.

FOR THE CRUMBLE MIX
- 170g (6oz) self-raising flour
- ½ tsp ground nutmeg (or use cinnamon, mixed spice or ginger if you make rhubarb)
- 90g (3oz) butter, at room temperature
- 40g (1½oz) porridge oats
- 40g (1½oz) demerara sugar
- 2 tbsp whole milk

FOR THE FRUIT
- 300g (10½oz) cooking apples (peeled weight) – about 3 or 4 large apples
- 100g (3½oz) blackberries (I used frozen)
- 2–3 dessertspoons caster sugar

Equipment: ovenproof dish (mine measures 23 × 15cm and 6cm deep/9 × 6 inches and 2 inches deep)

Put the flour, spice and butter in a roomy mixing bowl then rub with your fingertips until the mixture resembles breadcrumbs. Stir through the oats and sugar then spoon over the milk. Use a knife to stir the mixture around and you will see lumps will form as the mixture starts to stick together because of the addition of the milk. Pop the bowl into the fridge or freezer until you prepare the fruit.

Preheat the oven to 200°C/180°C (fan)/400°F/gas 6.

Peel, core and slice the apples into the ovenproof dish, scatter the blackberries around among the apple then sprinkle over the sugar. You may want to add a little ground cinnamon or nutmeg if you really love it. Take the crumble mix from the fridge and use a large spoon to carefully cover the fruit. Don't be tempted to push the crumble down over the fruit.

Bake in the oven for 30 minutes until the crumble is dark golden in colour. Remove from the oven and serve with custard, cream or ice cream.

Make extra crumble mix, put it in a freezer bag and store in the freezer. When you need a handy pudding, put fruit (fresh or frozen) in an ovenproof dish, sprinkle some sugar and the frozen crumble and pop it into the oven for 30 minutes!

LET ME SHOW YOU . . .

My Fruit Crumble Video

RICE PUDDING

I love rice pudding. I always used to make it in the oven but often found it to be either too dry (as it had baked for too long) or a bit sloppy, with gritty rice (when I had tried to rush it along). I now make it on the hob, leave it to stand, then reheat it and I it works perfectly every time. It's so simple.

30g (1oz) butter

150g (5½oz) pudding rice or short-grain rice, washed in a
    sieve under cold running water then drained

50g (1¾oz) granulated or caster sugar

1 litre (34fl oz) whole milk

1 tsp vanilla extract

1 tsp freshly grated nutmeg

400ml (14fl oz) tin of evaporated milk

Rub the base of a large saucepan with some of the butter to help avoid the milk burning on the bottom. Better still, use a non-stick pan.

Put all the ingredients in the saucepan, place over a low heat and stir well until the butter has melted and the sugar has dissolved. Bring to a very gentle simmer then turn down to the lowest heat and allow it to just tick over for 30 minutes, stirring every 5 minutes or so, so that it doesn't burn on the bottom and the rice doesn't clump together. The rice should be al dente and almost cooked through. Remove from the heat, cover with a lid and leave to cool.

When cool the rice should be thick, creamy and fully cooked. Give a good stir and a taste. To serve either reheat in the pan or microwave in individual bowls.

If you cook on a gas hob, place an upturned metal pie plate over the smallest burner on the lowest flame. Once your rice pudding is simmering gently, pop the pan onto the upturned metal plate. This will diffuse the heat and your pudding will cook perfectly without burning.

LET ME SHOW YOU . . .

My Rice Pudding Video

MERINGUE CROWN

SERVES: 8–10

With a crispy outside and soft light centre, this meringue crown attractively adorned with fruit jewels of the season is my elevated pavlova!

FOR THE CROWN
- 3 egg whites
- 150g (5½oz) caster sugar
- 1 tsp cornflour

FOR THE FILLING
- 300ml (10fl oz) double cream

selection of seasonal fruits

Equipment: tabletop (stand) mixer or hand-held electric whisk, piping bag fitted with a wide nozzle, baking sheet lined with non-stick baking parchment

Preheat the oven to 200°C/180°C (fan)/400°F/gas 6. Make sure your bowl and whisk are completely grease free, otherwise your egg whites will not whisk up to their full potential.

Put the egg whites in a large roomy mixing bowl or the bowl of a tabletop (stand) mixer.

Mix the caster sugar with the cornflour in a separate bowl. If you have time, pass the two through a sieve to ensure you have no lumps.

Whisk the egg whites with the whisk attachment of the mixer or a hand-held electric whisk until white and foamy and starting to form soft peaks (you want to start on a low speed, see page 336), then add the sugar/cornflour mix a tablespoon at a time, whisking for about 1 minute after each addition. Don't be tempted to rush – the whisking should take about 15 minutes. The meringue mix should be stiff and shiny and luscious. Fill a piping bag with the mix: I find it easier to suspend the bag inside a large jug then I can use both hands to spoon the meringue inside.

Draw a 20cm (8 inch) circle on the baking parchment with a marker pen or dark pencil – I use the loose bottom from a cake tin as a template. Turn the paper over so that the ink/pencil is not in contact with the meringue, place it on the baking sheet then start to pipe the meringue. (You may find it useful to secure the paper onto the sheet with a blob of meringue mix before you start.) Keeping within the line of your circle, start to smooth the meringue top and sides. I found this meringue bakes without cracks if the meringue is piped onto the paper in circles, starting in the centre and working outwards. There are then fewer air pockets. Use an angled palette knife or bench scraper to smooth the top and sides then you can use the back of a teaspoon or your palette knife to make ridges in the walls of your meringue. When you are happy with the finished design, pop it into the oven and immediately reduce the oven temperature to 140°C/120°C (fan)/275°F/gas 1. Bake for 2¼ hours. When the baking time is over, turn off the oven and wedge open the oven door with a wooden spoon. Leave the meringue overnight to completely dry out.

When ready to fill, peel the cooled meringue crown from the parchment, place onto your display plate, whip the cream then fill the crown with the freshly whipped cream and a selection of seasonal fruits.

My meringue mix won't form soft peaks

The reason your meringue refuses to whisk up could be because there is grease present in the bowl or on your whisk. Always make sure your equipment is super clean. Also, egg whites will whip up quicker and to their full potential if they are at room temperature.

My meringue was very hard and almost biscuit like, but I wanted it crisp on the outside and fluffy in the centre

The addition of cornflour should help with this – I use it often when making meringue because it helps to bind the mixture and achieve a soft centre and a crispy outside. Meringue actually dries out in the oven rather than bakes: a very hard meringue may have been in the oven for too long. Bake for 30 minutes less next time, and check the amount of sugar you use – I usually work on 50g (1¾oz) sugar per egg white. Any more than that will produce a hard meringue which is perfect for meringue garnishes like 'kisses' but not for a crown or pavlova.

My baked meringues have little brown beads on them

The little brown beads on meringues have appeared because some of the sugar hasn't dissolved during the whisking and mixing. Use caster sugar (as it is fine) and add just 1 tablespoon of sugar at a time to ensure it has been well incorporated before moving on. Using room-temperature egg whites helps avoid the beads too, and mixing the whites and sugar for long enough so the sugar dissolves (you can check this: the meringue mix should no longer be crunchy with sugar when rubbed between your fingertips).

My meringue cracked when it cooled

There could be a couple of reasons for this. Whipping up the egg white on too high a speed too quickly can cause problems because large unstable air bubbles form which later collapse, causing cracks. Always start beating the whites on a low speed until they become frothy. If your recipe calls for lemon juice, vinegar or cream of tartar, add this before the sugar. These little acidic additions strengthen the proteins in the egg white, making for a more stable meringue. Add the sugar 1 tablespoon at a time, whisking well after each addition. The meringue will become smooth, thick and glossy. Too much mixing will cause the meringue to collapse and separate so stop mixing when your meringue peaks are shiny and stiff. A meringue can also crack because it cooled down too quickly, so to avoid this let it cool slowly in the turned-off oven with the door wedged open (I use a wooden spoon).

Can I make meringue ahead?

Meringue is a great 'get ahead' dessert.
Stored in a tin, it will keep for up to 1 week.

My meringue was perfect when it came out of the oven, but now it's gone soft!

Meringue suffers terribly if the atmosphere is humid. In fact, I remember reading an old French recipe book that suggested refraining from meringue-making if the weather outside was wet! Bear in mind that any dampness will find its way very quickly to your meringue and make it sticky and soft, so pop it in an airtight box or tin until ready to use. Even better, pop your gorgeous crisp pavlova, kisses or shapes in a tin or bag then throw in a Silica sachet (yes – that's right! One of those little bags that was found in the bottom of your handbag when you bought it). Silica gel absorbs any moisture and will keep your meringue perfectly crisp until you are ready to fill and decorate.

HALF-SUGAR ALMOND MERINGUES

MAKES: 6 MERINGUE NESTS

I'm always working to reduce the sugar content in my recipes. After various experiments, I have developed this great little meringue that contains half the sugar of standard recipes while maintaining a good structure, crispy on the outside and soft on the inside.

20g (¾oz) flaked almonds
60g (2¼oz) icing sugar
15g (½oz) cornflour
2 egg whites
¼ tsp almond extract (optional)

Equipment: food processor or coffee grinder, tabletop (stand) mixer or hand-held electric whisk, baking sheet lined with reusable baking parchment, piping bag fitted with a large star nozzle (optional)

Preheat the oven to 140°C/120°C (fan)/275°F/gas 1. Your bowl and whisks need to be completely clean and free from grease or your egg whites will not whisk up to their full potential.

Toast the flaked almonds in a dry frying pan over a medium heat until just turning golden brown. Transfer to a plate otherwise they will continue to cook and may burn. Once cool, blitz them to a fine crumb using a food processor or coffee grinder. Set aside.

Mix the icing sugar and cornflour in a bowl, then pass through a sieve to make sure there are no lumps.

Whisk the egg whites with the whisk attachment of the mixer or a hand-held electric whisk on a low speed to start with then increase as the whites thicken. Whisk until the whites form soft peaks, then start to incorporate the icing sugar and cornflour mix, adding it 1 tablespoon at a time and whisking well after each addition. After you've added all the sugar mix briefly fold in the nut crumb – don't whisk it in or you risk collapsing the meringue.

Either spoon or pipe the meringue mix onto the lined baking sheet – you will have enough for 6 small meringue nests. Transfer to the oven and bake for 30 minutes. Turn off the oven but leave the meringues inside overnight, with the door propped open with a wooden spoon.

The next day, peel the meringues from the parchment. They keep in a tin for up to 1 week. Fill with cream, crème pâtissière, seasonal fruits and a dusting of icing sugar.

LET ME SHOW YOU . . .

My Half-Sugar Almond Meringues Video

MERINGUE CAKE

SERVES: 6

I have called this a meringue cake but it is in fact a sublime
dessert, a real showstopper. This is a great recipe for the summer
and as with any meringue this bake can also be gluten free.

FOR THE MERINGUE
    30g (1oz) flaked almonds
    4 egg whites
    200g (7oz) caster sugar
    1 tsp cornflour

FOR THE LEMON CURD
    4 egg yolks
    75g (2½oz) caster sugar
    grated zest and juice of 1 lemon
    50g (1¾oz) butter

FOR THE FINISHED FILLING
    300ml (10fl oz) double cream
    125g (4¼oz) fresh berries

Equipment: food processor or coffee grinder, hand-held electric
whisk or tabletop (stand) mixer, piping bag fitted with a wide,
plain nozzle (optional), 2 × 18cm (7 inch) cake tins, base and
sides lined with greaseproof or baking paper

Preheat the oven to 140°C/120°C (fan) 275°F/gas 1.

Toast the flaked almonds in a dry frying pan over a medium heat until just turning golden brown. Transfer to a plate otherwise they will continue to cook and may burn. Once cool, blitz briefly to a coarse crumb using a food processor or coffee grinder. Set aside. You can use ground almonds, but I think more flavour is gained from toasting and grinding them fresh.

To make the meringue, whisk the egg whites in a clean grease-free bowl with a hand-held electric whisk (or use a tabletop/stand mixer) until they form soft peaks. Start to add the sugar 1 tablespoon at a time, whisking well after each addition. Don't be tempted to rush – the whisking should take about 15 minutes. The meringue mix should be stiff and shiny. Add the cornflour with the final spoon of sugar. Finally, fold in the ground/crumbed toasted almonds. I like to pipe the meringue mix into the tins, as it helps avoid air pockets: fill a large piping bag with the mix and pipe the mix into the tins, starting at the centre and working outwards, finishing at the edge of the tins.

Place the two tins in the oven and bake for 1½ hours. At the end of the cooking time turn off the oven and open the oven door very slightly – I wedge mine open with a wooden spoon. Leave the meringues to cool completely in the oven. I leave them overnight.

The next day, lift the meringues out of the tins using the paper then remove the paper from sides and base. If you want to get ahead, the meringue cakes will freeze perfectly and you can fill and decorate later. Alternatively, place them in a tin and they will keep for at least 3–4 days.

To make the lemon curd, mix the egg yolks in a small saucepan (off the heat) then add the sugar and mix well. Add the lemon zest and juice and finally the butter. Place over a low heat, stirring continuously until the butter melts. The curd will then start to thicken after 3–4 minutes – when you see the first bubble appear, take off the heat, give a really good beating then transfer to a heatproof bowl to cool. The lemon curd can also be made in advance and stored in the fridge for at least 3–4 days.

To assemble the meringue cake, first whisk the double cream in a large mixing bowl to soft peaks. Loosen the cold lemon curd with a little of the cream, give it a good mix, then pour the lemon curd mix into the whipped cream, folding just enough to incorporate but leaving some lemon ripples. Use half the mixture to sandwich the cake together, along with a few berries, then pile the rest onto the top and decorate with the rest of the fruit. Serve straight away (it's best eaten the same day it's assembled).

LET ME SHOW YOU . . .

My Meringue Cake Video

SUMMER LEMON AND ELDERFLOWER CHEESECAKE

SERVES:10–12

This fantastic summer dessert can, with a little thought about decoration, really impress your friends. It is easy to make and can be made ahead of time – up to two days before. Fresh, seasonal and colourful fruits, a smooth lemon filling, thin base and a topping of elderflower jelly make for sheer elegance!

FOR THE BASE
  110g (4oz) digestive biscuits (about 9 biscuits)
  50g (1¾oz) butter
  ½ tsp Chinese five spice

FOR THE CURD
  4 gelatine leaves
  2 eggs
  75g (2½oz) caster sugar
  50g (1¾oz) butter
  grated zest and juice of 1 lemon

FOR THE FILLING
  500g (1lb 2oz) mascarpone cheese, at room temperature
  180g (6¼oz) icing sugar, sifted
  170ml (5¾fl oz) whole milk
  grated zest and juice of 1 large lemon (or 2 small lemons)
  selection of colourful fruits, such as strawberries, raspberries,
    blueberries, melon, sliced, chopped or left whole (optional)

FOR THE ELDERFLOWER JELLY GLAZE

2 gelatine leaves

140ml (4¾fl oz) cold water

4 tbsp elderflower cordial

tiny amount of lemon-yellow food colour

FOR THE DECORATION

mixed seasonal fruits

Equipment: 23cm (9 inch) round springform cake tin – I remove the metal base and replace it with a thin cake board of the same size (see Tip)

Start by making the base mix. Crush the biscuits in a large freezer bag using a rolling pin (or pop them in the bowl of a food processor and blitz to a crumb). Melt the butter in a small saucepan over a low heat then add the biscuit crumbs and five spice and stir well to combine. Transfer the buttery crumb to the base of the prepared tin and press down firmly using the back of a spoon or small angled palette knife. Chill in the fridge for about 1 hour.

Soak the 4 gelatine leaves for the curd in cold water for at least 10 minutes.

To make the curd, beat the eggs in a small saucepan and then add all the other ingredients. Place over a low heat and stir until the butter has melted. Turn up the heat slightly, still stirring all the time, and when the curd starts to thicken, remove it from the heat and give it a really good stir with a wooden spoon or whisk to make sure it is smooth and silky. Take the 4 softened gelatine leaves from the soaking water and drop them into the curd while it is still hot but not boiling. Stir until dissolved then set aside in the pan.

If you want to decorate the sides of your cheesecake with fruits, it's best to line the sides of the tin with a strip of acetate. The acetate will hug the sides of the tin and the fruits will stick to it and stay in place. Decorate the sides with your fruits then pop it all back into the fridge while you prepare the filling.

To make the filling, whisk the mascarpone cheese with the sifted icing sugar in a large bowl until smooth then gradually whisk in the milk a little at a time. Add the lemon juice and zest and stir well. Pour in the lemon curd and gelatine from the pan and whisk the whole lot together. Take the chilled cheesecake base from the fridge and pour the filling over, smooth over the top then pop it back into the fridge to set for at least 3 hours.

While the cheesecake is setting, make the jelly glaze. Soak the 2 gelatine leaves in cold water for at least 10 minutes. Put the cold water and elderflower cordial in a small saucepan and heat gently – do not boil. It is worth tasting the mixture to make sure it is flavoursome enough, adding a little more cordial if required. It needs to be slightly stronger than a drink would be. Add the drained, softened gelatine leaves to the warm liquid and stir until dissolved and the mixture is completely clear. Add then the tiniest amount of lemon-yellow food colour to tint the jelly then transfer to the fridge in a microwave jug and leave to set.

When the cheesecake and jelly have set, take the jelly from the fridge and microwave it in 10-second bursts, stirring after each burst. You want to dissolve the jelly just enough for it to have turned back to liquid and be lukewarm and not hot.

Take the cheesecake from the fridge and spoon over the jelly – sufficient to cover the filling. You may not need all of the jelly, you just want a light glaze to cover. Pop back into the fridge to set for about 2 hours.

About 2–3 hours before serving, decorate with more fresh fruits. I like to take my cheesecake from the fridge about 1 hour before serving to take the chill off and release the lovely fruity flavours.

LET ME SHOW YOU . . .

My Lemon & Elderflower
Cheesecake Video

Easy-out cheesecake
A cake board fitted into the bottom of the cake tin in place of the metal base will give you a perfect easy-out cheesecake that can be taken straight to the table.

Working with gelatine

Some people are fearful of working with gelatine but once a few basic rules are understood it is a great ingredient to use in cold desserts. First and foremost, gelatine doesn't like extreme temperatures – bit like us, really! It will fail if it is brought to the boil and it will fail if it is frozen, and that's it! Bear those two things in mind and your gelatine will set.

Should I use powder or leaf gelatine?

I use both but tend to choose leaf gelatine because of its ease of use, and I know that when calculating recipes 1 leaf will set 100ml (3½fl oz) liquid. If you prefer powdered gelatine, 1 tablespoon powder (usually 1 sachet) will equal 3 sheets. There are vegetarian options for gelatine on the market which work extremely well.

My cheesecake, mousse or dessert had little shards of gelatine in it

This will have happened because the gelatine wasn't fully dissolved before it was added to the cold mixture. Gelatine leaves need to be softened in cold water for at least 10 minutes and then dissolved using heat before stirring through a cold mixture. I tend to drain my soaked gelatine leaves into a small pan and then put over the gentlest heat for a few seconds (do not boil) until you see those wobbly leaves completely dissolve and a clear liquid appear. At this stage your gelatine can be safely poured and quickly mixed into your main liquid.

PIÑA COLADA COCKTAIL DESSERT

MAKES: 8 INDIVIDUAL DESSERTS OR 1 LARGE CHEESECAKE

Piña colada is of course a delicious Caribbean cocktail flavoured with coconut, rum and pineapple and these are the flavours in these little, light no-bake desserts. They can easily be made to be gluten free if you use gluten-free biscuits, and can be made ahead and decorated just before serving – they will keep for up to 4 days in the fridge.

FOR THE BISCUIT BASE
  170g (6oz) digestive biscuits (about 14 biscuits)
  70g (2½oz) butter
  ½ nutmeg, finely grated

FOR THE COCONUT CREAM FILLING AND JELLY LAYER
  2 eggs
  120g (4¼oz) caster sugar
  400g (14oz) tin coconut milk, refrigerated overnight (upside down)
  30g (1oz) coconut milk powder (optional)
  120ml (4fl oz) double cream
  75ml (2½fl oz) dark or white rum
  5½ gelatine leaves
  A packet of pineapple jelly

TO SERVE
  fresh fruit, to decorate
  chocolate shards

Equipment: 8 × 8cm (3½ inches) wide × 5cm (2 inches) deep metal ring moulds, lined with acetate strips, or a 23cm (9 inch) loose-bottom cake tin lined with an acetate strip, baking sheet, baking parchment, hand-held electric whisk

Start by making the base mix. Crush the biscuits in a large freezer bag using a rolling pin (or pop them in the bowl of a food processor and blitz to a crumb). Melt the butter in a small saucepan over a low heat then add the biscuit crumbs and add the grated nutmeg and stir to combine. Place the lined ring moulds on individual pieces of baking parchment (this is so that you can slide a knife underneath and move them easily) on a baking sheet. Divide the buttery crumb among the moulds or cake tin, press down with the back of a spoon and chill in the fridge for at least 30 minutes.

To make the coconut cream filling, first whisk the eggs and the sugar together in a heatproof bowl with a hand-held electric whisk over a saucepan of simmering water until the mixture is pale, light and doubled in volume – by this time the eggs will be cooked through. Remove from the heat and set aside.

Carefully open the tin of coconut milk and pour off the water which will have risen to the top of the tin as the coconut milk sat in the fridge. Put the coconut milk in a separate bowl and whisk with the coconut milk powder (if using) until smooth. Add the double cream and whisk until thick, then gradually add the egg and sugar mix and finally the rum. Taste the mixture and add more rum if desired.

Soak the gelatine leaves in cold water for at least 10 minutes, then drain and dissolve the gelatine in the warm pan after pouring away the warm water which was used under the eggs and sugar bowl. When the gelatine has dissolved, whisk this into the coconut cream. Transfer the mix to a jug and carefully fill the chilled moulds. Leave to set in the fridge for 3 hours or overnight.

Make up the pineapple jelly according to the packet instructions then leave to cool before pouring a thin layer over each set dessert. Leave the jelly to set for about 4 hours then remove from the moulds directly onto a serving plate and remove the acetate, then decorate with a selection of fresh fruit, pineapple, chocolate shards or berries.

LET ME SHOW YOU . . .

My Pina Colada Dessert Video

RASPBERRY AND WHITE CHOCOLATE BUNDT

SERVES: 6–8

This is a real stunner. A delicious light dessert which can be served any time of the year as I have used frozen berries throughout. A fatless almond sponge supports a white chocolate panna cotta then topped with a berry-filled jelly. It can be dressed up to look irresistible and then served at any dinner party or family gathering.

FOR THE SIMPLE SYRUP
    200ml (7fl oz) water
    120g (4¼oz) caster sugar
    strip of lemon peel
    2.5cm (1 inch) vanilla pod

FOR THE JELLY
    5 gelatine leaves
    250ml (8fl oz) fresh fruit puree (I used a 300–400g/
        10½–14oz mix of frozen raspberries and strawberries,
        thawed)
    300ml (10fl oz) Simple Syrup (above)
    200g (7oz) frozen raspberries

If you want to speed up this dessert, instead of making
your own jelly make up 1 pint (570ml/16fl oz)
strawberry or raspberry packet jelly to use along with
the frozen raspberries.

FOR THE PANNA COTTA
    2 gelatine leaves
    100g (3½oz) white chocolate, broken into pieces
    120ml (4fl oz) whole milk
    200ml (7fl oz) double cream
    50g (1¾oz) sugar
    1 tsp vanilla extract

FOR THE ALMOND SPONGE
    2 eggs
    50g (1¾oz) caster sugar
    ½ tsp almond extract
    50g (1¾oz) plain flour (or gluten-free flour)
    1 tbsp flaked almonds (optional)

Equipment: hand-held electric whisk, 22cm (9 inch) bundt tin,
baking parchment, greaseproof paper or reusable baking
parchment

First, make the simple syrup: boil the ingredients together in
a saucepan for 2–3 minutes until the sugar dissolves then
remove from the heat and set aside.

Soak the gelatine leaves for the jelly in cold water for 10 minutes.

Now make a template for the sponge. Using the bundt tin, draw a circle on a piece of baking paper and mark the hole in the middle also. Cut out the shape as this will be used later when cutting the sponge.

To make the jelly, first pass the thawed fruit through a sieve to remove the seeds then pop into a jug. While the simple syrup is still warm, drop in the drained, softened gelatine leaves and stir well until dissolved. Combine the fruit puree and simple syrup plus gelatine and mix well.

There are two jelly layers in this dessert, so put aside half of this jelly mixture you have made for the second layer. For the first layer of jelly: place a quarter of your frozen berries in the bottom of the tin and pour over sufficient jelly to only just cover the fruits so that they remain in place. Pop into the fridge to set for 1–2 hours. The rest of the jelly will remain at room temperature in a jug and shouldn't set.

When the first layer of fruit has set, take from the fridge, add another quarter of berries and pour over the rest of the jelly for this first layer. The whole of this jelly layer can now be popped into the fridge to set completely ensuring an even distribution of fruits and an attractive layer of presentation berries at the base of the tin.

Soak the gelatine leaves for the panna cotta in a bowl of cold water for 10 minutes.

Put the broken chocolate in a heatproof bowl. Bring the milk, cream and sugar to a gentle simmer in a saucepan then pour it over the chocolate and add the drained, softened gelatine. Stir until the chocolate melts and the gelatine is dissolved, then pass the mix through a sieve (to remove any remaining chocolate solids) into a jug. Leave to cool at room temperature – don't put it in the fridge at this stage otherwise it will set.

When the jelly has set, remove it from the fridge and spoon over the panna cotta. The whole lot can now be transferred to the fridge for at least 2 hours to firm up completely.

Layer the remaining frozen berries over the panna cotta and add the rest of the jelly. If the second half of the jelly in its jug has set, simply pop it into the microwave in 15-second bursts until it turns to liquid but is not hot. If it is hot, allow it to cool down, otherwise it will melt your panna cotta as it is added. Spoon the jelly over the panna cotta until you have an even layer. Don't be tempted to pour it over as the weight of the jelly may penetrate the panna cotta and you will breach the surface. Leave to set in the fridge for a further 2 hours.

Preheat the oven to 200°C/180°C (fan)/400°F/gas 6. To make the fatless sponge, whisk the eggs and caster sugar in a bowl with a hand-held electric whisk until doubled in size and the whisk leaves a trail when lifted. Add the almond extract, sift over the flour and fold it in. Spread onto greaseproof paper or reusable baking parchment, making sure the sponge is larger than the paper template made earlier. Scatter over the flaked almonds (if using) and bake in the oven for 8–10 minutes. Leave to cool then, using the template, cut out the shape of the bundt tin. Carefully peel the baked sponge from the paper before cutting out – it's easier that way.

When the jelly has set, lay the sponge over the top, almond side facing up, then turn out onto a serving plate: briefly place the chilled bundt tin into a bowl of hot water for about

30 seconds. Your jelly will then release easily. Decorate with fresh fruit, mint leaves, chocolate curls etc., if you wish.

Fruit will automatically float in the jelly so if you want to be able to see fruit at the top of your finished dessert simply place a few presentation berries at the bottom of the tin before adding the first half of the jelly then spoon over 1 teaspoon of jelly to help keep them in place. Pop in the fridge for about 20 minutes to set. Take from the fridge and top up with the rest of the half of the jelly.

Gelatine will refuse to set if it is boiled or frozen so don't be tempted to speed things up by placing the bundt in the freezer.

LET ME SHOW YOU . . .

My Raspberry & White Chocolate
Bundt Video

CHOCOLATE AND ORANGE DELICE

SERVES: 8–10

Beautifully rich, dark, decadent and delicious, this delice is a treasure for chocolate lovers and can easily be adapted to be gluten free, too! This top-end patisserie comprises a praline base then a tangy orange layer topped off and decorated with dark chocolate. The chocolate sets with no gelatine in sight.

FOR THE PRALINE BASE

40g (1½oz) whole blanched hazelnuts
40g (1½oz) caster sugar
1 tbsp cold water
40g (1½oz) Shreddies or gluten-free cereal

FOR THE ORANGE LAYER

3 tbsp marmalade
finely grated zest of 1 orange

FOR THE CHOCOLATE LAYER

140ml (4¾fl oz) whole milk
300ml (10fl oz) double cream
3 eggs
360g dark chocolate, broken into pieces
1 tsp instant espresso coffee powder
½ tsp vanilla paste
¼ tsp ground star anise or Chinese five spice (optional)

Equipment: baking sheet lined with reusable baking parchment or foil, food processor, 18cm (7 inch) square loose-bottom cake tin, sides lined with baking paper or acetate strip

---

For easy cutting, pop the delice into the freezer for 1 hour and your portions will be incredibly neat and clean.

Start by making the praline. Toast the hazelnuts in a dry frying pan over a medium-low heat for about 5 minutes, swirling the around, until evenly golden. Remove from the pan immediately and set aside.

Put the sugar and cold water in a medium saucepan and place over a low heat. Do not be tempted to stir – just leave it to gradually dissolve, gently moving the pan from side to side. Once the sugar has dissolved, turn up the heat and cook until the syrup is pale yellow. Drop in the nuts, swirl the pan gently and cook until the nuts and syrup darken to the colour of golden syrup. Turn the mixture out onto the baking sheet lined with baking parchment or foil and allow to go completely cold.

In the bowl of a food processor with the blade attached, roughly blitz the Shreddies (or gluten-free cereal) until they form a rough crumb. Transfer to a bowl.

Break the nutty caramel into pieces then blitz them in the food processor until the praline has formed a thick paste. Transfer this paste to the bowl with the Shreddies and mix together. Transfer this mix to the cake tin and spread it over the base, pressing down firmly and evenly. Transfer to the fridge and allow to chill for 1 hour.

Mix the marmalade and orange zest then spread this over the firm base – pop back into the fridge.

Put the milk and cream in a medium saucepan and bring to the boil.

Beat the eggs in a separate large bowl then pour the recently boiled milk and cream mixture over the eggs in a thin steady stream, whisking all the time with a hand whisk. The heat from the liquid will cook the eggs. Add the chocolate, coffee, vanilla and spice (if using) and stir slowly until the chocolate has completely melted and the mixture is thick, dark and smooth.

Remove the tin from the fridge and pour on the chocolate mixture, then pop back into the fridge and allow to set for 6 hours or better still overnight. As this dessert doesn't contain gelatine it will freeze very well.

Decorate as desired but I think something simple is all that is required. Cut into tidy portions and serve! I like to serve this delice lightly chilled.

LET ME SHOW YOU . . .

My Chocolate and Orange
Delice Video

CRÈME CARAMEL

SERVES: 6

People tell me they find this traditional dessert hard to get right. Indeed, I had many unsatisfactory results myself to begin with: I was baking them too hot and for too long. They looked fine, but as they cooled the surface cracked. Crème caramel needs to be taken from the oven when there is still a slight wobble in the centre. As they cool, they firm up to the perfect consistency. This is a great dessert for entertaining as it has to be made ahead. These crèmes will in fact keep well in the fridge for 3–4 days.

FOR THE CARAMEL
    50ml (1¾fl oz) water
    150g (5½oz) caster sugar

FOR THE CUSTARD
    ½ vanilla pod (split and seeds scraped) or 1 tsp vanilla paste
    550ml (18½fl oz) whole milk
    3 eggs plus 3 egg yolks
    100g (3½oz) caster sugar

Equipment: 6 x ramekin dishes 9cm wide and 5cm deep (3½ inches wide and 2 inches deep) ramekin dishes, a small saucepan (preferably without a non-stick coating, as you need to be able to see the sugar change colour – a non-stick pan with a black interior will make this tricky) roasting tin large enough to hold the ramekins

To make the caramel, put the water and sugar in a saucepan and allow the sugar to dissolve over a low heat. Don't be tempted to mess with it, stir it or introduce any forks, spoons etc., as any grease whatsoever will cause the sugar to crystallize. I tend to swirl the pan from side to side gently to help the sugar to dissolve. Once you have a clear liquid in the pan, increase the heat and allow the sugar to boil. Once all the water has evaporated the sugar will start to colour. When the sugar is the colour of golden syrup, remove it from the heat and divide among the ramekin dishes. Set aside.

To make the custard, first split the vanilla pod in half lengthways (if using), scrape out the seeds and place the seeds and pod in the milk. Bring the milk to a simmer then remove from the heat and allow to infuse a short time while you mix the eggs and sugar. If you are using vanilla paste, simply add this to the milk at the outset.

Mix the eggs and egg yolks with the sugar in a large mixing bowl. Slowly pour the vanilla milk over (removing the vanilla pod) and whisk thoroughly. Transfer the custard mix to a large jug through a sieve to remove any egg solids and disperse any bubbles. Divide the custard mix evenly among the ramekins then place them on a piece of kitchen paper in the bottom of a roasting tin. The kitchen paper prevents the bowls from sliding around in the tin.

Preheat the oven to 150°C/130°C (fan)/300°F/gas 2.

Fill the roasting tin with tap-hot water so that it comes just below the level of the custard in the ramekin and bake the custards for 30 minutes. They should still have a tremble when you take them from the oven.

Remove immediately from the roasting tin and water and allow to cool.

When cold, lay the ramekins side by side on the fridge shelf and lay over a beeswax wrap or flat plate. Leave them to chill for 24 hours.

When ready to serve, slide a knife around the custard then invert onto a dish or serving plate. The caramel sauce will surround your lovely crème. Serve as they are or with a little fresh fruit garnish on the side.

LET ME SHOW YOU . . .

My Crème Caramel Video

My crème caramels tasted delicious but most of the caramel was left in the ramekin

It is unlikely you will remove every trace of caramel when you invert your dessert, but the more there is the better. Take your caramels from the fridge and gently run a knife around the side of the custard to loosen it then leave them to come to room temperature before serving. The caramel will run more freely from the ramekin if it is not chilled.

My crème caramels had little bubbles in the custard

This happened to me many times and I followed so many recipes to try and get them right. Every photograph in every book looked perfect but mine had bubbles! After many attempts and different experiments, I finally discovered that boiling water in the roasting tin was too hot for the custard, and caused the bubbles to form. I now use hot water from the tap and this is gentle enough to cook the custard perfectly.

Don't throw away your egg whites

In addition to 3 whole eggs, you need 3 egg yolks for this recipe, which leaves 3 egg whites. Pop them into a plastic container with a lid (I save yoghurt and cream cartons for this), mark clearly then freeze. These egg whites can be defrosted and used for a number of recipes in this book, including my Coconut and Passion Fruit Angel Cakes on page 170, Meringue Crown on page 333 as well as the Italian Meringue and Swiss Meringue Buttercreams (page 188 and 191).

CRÈME BRÛLÉE

SERVES: 4

This classic dessert is said to have its origins in France, or Spain and there are those who believe it was invented in England at Trinity College, Cambridge, where it was known as Burnt Cream. Whoever invented this beauty should be applauded – it is one of my favourite desserts. Smooth, creamy custard topped off with a thin caramel crunch. This one is easy, great for entertaining because you can get ahead the day before and it looks amazing when presented with just a few fresh berries. It's gluten free, too!

FOR THE CUSTARD
    300ml (10fl oz) double cream
    300ml (10fl oz) whole milk
    1 vanilla pod (split and seeds scraped) or 1 tsp vanilla extract
    4 egg yolks
    30g (1oz) caster sugar
    1 tsp cornflour

FOR THE CRACKING CARAMEL TOP
    4 tsp demerara sugar

Equipment: I have perfect little dishes – wider and shallower than ramekins – that are 12cm wide and 3cm deep (4½ inches wide and 1 inch deep, the French serve crème brûlée in such a dish. You can also use 4 × 7.5cm (3 inches) ramekins, cook's blowtorch

Put the cream, milk and vanilla pod and seeds (or extract) in a medium saucepan and slowly bring to the boil.

Put the egg yolks, sugar and cornflour in a medium bowl and stir thoroughly. Slowly pour the hot cream and milk over the egg mix, stirring all the time, then transfer it all back into the pan over a low heat. Stir continually until the custard thickens, then remove the vanilla pod (if used) and divide evenly among the ramekin dishes. Allow to cool then pop into the fridge and leave for at least 6 hours and preferably overnight.

When ready to serve, sprinkle 1 teaspoon of demerara sugar over each pudding and tilt from side to side to spread it out. Use the cook's blowtorch to caramelize the top of each pudding until the surface is golden brown and crunchy. This caramel will stay crisp for about 1 hour.

I would love to make this dessert, but I do not have a blowtorch

Try instead making a caramel to pour over the custard. Put 125g (4¼oz) sugar (caster or granulated) in a clean small saucepan and set over a low heat. Do not stir, just gently swirl the pan from side to side to help the sugar dissolve evenly. When the sugar has dissolved, and turned from a clear liquid to the shade of golden syrup, remove from the heat, keep your pan swirling around, then pour 1–2 tablespoons over each chilled crème and quickly swirl it around to make sure it runs to the edges of the custard before it quickly sets. You need to be swift so do one at a time. Let the caramel set and take

---

on its classic hard top. This caramel will stay
crunchy for about 2 hours but then will start to
suffer from the humidity and turn sticky even though
it will still taste good!

LET ME SHOW YOU . . .

My Crème Brûlée Video

CITRUS POSSET WITH BLUEBERRIES

SERVES: 6

Possets are steeped in history – William Shakespeare even gives the good old posset a mention in *Hamlet*, yet back then a posset was a dessert or drink made from curdled milk enriched with sugar and alcohol. It was often used for medicinal purposes, and it is mentioned in the *Journals of the House of Lords* that King Charles I was given a posset drink by his physician. Nowadays presented as a dessert, this little beauty is much underrated. No cornflour, eggs or gelatine are required to set this traditional English delight.

350ml (12fl oz) double cream
100ml (3½fl oz) single cream
130g (4½oz) granulated sugar
finely grated zest of 1 lemon, plus extra to serve
finely grated zest of 1 lime
finely grated zest of 1 orange
90ml (3fl oz) juice from the zested fruits
fresh blueberries, to decorate

Equipment: 6 × 120ml (4fl oz) glass tumblers (or similar capacity dishes/glasses)

Put all the ingredients except the juice and decorative blueberries in a medium saucepan and place over a low heat, stirring constantly until the sugar has dissolved. Increase the heat and bring to the boil, then reduce the heat and simmer, stirring regularly, for 10 minutes exactly. The cream mixture should be thick and bubbling – my grandson said it looks like frog spawn. The mixture needs to have reduced by one third.

Remove from the heat, stir in the juice, then transfer to a cold bowl and leave for 20–30 minutes to cool. A skin will form.

Push the cooled mixture (and skin) through a fine mesh sieve then transfer to glass tumblers and leave to go completely cold. Cover and chill for 3 hours or overnight.

Remove from the fridge about 1 hour before serving, then decorate with blueberries and some lemon zest.

These possets will keep in the fridge for 3–4 days.

LET ME SHOW YOU . . .

My Citrus Posset Video

ICE CREAM

A section on cold desserts just has to include ice cream. There are so many ice creams on the market that you may think it is not worth making it yourself, especially if it involves having to invest in an ice cream maker – I tend to agree. However, there will be times when maybe you find yourself with a surplus of egg yolks, or have been alarmed by the list of ingredients on your ice cream tub and want to make your own. The taste of home-made ice cream is worlds apart from shop bought. It is delicious! No ice cream maker is required for the recipes that follow.

VANILLA ICE CREAM

MAKES: 2 PINTS (1 LITRE/34FL OZ)

Most of us adore vanilla ice cream and a home-made one is the best. This recipe is ultra simple, tastes delicious and is inexpensive. If you have an ice-cream machine, the results are smooth and luscious, but if not I can explain how to get a very good result.

2 eggs
50g (1¾oz) caster sugar
1½ tsp vanilla extract (if you want to make your ice-cream really special, use ½ vanilla pod, split and seeds scraped)
400ml (14fl oz) tin of evaporated milk, chilled overnight in the fridge

Equipment: hand-held electric whisk, ice-cream machine (optional)

Put a large, clean bowl in the fridge for an hour before you start.

Bring a small pan of water to the boil then turn off the heat.

Whisk the eggs, sugar and vanilla together in a heatproof mixing bowl with a hand-held electric whisk. Place over the pan of boiled water and whisk continually for about 10 minutes until the mixture thickens, turns pale in colour and when the whisks are lifted out they leave a ribbon trail on the mixture. Whisking over the hot water will ensure the eggs are cooked. Remove the bowl from the heat and set aside.

Take the chilled bowl from the fridge and pour into it the chilled evaporated milk. With the same whisks, whip up the evaporated milk until thick and doubled in volume. Again, the whisks will leave a ribbon trail in the mixture as they are lifted out.

Stir the two mixes together then transfer to an ice-cream machine and churn until thick, smooth and iced. Transfer to a plastic tub and place in the freezer or eat at once! If frozen hard, leave to soften in the fridge for between 30 minutes and 1 hour before serving.

IF YOU DO NOT HAVE AN ICE CREAM MACHINE

Transfer your whipped-up mixture to a roomy plastic bowl (maybe a saved and washed-out ice-cream tub) which has a lid. Transfer to the freezer for 1½ hours. Remove from the freezer and whisk either by hand or with an electric whisk. This breaks down any ice particles that may be forming and incorporates some air into the mixture. Place back into the freezer. After another hour, repeat as above. Your ice cream should be setting and by giving this final whisk you should have a light delicious vanilla ice cream. This home-made ice cream will set very hard, so remember to take it out of the freezer and pop it into the fridge about an hour before serving to allow it to soften and make easier to scoop.

LET ME SHOW YOU . . .

My Vanilla Ice Cream Video

PASSION FRUIT ICE CREAM

MAKES: 800ML (27FL OZ)

The distinctive flavour of passion fruits makes this ice cream simply heavenly. It's easy to make and even easier to eat. My favourite way to serve it is to set the ice cream in silicone moulds – soften in the fridge for about an hour before serving then turn out onto serving plates with fresh fruits.

8 passion fruits
20ml (3/4 fl oz) passion fruit liqueur
250ml (8fl oz) cold condensed milk
300ml (10fl oz) cold double cream

Equipment: hand-held electric whisk or tabletop (stand) mixer

Juice the passion fruits (see Tip on page 372) and set aside 150ml (5fl oz) juice.

Put the condensed milk, fruit juice and double cream in a large bowl and whisk with a hand-held electric whisk (or use a tabletop/stand mixer) until thickened. Transfer to a plastic tub with a lid to freeze or alternatively fill silicone moulds and freeze until required.

Remove from the freezer 30 minutes before required and pop the tub or moulds into the fridge to soften. This ice cream is unbelievably good!

How to juice a passion fruit

Cut each fruit in half, scoop out the seeds, then either push through a metal sieve with a metal spoon or pop the fruit pulp into the goblet of a food processor along with the alcohol (passion fruit liqueur) and blitz for a minute. The juice will then pour through the sieve easily.

LET ME SHOW YOU . . .

My Passion Fruit Ice Cream Video

NO-CHURN RASPBERRY RIPPLE ICE CREAM

MAKES: 1.5 LITRES (50FL OZ)

This ice cream is super easy to make, and no ice-cream maker is required. Raspberry ripple is a nostalgic favourite and, with its real-fruit ripples, children and adults adore it. Remember to soften it in the fridge for about an hour before serving and enjoy it on its own or as a summer dessert with fresh berries.

400g (14oz) fresh raspberries
2 eggs, separated
120g (4¼oz) caster sugar
few drops of vanilla extract
300ml (10fl oz) double cream
1 tbsp lemon juice

Equipment: food processor, hand-held electric whisk 2 x 1 litre (34fl oz/2 pint) plastic containers

Blitz the raspberries to a pulp in a food processor then pass through a sieve. I like to reduce the raspberry puree to a fairly thick sauce that has a similar consistency to tomato ketchup. Just place the puree in a small saucepan and boil rapidly for about 6 minutes. Transfer to a cold bowl and allow the puree to cool completely.

Whisk the egg whites in a spotlessly clean bowl with half of the sugar with a hand-held electric whisk until the whites have increased in size and formed stiff peaks.

Put a second (heatproof) bowl over a pan of hot water (off the heat). Add the egg yolks, the remaining sugar and the vanilla and whisk constantly until the mixture has doubled in size and has taken on a pale straw colour. Remove the bowl from the pan of water and set aside.

In a third bowl, whisk the double cream to very soft peaks – be careful, you don't want to over-whip the cream.

Fold the egg whites into the egg yolk and sugar mix, then add the double cream and lemon juice. Make sure all is well combined then briefly fold in the thickened raspberry puree – giving just a few turns. You want a ripple effect, not a pink ice cream.

Transfer to 2 × 1 litre (34fl oz/2 pint) plastic containers, place lids on and put in the freezer for at least 4 hours. Remove from the freezer and place in the fridge to soften about an hour before serving.

LET ME SHOW YOU . . .

My Raspberry Ripple Ice Cream Video

LEMON AND RASPBERRY ARCTIC BUNDT

SERVES: 14–16

I couldn't close the Puddings and Desserts chapter without including this showstopper dessert. It has so many assets: it can be made ahead – weeks ahead, in fact! both children and adults adore it, and it is easy to make, not expensive and looks very impressive.

FOR THE SPONGE
- 150ml (5fl oz) whole milk
- finely grated zest and juice of 1 lemon
- 250g (9oz) margarine or butter, at room temperature
- 250g (9oz) caster sugar
- 5 eggs, separated
- 250g (9oz) self-raising flour, sifted
- 1 tsp cream of tartar

FOR THE ICE CREAM
- 200ml (7fl oz) cold double cream
- 200ml (7fl oz) cold condensed milk
- 100g (3½oz) frozen raspberries

TO DECORATE
- fresh berries (I used strawberries and blueberries)
- icing sugar, for dusting

Equipment: hand-held electric whisk, bundt tin about 22cm (9 inches) diameter, greased or lined with lining paste

First, put a roomy mixing bowl in the fridge to chill (this is for making the ice cream later). Preheat the oven to 190°C/170°C (fan)/375°F/gas 5.

To make the sponge, pour the milk in a measuring jug then, after zesting the lemon into a large mixing bowl, add the juice to the milk and set aside to thicken.

Add the margarine (or butter) and sugar to the large bowl containing the zest and whisk with a hand-held electric whisk until light and fluffy. Add the egg yolks one at a time, whisking well after each addition. Fold in the sifted self-raising flour until well combined then fold in the thickened milk a little at a time until all is well incorporated.

Put the egg whites and cream of tartar in a separate clean bowl and whisk vigorously with clean whisks until the whites are thick, shiny and standing in soft peaks. Fold the whites into the sponge mixture one very large spoonful at a time then transfer the whole lot into the prepared bundt tin. Bake in the oven for 40–45 minutes until the top is dark golden in colour and firm to the touch.

Remove from the oven and leave on a cooling rack for 5–10 minutes until cool enough to handle, then turn out and allow to cool completely.

Once completely cold, slice off the bottom 2cm (¾ inch) of the bundt with a bread knife. Use a basin that fits the bundt comfortably then cover and flip the whole lot over so that the cake is contained within the basin and you can remove the recently sliced lid. Remove the lid and set aside. Use a sharp vegetable knife to cut a trough out of the remaining sponge – this will be filled with ice cream. Children love to eat up all the offcuts!

To make the ice cream, take the chilled mixing bowl from the fridge and pour in the double cream and condensed milk which are both well chilled. Whisk with a hand-held electric whisk at high speed until the mixture becomes very thick, then fold in the frozen raspberries – I find the finish much more effective if the raspberries have been broken into frozen crumbs, but that is up to you. Spoon the ice-cream mixture into the cake trough, replace the lid then pop into the freezer for at least 6 hours but preferably overnight.

The next day, take the basin from the freezer and turn out onto a cake board or presentation plate (that will fit back into your freezer). If the bundt seems stuck in the basin, do not worry. Place warm towels around the outside of the basin and in no time the bundt will release. Return the bundt to the freezer until 2 hours before you want to serve it.

When ready to prepare your dessert, remove it from the freezer and fill the central cavity with a selection of fresh berries. Pop the whole lot into the fridge and allow to soften for 2 hours. When ready to serve take from the fridge, dust all over with icing sugar, slice and enjoy! If you have any left, pop it in the freezer for later!

LET ME SHOW YOU . . .

My Lemon and Raspberry Arctic Bundt Video

HOME TIME

GROWING YOUR OWN FOOD

This book is by no means a gardening book, but for those who want to try just a little 'home growing', here are a few ideas.

CONTINUAL SALAD LEAVES, MICRO HERBS, CRESSES AND GARNISHES

A packet of mixed salad leaves or herbs has so many uses. Sprinkle seeds into a tray of potting compost every three weeks or so through the summer months and you will be rewarded with a regular supply of leaves. 'Cut and come again' salad leaves are also available – use them when they are tiny, as micro herbs to garnish the most delicate of bakes or dishes, or grow them to full size for salads and cooking, and when you have finished your tray the chickens will nibble at the rest (or leave them out for the wild birds before then tossing the whatever is left into the compost bin to be recycled).

MARROWFAT PEAS

If you just want to grow pea shoots for garnishing, there is absolutely no need to purchase pea seeds that will be grown into full crops. A handful of marrowfat peas placed in a pot of compost will germinate and you will be rewarded with perfect little pea shoots to decorate your risotto or salad.

PERENNIAL HERBS

Whatever the size of your garden – even if you only have space for a few pots – I urge you to invest in a few perennial herbs. Herbs add so much flavour to dishes, and if you can get your hand on fresh herbs, that's even better. That said, don't be worried about using dried herbs by the way – I use them a lot during the winter months.

If you are thinking of investing in just a few year-round herbs that need little or no care, can be grown in a pot, these will save you pounds in the long run as you'll become self-sufficient and won't need to call on the supermarket for a bag:

ROSEMARY this woody plant has fragrant evergreen needle-like leaves and edible (often blue) flowers in the spring. It's delicious with pork, lamb or chicken, and roasted with vegetables. I use it with cranberries dusted in icing sugar to decorate my chocolate tart at Christmas, and they add a little interest as leafy decorations on my Carrot and Orange Cake (page 167).

SAGE Sage leaves are greyish green and soft and velvety to the touch, and have so many uses. I use it chopped in sausage meat for sausage rolls and pork pies, and a real favourite is to chop them up really small along with chives and stir them through mashed potato.

MINT A pot of fresh mint is a must. Nothing beats the smell of home-grown new potatoes boiled with a sprig of fresh mint. Use chopped leaves in salad dressings and try very finely chopped mint leaves in a chocolate traybake.

THYME This small bushy plant with tiny leaves will provide tiny edible lilac-coloured flowers in the spring. Use the flowers as a garnish or stir them into butter to give a lemony flavour to foods. Thyme leaves can be used all year round with roast meats such as chicken, roast vegetables, soups, stews and – a favourite of mine – duck. Lemon cakes and puddings enhanced with a little thyme are always popular in my house.

There are so many herbs and aromatics to choose from and once you have these available at your fingertips you will want to have more.

PRESERVING FOOD

Historically, a whole range of produce was preserved, pickled, smoked and cured so that it could feed us during the dreary winter months. The necessity to preserve food is no longer so pressing, but for me the pleasure still remains. Home-made jam spread on a freshly baked scone can present a memory of cream teas in sunny June even though it may be a dreary foggy November day. My home-made 'end of season' chutney served with cold meats at Christmas always reminds me of my greenhouse packed with fresh tomatoes in August.

Anyone who cares about the food that they eat and has put the effort into growing it will want to savour every last berry or bean – and preserving does just that. Once you have made your own jam, pickles, bottled fruits or chutney you will realize that bought equivalents are often overly sweet and lack any real substance.

STRAWBERRY JAM

Home-made strawberry jam is more than delicious! It is afternoon tea, cream tea, Victoria sandwich cake, fresh bread . . . it's fabulous.

Making a tasty jam is not difficult, and if you grow your own fruit and have plenty to use, what better solution than to preserve them for the months to come. The main problem with soft fruits is that they can easily be destroyed by over-stirring, boiling and handling. I avoid washing the fruits and pick them when the weather is dry – we don't want any extra moisture going on as there is plenty contained within the fruits.

2kg (4lb 8oz) fresh strawberries
finely grated zest and juice of 1 lemon
1kg (2lb 4oz) granulated sugar

Equipment: preserving pan (I like to rub butter on the base of the pan to prevent sticking), 5 or 6 x 450g (1lb) jars

The night before you want to make your jam, remove the hulls (the green leaves and little core) from your strawberries and place in the buttered preserving pan. Finely grate over the lemon zest and add the juice. Sprinkle over the sugar then leave at room temperature until the next day.

Preheat the oven to 120°C/100°C (fan)/250°F/gas ½ and put two or three saucers or tea plates in the freezer. Heat your jars (to sterilize them) without their lids in the warm oven while you start to make your jam.

When you return to your pan the sugar will have started to dissolve around the fruit. Place the pan over a low heat and gently stir from time to time until all of the sugar has fully dissolved. Wait until the grittiness of the sugar has disappeared – you can feel this with a wooden spoon on the base of the pan. Turn up the heat and bring the mix to a fast boil. Time the boiling period for 20 minutes then remove it from the heat.

Take one of the saucers from the freezer and put a tablespoon of your jam onto the freezing cold plate. Pop the plate in the fridge for 2–3 minutes. Take out the plate, then push the jam from one side with your finger. If it is still liquid and the track made by your finger immediately fills with jam, then boil for another 5 minutes and repeat. If, however, when you push the jam it wrinkles and has formed a thin skin and your finger leaves a trail, it is cooked perfectly and will set when it is cold. If a scum forms when cooking, simply add a knob of butter when the jam is ready, stir it through and it will disappear.

Take your warm jars from the oven and fill them with the hot jam. The heating of the jars not only sterilizes them, it also prevents them from cracking when the hot jam is poured in. Seal the jars immediately and label them when cold.

LET ME SHOW YOU . . .

My Strawberry Jam Video

SUGAR-FREE 'FREEZER JAM'

MAKES: 3 450G (1LB) JARS

This is simply fantastic: summer strawberries, fresh in flavour, that can be enjoyed all the year round. I have used honey as a sweetener here. As there is no boiling of sugar, this jam is thinner in consistency than standard jam, but it tastes amazing. Serve it with breakfast, alongside desserts, on ice cream, rice pudding – you have lots of options!

450g (1lb) fresh strawberries, leaves and hulls removed
finely grated zest and juice of 1 lemon
finely grated zest and juice of 1 orange
45g (1½oz) honey
1 tsp vanilla paste
1 tsp ground cinnamon

Equipment: stick blender (optional), 3 x 450g (1lb) jars

Put the hulled strawberries in a roomy bowl and use a potato masher to break them down. I then finish mashing them with a stick blender but don't blend them down to a pulp – you still want some good strawberry lumps.

Put the lemon and orange zests and juice, honey and 200g (7oz) of the strawberry pulp in a small saucepan. Place over a medium heat and bring to a fast boil, stirring all the time, then let it bubble away for 3 minutes, stirring from time to time. The mixture will thicken considerably – make sure it doesn't burn!

Remove from the heat and add to the remaining strawberries in the bowl. Stir in the vanilla and cinnamon then transfer to 3 clean jars with screw-top lids or plastic containers if you prefer. Do not fill to the top of the jar – allow some headroom as the jam will expand as it freezes. Label the jars when cold.

This jam keeps well in the freezer for up to 1 year. When ready to use, take from the freezer, thaw overnight in the fridge and then it will keep for at least a week.

LET ME SHOW YOU . . .

My Sugar-Free Freezer Jam Video

REDCURRANT JELLY

MAKES: 2 X 200G JARS

If you grow your own redcurrants (and I urge you to do so), one little bush will yield pounds and pounds of fruit if looked after properly. Home-made redcurrant jelly is far superior to any shop-bought version and I use it in all sorts of recipes, especially at Christmas time. It is delicious served with cheese and cold meats, and I add a spoonful to savoury pie fillings, stews and casseroles (a spoon of jelly instantly rescues an over-salted gravy or sauce). You will need a jelly bag, a fine nylon bag that comes with its own stand.

900g (1lb 15oz) redcurrants – stalks and all
granulated sugar (see method for quantity)

Equipment: jelly bag, large casserole dish or preserving pan,
2 jars

Attach the jelly bag to the stand and suspend it over a large pan or heatproof jug.

Put the berries in the large casserole dish or preserving pan. Place over a low heat and let the fruits break down. As the cooking progresses, I use a potato masher to help burst the berries. Bring to the boil then turn off the heat and pour the hot puree into the jelly bag. Leave it undisturbed overnight, for the juice to drip through slowly. (If you squeeze the bag to try and rush things along, you will not get a clear jelly.)

The next day, measure how much fruit juice you have produced and weigh out the same weight in granulated sugar. For this recipe I had a yield of 200ml (7fl oz) juice which I poured into a clean saucepan before adding 200g (7oz) granulated sugar.

Preheat the oven to 120°C/100°C (fan)/250°F/gas ½. Heat your jars (to sterilize them) without their lids in the warm oven while you start to make your jelly.

Dissolve the sugar with the fruit over a low heat then increase the heat and allow the jelly to reach a fast boil. Boil for 1 minute only, then turn off the heat. You will have a scum over the jelly but drop a knob of butter into the pan, stir and this will disappear. Quickly transfer the jelly into the hot clean jars before it sets. Place the lids on the jars and store until required. Label the jars when cold.

LET ME SHOW YOU . . .

My Redcurrant Jelly Video

SEVILLE ORANGE MARMALADE

Allow four hours for marmalade making. The first time I made it I started early evening and then couldn't go to bed because I was waiting for it to reach a set! Seville oranges are in season in January and early February and that's the only time you can buy them, so I make enough marmalade for the whole year. The house will be filled with a lovely orange smell but if it is particularly cold outside your windows will steam up – choose a windy day and the condensation won't be so bad. I am lucky enough to have an outside hob for frying fish and the marmalade is made outside too.

1kg (2lb 4oz) Seville oranges
1 lemon
2 litres (68fl oz) water
2kg (4lb 8oz) granulated sugar

Equipment: very large saucepan, square of muslin (if you don't have one, use a brand-new double-layered dishcloth and cut it open at one end), 6 × 450g (1lb) glass jars with screw tops

First, juice the oranges and lemon. I use the juicing attachment on my food processor, but if you don't have this, just squeeze out as much juice as possible by hand and put it into the pan containing the 2 litres (68fl oz) water.

Next, scrape out the pith and pips from the fruit with a teaspoon and place into the pocket of the dishcloth or on a piece of muslin. It is important to keep these scraps as they contain the pectin which will set the marmalade. Tie the pips and pith in the cloth or muslin with string and then tie the string to the handle of the pan, allowing the pips and pith to sit in the water.

Cut all the orange and lemon fruit shells into thin strips. This can seem tiresome but the thinner the strips, the lovelier the marmalade with be. Put the fruit strips in the pan then place the pan over a high heat, bring to the boil, then turn the heat down and simmer for 2 hours – yes 2 hours! The mixture should just simmer very gently.

At the end of the cooking time, check the strips of peel are tender and soft. In the meantime, put the sugar in a large mixing bowl and place in a low oven at 100°C/80°C (fan)/200°F/gas ¼ (or put the unopened bags of sugar on a warm radiator) to warm it through – this will prevent the marmalade being cooled down too much when the sugar is added.

After the 2 hours, remove the bag of pith and pips, place in a bowl and allow to cool down slightly. Wearing a pair of rubber gloves, carefully squeeze the bag between two large plates and then between your hands to extract the lovely gooey pectin. Put the pectin mix in the pan with the now-tender orange peel and keep squeezing until you cannot extract any more, then discard the cloth bag.

Carefully add the warmed sugar to the pan and stir over a gentle heat until completely dissolved. Put 2 tea plates in the freezer and your clean jars into the warm oven that had the sugar. Bring the marmalade mix to a fast boil and keep it there for about 20 minutes. Stir from time to time to avoid sticking. If you have a sugar thermometer, the marmalade needs to reach 104°C. If you don't have one, then take your plate from the freezer and put a spoonful of the marmalade onto it. Put the plate in the fridge for 3–4 minutes until the marmalade is cool, then push the cooled liquid from one edge with your finger. If it crinkles, the marmalade is done – if it is still liquid then boil for another 10 minutes then try again with the other clean chilled plate.

When the marmalade is done, remove from the heat and leave to stand for 20 minutes. This is important as the mix will start to thicken and then when placed in the jars the rind will not float to the top.

Take the warm jars from the oven and pour the marmalade from the pan to the jar (I use a Pyrex jug). Screw the tops on while still hot. Label the jars when cold.

LET ME SHOW YOU . . .

My Seville Orange Marmalade Video

END OF SEASON CHUTNEY

MAKES: 8–10 450G (1LB) JARS

This chutney makes excellent use of all of my leftover tomatoes; green, red and yellow at different stages of ripeness. I have a few windfall apples in there too, plus onions, dried fruit and garlic. So often chutney is brown, but I make this one with granulated sugar and distilled white vinegar which results in a chutney that is colourful and vibrant . . . Autumn in a jar!

Give yourself a good few hours if you decide to make this chutney, as it needs to simmer away gently for quite a while! But it's worth it.

FOR THE SPICE PASTE

1½ tsp ground allspice

1 tsp ground coriander

½ tsp chilli powder

1 tsp ground ginger

1 tsp ground cinnamon

1 tbsp ground turmeric

1 tbsp mustard seed

FOR THE CHUTNEY

1.5 litres (50fl oz) distilled white vinegar

1kg (2lb 4oz) tomatoes (all sizes and colours)

1kg (2lb 4oz) onions, peeled and roughly chopped

6 garlic cloves, peeled and finely chopped

500g (1lb 2oz) granulated sugar

200g (7oz) ready-to-eat dried apricots, finely chopped
200g (7oz) golden sultanas
1 tbsp salt
1kg (2lb 4oz) apples (dessert or cooking), washed and
  dried

Equipment: preserving pan or large casserole dish (I like to rub butter on the base of the pan to prevent sticking), food processor (optional), 8–10 x 450g (1lb) jars

Prepping this chutney will be speedy
if you have a food processor.

Start by making the spice paste. Mix all the paste ingredients together in a bowl with enough vinegar (taken from the measured amount for the chutney) to make a smooth mixture about the consistency of single cream. Set aside.

Cut the large tomatoes into quarters and small ones in half, then chop roughly in your processor fitted with the blade attachment (or chop by hand). Transfer to the preserving pan or casserole dish and add the roughly chopped onion and the garlic. Add the sugar, dried fruit, salt, spice paste and remaining vinegar and give everything a good stir.

Quarter and core the apples, then cut the quarters in half and chop in the processor (or by hand) too. Transfer them to the pan and stir well. (I leave the apples until the last because I don't want them to brown.)

Bring to the boil then reduce the heat and leave on a steady simmer for 3½ hours, stirring from time to time, until thick – a wooden spoon should leave a brief trail in the mix when stirred. If the chutney is sticking to the base of the pan, reduce the heat a touch.

Heat the oven to 120°C/100°C (fan)/250°F/gas ½. Put your jars (to sterilize them) without their lids in the warm oven.

Remove from the heat and leave to cool a little, then transfer to the clean, hot jars and place a lid on immediately. Label the jars when cold.

LET ME SHOW YOU . . .

My End Of Season Chutney Video

PICKLED ONIONS

If you have grown your own shallots or find them cheap in the shops, try making your own pickled onions! I've provided two recipes – one is easy and quick, the other is more traditional and not as quick, but still easy.

LET ME SHOW YOU . . .

My Pickled Onions Video

EASY PICKLED ONION RECIPE

MAKES: 4 450G (1LB) JARS

1kg (2lb 4oz) shallots
25g (1oz) pickling spice
1 litre (34fl oz) malt vinegar or distilled white vinegar

Equipment: 4 × 450g (1lb) sterilized jars

Put the shallots in a roomy heatproof bowl, pour over hot water to cover and leave for 5 minutes, then peel.

Put the peeled shallots in jars, sprinkle over the pickling spice then pour over the vinegar, making sure the shallots are covered. Pop on a screw-top lid and leave for 2 months before eating. These quick pickles will keep for 3–4 months.

TRADITIONAL PICKLED ONION RECIPE

MAKES: 4 450G (1LB) JARS

1kg (2lb 4oz) shallots
25g (1oz) pickling spice
1 litre (34fl oz) distilled white vinegar or malt vinegar

FOR THE BRINE
120g (4¼oz) table salt
1 litre (34fl oz) cold water

Equipment: 4 × 450g (1lb) sterilized jars

Put the shallots in a roomy heatproof bowl, pour over hot water to cover and leave for 5 minutes, then peel.

Put the salt for the brine in another bowl, pour over the cold water then pop the peeled shallots into the brine. Cover with a plate to make sure all the shallots are submerged then leave at room temperature until the next day.

Put the pickling spice in a saucepan and add the vinegar. Bring to a fast boil and cook for 3 minutes then take off the heat and allow to cool completely.

Strain the shallots from the brine and dry on tea towels then pack into four jars. Pour the cold spiced vinegar over the shallots and divide the spices left behind among the jars. Cover with a screw-top lid and keep a month before eating. These pickled shallots will keep for a year.

FRESH TOMATO SAUCE

MAKES: 1.5KG (3LB 5OZ) SAUCE

If you grow your own tomatoes and by the middle of August you have a glut, make a batch of this delicious, thick tasty sauce. It can be frozen in clean 300ml (10fl oz) plastic cream or yoghurt containers then used as a base for pizzas, bolognese, lasagne, moussaka or any recipes that call for a tin of tomatoes. I include wine or vinegar for a little acidity and extra flavour, but you can leave it out if you like.

2kg (4lb 8oz) fresh tomatoes
3 tbsp olive oil or rapeseed oil
2 onions, peeled and roughly chopped
1½ tbsp dried mixed herbs
2 tbsp granulated sugar
4 garlic cloves, peeled and roughly chopped
100ml (3½fl oz) red wine or malt vinegar (optional)
salt and pepper

Equipment: very large casserole dish

Start by skinning the tomatoes. This may seem tedious with so many tomatoes, but it is worth it because the skins are tough and unpleasant. Slit a cross into each tomato at its base with a sharp knife. Place the tomatoes in a large heatproof bowl then pour over boiling water. Leave for 2–3 minutes then pour off the water. Starting at the base of each tomato, where you have made the cross, carefully peel off the skins. They should come off easily, especially if the tomatoes are really ripe. I tend to cut the tomatoes in half.

Heat the oil in the casserole dish, then add the chopped onion and fry gently for about 10 minutes until softened. Add the herbs, sugar and garlic and stir well then add the red wine (if using), some salt and pepper and, finally, the tomatoes. Increase the heat and bring everything to a bubble, then reduce the heat and cook at a gentle simmer, uncovered, for 1½ hours. Stir occasionally. By the end of the cooking time you should have a very thick sauce.

If you want a really smooth passata, give it a quick blitz with a stick blender. Taste for seasoning and leave to cool in the casserole dish, then freeze in containers as described in the introduction above.

LET ME SHOW YOU . . .

My Fresh Tomato Sauce Video

ACKNOWLEDGEMENTS

This book – in its original form – took some significant time to plan, structure and write. It was my first book and it saw me feel and express many things, from frustration, fatigue and fear, to fun and now friendship. I adore it.

I self-published it and had it printed in small, affordable numbers – 1000 at a time – until I had sold a total of 12,000 copies. Each and every copy was handled by me, from personally unloading them from a lorry on arrival from the printer, to stacking them under the stairs, addressing, labelling and bundling them up to be taken down to the Post Office. In the end, despatching every single copy from my dining room became a huge, ever-growing, uphill task. The book consequently just had to go out of print.

I have had many requests for a reprint and have seen copies being sold second hand for ridiculous prices. Thankfully, my friends at Pan Macmillan (One Boat who have since gone on to publish my *Sunday Times* bestselling *Clean and Green*, *Green Living Made Easy*, *The Green Gardening Handbook* and *The Green Budget Guide*) offered to print a second edition of my very first piece of work and for that I am so appreciative and delighted. *Sizzle and Drizzle* is once again in circulation!

The publishing team have gone through every page, picking up points I had failed to notice. I realize being author, copy editor and proof-reader, video maker, illustrator and photographer is maybe not a job for one person.

There are a number of other people I have to thank – without them my thoughts, aspirations and instincts could not have materialized.

My agent and most of all friends at Yellow Poppy Media. They have supported, advised and signposted me for many years and continue to instil in me the fact that quality counts.

My website and IT support at Codebase Consulting. Patience is required when dealing with me and IT. My raw thoughts and aspirations and the need to be able to incorporate video access for each recipe in this book, integrate my website and generally make everything work was done seamlessly.

My social media followers: without their continued support, engagement and encouragement I doubt a book would have ever materialized. This edition of my book has been reindexed but thank you to Curtis Duffett, a super-kind follower of mine in the US, who created the index for my self-published, original edition of *Sizzle & Drizzle*.

My Instagram 'bestie', Jonathan Van Ness, for taking the time out of his epic schedule and engagements to have a look at my posts every day, offering the best feedback and writing the most amazing Foreword. I will be forever grateful for his support at the beginning of my journey.

My family members and close friends – they are always there for me!

Last but by no means least – him indoors! Tim has that ability to never lose sight of what is important in life. He takes away the stresses, carries the bags, does the washing up, upgrades computers and phones, manages the paperwork – enabling me to do what I do!

Thanks everyone x

INDEX